From Sin to Disease

From Sin to Disease

*The Medicalization of Addiction and Its Influence on How
The Southern Baptist Convention Approaches Ministering
to Those Who Struggle with Mind Altering Substances.*

JONATHAN K. OKINAGA

WIPF & STOCK · Eugene, Oregon

FROM SIN TO DISEASE
The Medicalization of Addiction and Its Influence on How The Southern Baptist Convention Approaches Ministering to Those Who Struggle with Mind Altering Substances

Copyright © 2022 Jonathan K. Okinaga. All rights reserved. Except for brief quotations in critical publications or reviews, no part of this book may be reproduced in any manner without prior written permission from the publisher. Write: Permissions, Wipf and Stock Publishers, 199 W. 8th Ave., Suite 3, Eugene, OR 97401.

Wipf & Stock
An Imprint of Wipf and Stock Publishers
199 W. 8th Ave., Suite 3
Eugene, OR 97401

www.wipfandstock.com

PAPERBACK ISBN: 978-1-6667-0649-9
HARDCOVER ISBN: 978-1-6667-0650-5
EBOOK ISBN: 978-1-6667-0651-2

To Nicole, God blessed me with a wife that supported me unconditionally.
You exemplified what a Proverbs 31 wife should be: faithful, reverent, strong, enduring, charitable, a provider, honorable, wise, kind, praiseworthy, excellent, and, most importantly, one who fears the Lord.
Tait, Jeff, John M., Reza, Vanessa, Nicole,
Becca, Joey, McNeil, Adyson, Ryan, Colin,
Derek, Annie, Kyle, Lenny, Kevin, CJ.
This is my opus to each of you. I never had the chance to say goodbye; your lives were not lost in vain.

Contents

List of Tables ix
Acknowledgements xi

Chapter 1: Introduction 1
  Background 3
  Statement of the Problem 4
  Thesis Statement 5
  History or Relevant Research 5
  Definition of Terms 15
  Research Methodology 16

Chapter 2: Historical Shifts in Addiction Ideology and Treatment 17
  Introduction 17
  Ideological Shifts of the 1700s 18
  Ideological Shifts of the 1800s 21
  Ideological Shifts of the 1900s 26
  Ideological Shifts of the 2000s 33
  Conclusion 35

Chapter 3: Alcoholics Anonymous and Its Influence on the Church 36
  Introduction 36
  History of Alcoholics Anonymous 38
  Evaluation of Alcoholics Anonymous 42
  The Influence of A.A. in the SBC through Celebrate Recovery 66
  Conclusion 76

Chapter 4: The DSM's Influence on the Medicalization of Addiction in America 78
  Introduction 78
  History of Changes to Addiction Classifications in the DSM 81

Contents

    Evaluation of the DSM 85
    Questionable Methodology and Classifications 91
    Pharmaceutical Companies' Influence on the DSM 97
    The DSM's Influence on How the SBC Approaches Addiction and Its Co-Occurring Disorders 102
    Conclusion 106

Chapter 5: Conclusion 107
    Summary 107
    Three Views of Addiction 108
    From Sin to Disease 111
    Implications 113

Bibliography 117

Tables

Table One: Distribution of categories in entire book
    by number and frequency 50

Table Two: Distribution of categories in teaching section
    by number and frequency 51

Table Three: Distribution of categories in testimonial section
    by number and frequency 51

Table Four: Distribution of categories with Higher Power
    by number and frequency 57

Table Five: Distribution of God and Higher Power
    by number and frequency 58

Acknowledgements

Writing this book was a challenge due to fact that I have seen AA doing the job of the "church." I challenge my students with a few simple questions.

1. Does your church have a 24/7 hotline to take phone calls from those struggling with staying sober? If you don't, AA does.
2. Does you church have members who are willing to open up their homes to those who need a place to sleep while they are detoxing? If you don't, AA does.
3. Does your church welcome the smelly drunk and encourage them to keep coming back no matter how unkept and dirty they are? If you don't, AA does.

I have over fifteen years in the recovery field and have sadly seen a program that is unbiblical treat those who struggle with addiction better than most churches. My argument is that the church has to reclaim soul care and when it does, it has to have the foundation on the Word of God. As you read my book, know that I have lifelong friends who subscribe to the AA or CR models. We are able to have calm and honest conversations about treatment because of a common goal, to stop seeing our friends die. However, we are worlds apart on what we feel is the best solution. I hold firm that the Word of God is sufficient for all things, without Christ any change is solely behavior modification. I realize what I have written will ruffle some feathers and be uncomfortable for some in ministry. Those who follow Christ need to know that we can offer something that AA cannot, hope. Most importantly, if the addict chooses to have Christ as the center of their life, salvation.

The completion of this book was not done on my own. I would like to take the time to thank those that were integral on this journey. Eight years

Acknowledgements

ago when I moved to Fort Worth to pursue my master's degree, I would have told you there was no way I would ever get a PhD. With the help and guidance of John Babler, this accomplishment became a reality. He and his family have embraced me as one of their own over the years, and I am so grateful for being the adopted twelfth child.

Alcoholics Anonymous is very secretive in nature, with anonymity as a foundational pillar which keeps their fellowship going. Persuading long-time members to speak about the inner workings formed between A.A., drug and alcohol treatment centers, and the church can be very difficult. I am very grateful for Tim P. and Frank B., who both took the time to offer background information and insight from decades of working in the recovery field. While we may not always agree on how to treat addiction, we all agree that Christ should be the center of recovery.

To my numerous colleagues that gave input during seminars and also sat with me as I fleshed out through discussions what this book would look like, thank you. I am especially thankful for Sam Stephens who offered much needed encouragement during my first semesters of PhD work when I wanted to quit. Daniel Bollen, who allowed me to visit him in his office to discuss ideas, and Cody Barron who not only gave feeback and critiques but also had the momentous task of editing my work.

To my friends and family that have supported me since I left for drug and alcohol treatment fifteen years ago, the love of Christ was evident in how you embraced me despite my struggles. There are too many names to list, but you are all part of this story. For my Hawaii friends who helped me those first years of sobriety, you took the time to spend time with me when I was feeling alone; I love you all. Pastor Robert, Pastor Dave, and Pastor Kaala, without you showing Christ I would not be here today. For my California faith community at Sanctuary and theeffect, I learned so much about unconditional love with my time with you. Jim Burns and Bill Dogetrom, thank you for encouraging me to get my degree and to leave the comfort of California to expand my horizons in Texas. To my boys, you know who you are. For almost seven years you were my sons. I pray that you are walking with God and living a life that makes me proud. Steve and Tina Henningson, you adopted me into your home for two years and allowed me to rest and finish my undergraduate degree. Words cannot express my gratitude. Mom, Dad, Marissa, Shelby, Ellie, Ben, and Jessa, thank you for putting up with me while I finished my PhD. You have always supported me and loved me.

Acknowledgements

Finally to my wife, there were countless weeks where I canceled date nights and evenings where I would ask you to retreat to the bedroom so I could research in quiet. Those are just two of the many sacrifices that you made while we completed the book as a team. You are the blessing that God granted me when I moved here years ago. Without you none of this would have been possible.

Chapter 1

Introduction

IN JUNE OF 2006, the Southern Baptist Convention (SBC) adopted the resolution *On Alcohol Use in America*. Part of the resolution stated, "That we commend organizations and ministries that treat alcohol-related problems from a biblical perspective and promote abstinence and encourage local churches to begin and/or support such biblically-based ministries." [1] The rest of the resolution focused on the opposition to the manufacturing, distribution, advertising, and consumption of alcohol. Furthermore, the resolution urged that the convention should not elect anyone who drinks

---

1. "RESOLVED, That the messengers to the Southern Baptist Convention meeting in Greensboro, North Carolina, June 13–14, 2006, express our total opposition to the manufacturing, advertising, distributing, and consuming of alcoholic beverages; and be it further
 RESOLVED, That we urge that no one be elected to serve as a trustee or member of any entity or committee of the Southern Baptist Convention that is a user of alcoholic beverages.
 RESOLVED, That we urge Southern Baptists to take an active role in supporting legislation that is intended to curb alcohol use in our communities and nation; and be it further
 RESOLVED, That we urge Southern Baptists to be actively involved in educating students and adults concerning the destructive nature of alcoholic beverages; and be it finally
 RESOLVED, That we commend organizations and ministries that treat alcohol-related problems from a biblical perspective and promote abstinence and encourage local churches to begin and/or support such biblically-based ministries." *Annual of the 2006 Southern Baptist Convention,* 108–109. Resolutions traditionally express a concern or opinion of the convention but do not compel any SBC entity to abide by it. However, resolutions pass at the annual SBC meetings when a plurality of messengers present vote in favor of the resolution.

alcohol to a position of authority within the convention. The resolution's added restriction for SBC leaders during the meeting in Greensboro, North Carolina, acknowledged the pervasiveness of addiction in society and the need for local churches to actively combat the detriments of alcohol decimating church congregations across the United States.

Importantly, the 2006 resolution represented a shift from the SBC's previous stance on how to address addiction by encouraging local churches to get involved. In 1988, the SBC resolution *A Resolution on Alcohol* stated, "That we commend organizations which treat alcohol related problems as well as those organizations which promote prevention, using scripturally-based principles."[2] While the 1988 resolution commended organizations for helping treat issues caused by alcohol use, it did not encourage local churches to begin working with or to actively support entities combating addictions.

The first mention of alcohol in SBC history occurred during an 1890 report in which the convention took a stand against the sale and manufacture of alcohol.[3] Later, at the 1955 SBC meeting, the convention deemed drugs and alcohol a "vicious evil" and placed them in the same category as communism as a threat against the stability of government.[4] Since 1845,

---

2. "Be it RESOLVED, That we encourage the United States Government to cease to assist these industries via trade talks; and

Be it finally RESOLVED, That Southern Baptists in their annual meeting, June 14–16, 1988, in San Antonio, Texas, declare their opposition to these hypocritical practices by the United States Government on behalf of the alcohol and tobacco industries." *Annual of the 1988 Southern Baptist Convention*, 73. The resolution did not mention any specific organizations that it commended.

3. "RESOLVED, By the Southern Baptist Convention assembled, that we are unalterably opposed to the sale of intoxicating liquor, as a beverage, either under high or low license." *Annual of the 1890 Southern Baptist Convention*, 40.

4. "THEREFORE, BE IT RESOLVED:

(1) That the Southern Baptist Convention express its unceasing opposition to the manufacture, sale, and use of alcoholic beverages, and

(2) That it approve a more intensified program along the following lines:

a. To inform our people of the true nature of alcohol as a beverage and the effects of its use as a beverage on the individual and in society.

b. To provide additional materials that are attractive in appearance, adequate in quantity, and accurate in statement that will make a greater impact on our people on a national scale.

c. To encourage and promote leadership training in the field of alcohol education.

d. To cooperate with the national and state temperance leagues in encouraging our people to vote and take part in political action on temperance issues.

(3) To this end the Convention requests the Christian Life Commission to seek

INTRODUCTION

the SBC adopted a total of seventy resolutions on substance abuse during its annual meetings.[5] Sixty-seven of these resolutions focused on the distribution and marketing of drugs or alcohol; one resolution persuaded church members to come alongside and encourage those who struggled with addiction during Fourth of July celebrations; and only one encouraged the local church to support biblically-based ministries aiming to combat substance abuse.[6]

Background

The SBC has historically taken a stance against the sale and distribution of alcohol and illicit drugs. But until 2006, the convention remained relatively silent for almost a century regarding how the local church should help individuals overcome addiction problems. Prior to 2006, the last time that an SBC resolution addressed the local church's role in helping those who struggle with addiction was in 1905.[7] After the 1905 SBC gathering in Kansas City, Missouri, a paradigm shift occurred in how the SBC approached addictions, coinciding with the popularity of psychology within the church.[8] The psychological understanding of addiction undermined the concept of addiction as a sin, and what became known as the "disease model" for addiction elevated to become the established "fact" in both the secular world as well as in the church.[9]

---

through the normal Convention channels ways and means to implement such a program." *Annual of the 1955 Southern Baptist Convention*, 61–62.

5. "Resolutions Search Results for: Alcohol," Southern Baptist Convention, accessed April 11, 2019, http://www.sbc.net/resolutions/about/alcohol.

6. "Resolutions Search Results for: Alcohol."

7. "RESOLVED, That we call upon our churches, Sabbath schools, and young peoples' societies everywhere to join with other religious organizations and temperance bodies in every community for a legitimate and wholesome celebration where patriotic temperance addresses shall be delivered, and appropriate and inspiring music rendered." *Annual of the 1905 Southern Baptist Convention*, 35.

8. "Alcoholics Anonymous and 12-Step programs have become the preferred replacement for church by the market-sensitive pastors. Many of these changes are motivated by a desire to keep pace with the rapidly changing currents of society, otherwise the church could appear hopelessly out-of-date and irrelevant. It is striking that for much of two thousand years of church history there does not seem to be the same concern for the church's irrelevancy as there is today." Street, "Market-Driven Madness," 19.

9. Powlison, *The Biblical Counseling Movement*, 101; Adams, *The Big Umbrella*, 109; Priolo, "Sin and Misery: Connecting the Dots," 97; Shaw, *The Heart of Addiction*, 515–20,

One of the earliest signs of the disease model's influence on the church occurred in 1946 when the SBC resolved, "That we urge the Baptists in the several states to co-operate with and support heartily the temperance organizations (or organization) in each state which are rendering worthy service in the fight against alcoholism and the liquor traffic."[10] Oddly, the church embraced the disease model at the same time that Alcoholics Anonymous (AA) gained popularity after its inception in 1935.[11] The 1968 SBC meeting in Houston, Texas, considered addiction a mental health issue:

> Therefore be it RESOLVED, That we express gratitude to our government for its actions attempting to protect the health of American citizens, and Be it further RESOLVED, That we request the Surgeon General of the United States to undertake a similar effort on the effect of alcoholic beverages on physical and mental health.[12]

The resolution passed at approximately the same time the American Psychiatric Association (APA) and the American Medical Association (AMA) declared that addictions were mental diseases.[13]

Statement of the Problem

Prior to the 1990s and the rise of Celebrate Recovery (CR), SBC churches generally helped those struggling with addiction by renting their buildings to AA, offering minimal assistance or soul care to addicts.[14] The follow-

Kindle; Playfair and Bryson, *The Useful Lie*, 26.

    10. *Annual of the 1946 Southern Baptist Convention*, 127.

    11. Alcoholics Anonymous, "Historical Data: The Birth of AA and Its Growth in the U.S./Canada,"

    12. *Annual of the 1968 Southern Baptist Convention*, 78.

    13. *Diagnostic and Statistical Manual of Mental Disorders: DSM-II*, 39. David J. Mersy wrote, "In 1956, the American Medical Association officially said alcoholism met three standard criteria for being declared a disease. First, it had an identifiable set of symptoms. Second, it followed a predictable and malignant progression if not treated, and third, it did respond to treatment. What this meant was that the insurance industry agreed to pay for treatment, just as if you came down with diabetes." Mersy, "Recognition of Alcohol and Substance Abuse," 1529.

    14. "Why is it that the power of personal transformation is facilitated by an organization external to the local church while the local church contributes only meeting space? If recovery ministry remains at the margins of congregational life, significant opportunities may be missed. Increasingly congregations are finding ways to retain AA-in-the-basement strategy, but they are also finding additional ways to supplement this strategy

Introduction

ing research question arises from this observation: What influence did the psychological redefinition of addiction from sin to disease have on the SBC churches' care for addicts?

Thesis Statement

Southern Baptist Convention churches adopted the new definition of addiction changed by Alcoholics Anonymous and the medical community to mean a life-long disease rather than a result of sinful behavior and consequently abdicated their responsibility to assist addicts through soul care by instead relying on unbiblical approaches and solutions for addictions.

History of Relevant Research

Addiction may be perceived in three distinct ways: as a sinful choice, as a disease, and as neither a disease nor sin.[15] Prominent individuals support each distinct category as the correct view.[16]

For centuries, society understood addiction as a moral issue—a result of the addict living a life of sin. Today's society sees addiction as a disease.[17]

---

with other resources in order to build a more comprehensive ministry." Franklin, *The Church Leader's Counseling Resource Book,* 34.

15. See Carroll, "Presuppositions One and Two: God's Sovereignty and Man's Responsibilities," 67–68; DiClemente, *Addiction and Change,* 3; Shaw, *The Heart of Addiction,* 515–20, Kindle; Vogel, "Finding the Whole Person," 181–82; Fingarette, *Heavy Drinking: The Myth of Alcoholism as a Disease,* 5. Rohan, "Comment on 'The N.C.A. Criteria for the Diagnosis of Alcoholism,'" 211; Mendelson *The Diagnosis and Treatment of Alcoholism*; Vaillant, *The Natural History of Alcoholism,* 20; Berg, *Changed into His Image,* 29.

16. Carroll, "Presuppositions One and Two," 67–68; DiClemente, *Addiction and Change,* 3; Shaw, *The Heart of Addiction,* 515–20, Kindle; Vogel, "Finding the Whole Person," 181–82; Playfair and Bryson, *The Useful Lie,* 33; Fingarette, *Heavy Drinking*; Rohan, "Comment on 'The N.C.A. Criteria,'" 211; Mendelson and Mello, *The Diagnosis and Treatment of Alcoholism*; Vaillant, *The Natural History of Alcoholism,* 20; Berg, *Changed into His Image,* 29; White and Crowley, *Slaying the Dragon,* 2–3;. Katcher, "Benjamin Rush's Educational Campaign against Hard Drinking," 275; Rush, *An Enquiry into the Effects of Ardent Spirits;* Warner, "'Resolv'd to Drink No More,'" 685.

17. Carroll, "Presuppositions One and Two," 67–68; DiClemente, *Addiction and Change,* 3; Shaw, *The Heart of Addiction,* 515–20, Kindle; Vogel, "Finding the Whole Person," 181–82; Playfair and Bryson, *The Useful Lie,* 33; Fingarette, *Heavy Drinking*; Rohan, "Comment on 'The N.C.A. Criteria,'" 211–18; Mendelson and Mello, *The Diagnosis and Treatment of Alcoholism*; Vaillant, *The Natural History of Alcoholism,* 20; Berg, *Changed into His Image,* 29.

From Sin to Disease

Generally, struggling addicts prioritize drugs and alcohol over God and turn mind-altering substances into idols. The idea that addiction should not be called sinful opposes biblical teaching.[18] The Bible presents several instances of the negative consequences of alcoholic behavior but never classifies alcohol addiction as a disease.[19] The biblical terms for "disease" in the original Greek (*nósos*) and Hebrew (*tachalu*) do not associate with or refer to problems of drunkenness.[20] Rather, a person willingly chooses to consume the mind-altering substance and live a life which neglects to bring praise and glory to God.[21] A disease does not separate from God, but sin does.[22] Biblical counselors propose that addicts fail to recognize their actions and thinking do not correspond with God's Word when they believe their addiction is a disease.[23]

When Benjamin Rush wrote *An Enquiry into the Effects of Spirituous Liquors upon the Human Body and Their Influence upon the Happiness of Society* in 1813, his work marked the beginning of a shift in attitude about addictions.[24] His view coincided with other physicians who examined medicine from a more scientific viewpoint.[25] He believed alcohol consumption possessed inherent medical hazards.[26] While Rush's stance for individuals to abstain from drinking alcohol remained primarily moral, he still

---

18. Playfair and Bryson, *The Useful Lie*, 33.

19. Genesis 9:20–23 describes Noah's drunkenness and his sons covering up his nakedness. Genesis 19:33–38 tells the story of Lot getting drunk and committing incest with two of his daughters. In Leviticus 10:1–9, two priests offered a "strange fire" to God while under the influence of alcohol. These examples represent just a few passages mentioning drunken behavior. The Bible issues no direct commands against drinking. Drinking alcohol is not the sin issue; drunkenness is the problem.

20. Bauer, *A Greek-English Lexicon of the New Testament*, 679; Brannan, *Lexham Research Lexicon*.

21. Carroll, "Presuppositions One and Two," 67–68; Shaw, *The Heart of Addiction*, 515–20, Kindle; Playfair and Bryson, *The Useful Lie*, 33; Berg, *Changed into His Image*, 29.

22. Kreeft and Tacelli, *Handbook of Christian Apologetics*, 202.

23. Priolo, "Sin and Misery," 97.

24. Rush, *An Enquiry into the Effects of Ardent Spirits*; Buschendorf, Franke, and Voelz, eds., *Civilizing and Decivilizing Processes*, 7.

25. White and Crowley, *Slaying the Dragon*, 2–3; Katcher, "Benjamin Rush's Educational Campaign against Hard Drinking," 275; Rush, *An Enquiry into the Effects of Ardent Spirits*, 17; Warner, "'Resolv'd to Drink No More,'" 685.

26. White and Crowley, *Slaying the Dragon*, 2–3; Katcher, "Benjamin Rush's Educational Campaign against Hard Drinking," 273; Rush, *An Enquiry into the Effects of Ardent Spirits*; Warner, "'Resolv'd to Drink No More,'" 689.

INTRODUCTION

proposed strictly scientific reasons to stay sober rather than moral or biblical reasons.[27] Rush's view marked the beginning of the removal of sin as the root cause of addiction, which was once regarded as a moral problem, in favor of medical intervention.[28]

The Society for the Study and Cure of Inebriety, a professional society in Great Britain, devoted itself to investigating alcohol and drug habituations.[29] The word "inebriate," derived from the Latin word *inebriatus* or "intoxicated," became the first scholarly term to describe a drunk.[30] The Society for the Study and Cure of Inebriety used the term "inebriety" to honor its founder, Norman Kerr, who proposed that drug and alcohol habituations were a physical and hereditary disease.[31] During the early 1900s, William Collins became the new leader for the Society for the Study and Cure of Inebriety and began using the word "addiction" instead of inebriety.[32] His decision to change the terminology aimed to push forward the new theory of the "disease of will," which proposed that the root problem of addiction dealt more with psychological issues rather than any physical malady.[33]

Before the Eighteenth Amendment to the United States Constitution, ratified on January 16, 1919, American society viewed addiction as a moral problem controllable by laws.[34] The concept of addiction as a disease was

---

27. Rush, *An Enquiry into the Effects of Ardent Spirits*, 13. Jürgen Rehm supported Rush's claim: "Alcohol consumption, particularly heavier drinking, is an important risk factor for many health problems and, thus, is a major contributor to the global burden of disease. In fact, alcohol is a necessary underlying cause for more than 30 conditions and a contributing factor to many more. The most common disease categories that are entirely or partly caused by alcohol consumption include infectious diseases, cancer, diabetes, neuropsychiatric diseases (including alcohol use disorders), cardiovascular disease, liver and pancreas disease, and unintentional and intentional injury." See Rehm, "The Risks Associated with Alcohol Use and Alcoholism," 135.

28. Carroll, "Presuppositions One and Two," 67–68; London, *The Modes and Morals*, 172.

29. Kerr, *Society for the Study and Cure of Inebriety*.

30. Crystal, *Words in Time and Place*, 58.

31. Winskill, *The Temperance Movement and Its Workers*, 152; White and Crowley, *Slaying the Dragon*, 49.

32. Blocker, Fahey, and Tyrrell, *Alcohol and Temperance in Modern History*, 38.

33. Blocker, Fahey, and Tyrrell, *Alcohol and Temperance in Modern History*, 564; Blumberg, "The American Association for the Study and Cure of Inebriety," 235; Nutt, *Drugs and the Future*, 472; Winskill, *The Temperance Movement and Its Workers*, 152.

34. The Eighteenth Amendment made illegal the manufacture, transportation, and distribution of liquor. See Levy, Karst, and Winkler, *Encyclopedia of the American*

still in its infancy but gaining traction in the medical field. Since the early 1900s, the medical field increasingly pushed the narrative that addiction is a disease, not a sin.[35] This way of thinking permeated not only the church but also pastors and counselors—the shepherds of the church.[36] Twelve-Step groups like AA played an instrumental role in encouraging followers of Christ to accept secular treatment options as the answer to addictions.[37] Previously recognized as a spiritual and moral dilemma, both secular psychology and the church now accepted addiction as a medical issue.[38]

Two of the early primary voices of the addiction-as-disease model are E. M. Jellinek and AA In his book *The Disease Concept of Alcoholism*, Jellinek demonstrated how AA's efforts and ideology rose to the forefront of pushing the addiction-as-a-disease narrative.[39] AA increased its influence due to their initial outreach to churches and the clergy.[40] By presenting their program as a spiritual program, AA's proponents convinced many clergy to acquiesce the care of souls to AA and other Twelve-Step groups.[41]

Constitution; Olson and Gerstein, Alcohol in America, 1–2.

35. National Institute on Drug Abuse, *Principles of Drug Addiction Treatment: A Research-Based Guide*, 2nd ed, Towns and Lambert, *Habits that Handicap*, 177; Towns, *The Work of the Charles B. Towns Hospital*; Abadinsky, *Drug Use and Abuse: A Comprehensive Introduction*; McCarthy, "Early Alcoholism Treatment," 60; Dubiel, *The Road to Fellowship*; Lombardo, *A Century of Eugenics in America*; Tobey, "Historical, Legal, and Statistical Review of Eugenical Sterilization in the United States," 725–726; Carroll, "Presuppositions One and Two," 67–68; DiClemente, *Addiction and Change*, 3; Shaw, *The Heart of Addiction*, 515–20, Kindle; Vogel, "Finding the Whole Person," 181–82; Playfair and Bryson, *The Useful Lie*, 33; Rohan, "Comment on 'The N.C.A. Criteria,'" 211–18; Vaillant, *The Natural History of Alcoholism*, 20; Berg, *Changed into His Image*, 29.

36. Playfair and Bryson, *The Useful Lie*, 26; Spickard and Thompson, *Dying for a Drink*, 41; Ganz, *Psychobabble*, 27; Rowe, "Getting Christ off the Couch," 74; London, *The Modes and Morals of Psychotherapy*, 172; Bowen, "Helping People Recover from Recovery," 71.

37. "After centuries of treating alcoholism as a moral weakness, most present-day medical opinion considers alcoholism a disease which, like diabetes, can be arrested but not cured. Many of the clergy, too, now accept alcoholism as sickness and not sin." Anonymous, *Al-Anon Family Groups*, 8; Street, "Market-Driven Madness," 19; Jellinek, *The Disease Concept of Alcoholism*,160.

38. Playfair and Bryson, *The Useful Lie*, 28; Rowe, "Getting Christ off the Couch," 74; Whitaker, *Anatomy of an Epidemic*, 43; Dunnington, *Addiction and Virtue*, 559–60, Kindle.

39. Jellinek, *The Disease Concept of Alcoholism*, 160.

40. Jellinek, *The Disease Concept of Alcoholism*, 171; Playfair and Bryson, *The Useful Lie*, 28; Lender, *Dictionary of American Temperance Biography*, 42.

41. "It is easy to let up on the spiritual program of action and rest on our laurels."

Introduction

Bill W. represented the center of the AA movement along with W. D. Silkworth, who shaped Bill's belief that alcoholism was not a moral issue.[42] AA visibly impacted the changing perception of addiction by the late 1950s. Elmo Roper and Associates surveyed the nation in 1958, asking, "Should alcoholics be considered morally weak or sick?"[43] Of the responses, "58 percent replied that they were sick, [and] only 35 percent said that they were morally weak."[44] This statistic changed in following decades. A Gallup poll in 2006 found that 76 percent of those polled viewed addiction as a disease.[45]

Today, the vast majority in the medical field along with many in the church view addiction as a disease.[46] Accordingly, those in the fields of psychology and psychiatry currently classify the consumption of mind-altering substances as a mental disorder.[47] Similarly, those in the neuroscience field

---

Bill W., *Alcoholics Anonymous: The Big Book: The Original 1939 Edition*, 113. See also Anonymous, *Al-Anon Family Groups*, 8.

42. Jellinek, *The Disease Concept of Alcoholism*, 160; McPeake, *William D. Silkworth, M.D.*; Anonymous, "Dr. Silkworth's Rx for Sobriety."

43. Jellinek, *The Disease Concept of Alcoholism*, 183.

44. Jellinek, *The Disease Concept of Alcoholism*, 183.

45. Jones, *Americans with Addiction in Their Family Believe It Is a Disease*. A newer poll by The Associated Press-NORC Center for Public Affairs Research in 2018 asked participants if they viewed prescribed opiate medication as a disease. 53 percent considered the opiate medication a disease. The poll did not ask what percentage of participants viewed drugs or alcohol addiction as a disease. This observation demonstrates that a segment of society does not view prescription medication as a drug abuse problem. In fact, some clinicians differentiate illicit drug use and pharmaceutical drug use. "Accordingly, there appear to be meaningful differences between prescription and illicit drugs of the same class. For example, cue-induced craving appears to be less robust among those abusing prescription opioids relative to those abusing heroin, and these groups may also have different responses to treatment. Stein found that prescription opioid- and heroin-dependent individuals report different life concerns, with those dependent upon prescription opioids less concerned about infectious disease, but more concerned about alcohol use relative to heroin users." McHugh, Nielsen, and Weiss, "Prescription Drug Abuse: From Epidemiology to Public Policy," 3.

46. McLellan, "Drug Dependence, A Chronic Medical," 1689–95; National Institute on Drug Abuse, *Principles of Drug Addiction Treatment*; DiClemente, *Addiction and Change*, 3; Whitaker, *Anatomy of an Epidemic*, 46; Potenza, "Neuroscience of Behavioral and Pharmacological Treatments for Addictions," 695–99; Davies, *Cracked*, 174; Playfair and Bryson, *The Useful Lie*, 35; Jellinek, *The Disease Concept of Alcoholism*, 37; Spickard and Thompson, *Dying for a Drink*, 41; Welch, *Addictions: A Banquet in the Grave*, 37.

47. *Diagnostic and Statistical Manual of Mental Disorders: DSM-V-TR*.

label addiction as a brain disease.[48] They regarded addiction as an uncontrollable action that the addict cannot stop even though life-threatening consequences may occur.[49] The literature produced from this perspective teaches that the brain will rewire after the body receives prolonged exposure to drugs and alcohol, and the addict will experience an onset of impaired learning, motivation, memory, and control.[50]

One reason for embracing the definition of addiction as a disease, stems from the medical profession's redefinition of what constitutes a disease:

> The third generation of diseases—addictions—strays still farther from the model of physical disorder to which the name disease was first applied by modern medicine. That is, unlike a mental illness such as schizophrenia, which is indicated by disordered thinking and feelings, addictive disorders are known by the behaviors they describe.[51]

Based on the understanding above, diseases are no longer classified solely by physical changes to the body, but they now include behavioral and mental issues. These changes to the definition of disease receive wide acceptance as truth despite the absence of tests to confirm a proper diagnosis.[52]

The rise of psychology and psychiatry also contributed to the decision for churches stepping away from the soul care of addicts. David Powlison's book *The Biblical Counseling Movement: History and Context* takes a historical look at the secularization of traditional pastoral counseling. Powlison's book details both how and why pastors abdicated discipling their

---

48. Leshner, "Addiction Is a Brain Disease, and It Matters," 45–47; Satel and Lilienfeld, "Addiction and the Brain-Disease Fallacy,"; Dentzer, "Substance Abuse and other Substantive Matters," 1398; Henningfield, Santora, and Bickel, *Addiction Treatment: Science and Policy for the Twenty-First Century*,13; American Society of Addiction Medicine, "The Definition of Addiction."

49. DiClemente, *Addiction and Change*, 3; Playfair and Bryson, *The Useful Lie*, 33; Jellinek, *The Disease Concept of Alcoholism*, 4; Fingarette, *Heavy Drinking*, 2; Shaw, *The Heart of Addiction*, 421–24, Kindle.

50. Szalavitz, *Unbroken Brain*, 3; Miller, "How Addiction Hijacks the Brain," 1–3; NIH, NIAA, "Neuroscience: Pathways to Alcohol Dependence," 3; Erickson, *The Science of Addiction*."

51. Peele, *Diseasing of America*, 364–67, Kindle.

52. Shaw, *The Heart of Addiction*, 515–20, Kindle; Davies, *Cracked*, 15; Peele, *Diseasing of America*, 774, Kindle.

INTRODUCTION

congregations.[53] Jay Adams, founder of the nouthetic counseling movement, wrote, "Biblical counseling, in contrast to Sigmund Freud and Carl Rogers, two of the main humanistic psychotherapists of the 20th century, assumes that problems stem from sin."[54] Pastors are competent to counsel, an important factor to consider when people suggest those with addictions should be sent to a licensed counseling professional rather than a pastor.[55] Theologically, pastors serve as shepherds of souls, not brain mechanics such as psychologists and psychiatrists. According to Adams, "[Pastors] are God's professionals."[56] Addicts may receive needed help from the church, rather than from trained counseling professionals, through proper theology preached from the pulpit as well as other preventative measures within the church which help the addict realize that addiction is a sin issue, not a disease.[57]

Secular thinkers find a correlation between the treatment of addiction and mental illness because of the similar anthropology in each approach.[58] Instead of accepting that the root cause of addiction usually entails disobedience to God and not following His instructions, the sciences place the

---

53. In an interview about the release of *The Biblical Counseling Movement: History and Context*, Dr. Powlison described "[the biblical counseling] history about the trajectory that we are part of. . . . Where do we come from? What are we? Where are we going? It's trying to capture that flow. From a significant to forecast script and call people to future choices to help make the church stronger . . . Wisdom is not timeless. Thinking through where is the church in relation to counseling? Where is the culture? What are the various conflicts, tensions, issues that have are playing both in the culture and the church?" CCEF Live, "The Biblical Counseling Movement: History & Context by David Powlison."

54. Adams, *The Big Umbrella*, 109.

55. Powlison, *The Biblical Counseling Movement*, 132; Adams, *Competent to Counsel*, 18.

56. Adams, *A Theology of Christian Counseling*, 310.

57. Playfair and Bryson, *The Useful Lie*, 62; Welch, *Addictions*, 287.

58. Singer stated, "The research and published literature on the anthropology of drug use has grown and diversified since the 1970s, found acceptance in the wider multi-disciplinary domain of alcohol and drug studies and developed beyond the socio-cultural model to include life-style, critical medical anthropology and experiential explanatory models. Anthropological research has helped to shape the field of addiction science, e.g. ethnographic studies show that the lived worlds and self-identities of drug users have cultural order and socially constructed purpose and meaning, and experiential research shows that some addictions or aspects of addictions can be affirmative, creative and sustainable." Singer, "Anthropology and Addiction: An Historical Review," 1747.

blame on disease.[59] However, an inherent problem exists with this viewpoint because the sciences have not proven how biology impacts addiction.[60] Furthermore, disease-focused treatment options rarely offer biblical principles to rehabilitate the addict, whereas an addict may receive biblical treatment uninfluenced by secular thought within the church.[61] Current treatment options seek to alleviate and help the addict abstain from the use of drugs or alcohol, not resolve moral or sinful issues.[62]

The introduction of the disease model influenced the way addicts view their life-dominating sins.[63] The belief that addressing addiction from

---

59. DiClemente, *Addiction and Change*, 3; Whitaker, *Anatomy of an Epidemic*, 46; Potenza, et al., "Neuroscience of Behavioral and Pharmacological Treatments for Addictions," 698; Davies, *Cracked*, 174; Playfair and Bryson, *The Useful Lie*, 35; Jellinek, *The Disease Concept of Alcoholism*, 37; Spickard and Thompson, *Dying for a Drink*, 41; Welch, *Addictions*, 37.

60. "Although the brain disease model of addiction has yielded effective preventive measures, treatment interventions, and public health policies to address substance-use disorders, the underlying concept of substance abuse as a brain disease continues to be questioned, perhaps because the aberrant, impulsive, and compulsive behaviors that are characteristic of addiction have not been clearly tied to neurobiology." Volkow, Koob, and McLellan, "Neurobiologic Advances from the Brain Disease Model of Addiction," 363–71. See also Peele, *Diseasing of America*, 364–67, Kindle; Shaw, *The Heart of Addiction*, 421–24, Kindle.

61. Playfair and Bryson, *The Useful Lie*, 62; Welch, *Addictions*, 287. According to Landry, despite the churches' attempt to provide a biblical approach to addictions, the starting point for addiction treatment has almost always built its foundation upon the unbiblical program of AA "The 12 step programs, such as AA, Narcotics Anonymous, Cocaine Anonymous are among the most widely used services used in addiction treatment and recovery." Landry, *Overview of Addiction Treatment Effectiveness*, 64.

62. "Tradition Three: 'The only requirement for AA membership is a desire to stop drinking.'" Anonymous, *Twelve Steps and Twelve Traditions*, 139.

63. Addicts have embraced the concept that they suffer from a disease rather than realizing that the root of their problems is sin. According to Hammer, "The majority of our interviewed patients found the disease model useful. Many believed that a disease diagnosis diminishes moral judgment while reinforcing the imperative that the sick persons take responsibility for their condition and seek treatment." Paige, one of the clients in treatment for alcoholism, said, "I think understanding that it is a disease is what helps me take control over my addiction. It helps me to understand it, and if I understand it, especially, it takes away the guilt and the shame processes that we go through, and it is hard to carry that around and get into recovery." Elise, a smoker, disclosed an ongoing argument with her husband: "He keeps telling me it is mind over matter and I keep saying 'no, when I'm having physical symptoms, that is not mind over matter.' . . . I would like to think that addiction is [a disease], again, to take some of the blame off myself for feeling horrible that I did this." Hammer, "Addiction: Current Criticism of the Brain Disease Paradigm," 27.

Introduction

a moral standpoint hindered efficient help for people achieving sobriety provided one of the primary reasons for the inception of the disease model.[64] Thus, a necessary question asks, "How effective is the current treatment compared to the success rate of treatments that predate modern secular techniques and therapies?"[65] Current treatment statistics boast, at best, a 60 percent success rate for rehab patients maintaining sobriety.[66] Treatment centers employ questionable methodology to obtain statistics on which to base efficacy claims.[67] For example, treatment centers send out questionnaires asking former clients if they are still sober, but the statistics do not include individuals who opted not to return the survey.[68] With so much faith put into the effectiveness of secular therapies, a deeper investigation into the real numbers of addicts who benefit from secular treatments must occur.

Several voices speak out against the addiction-as-disease model from a purely scientific perspective without using biblical support to reach their conclusions. Stanton Peele, James Davies, Robert Whitaker, and Herbert

---

"Addicts do not see their issue as a sin problem. They default that they have a disease which allows them to shift the blame of their problems from it being a choice to where it is the disease's fault they struggle with addiction." Tim P. is currently a missionary in Southern California. Previously, he was a Certified Alcohol and Drug Abuse Counselor III (the highest certification in California) and the clinical director at one of the premier Christian Drug and Alcohol Treatment Centers in the nation for over a decade.

64. "If one approached treatment from this moral perspective, it was inevitably viewed as ineffective. A moral defect is incurable; therefore, the alcoholic was typically punished." Miller, *Learning the Language of Addiction Counseling*, 330; Lewis, *The Biology of Desire*, 1.

65. The author uses this argumentation from a statistical viewpoint to prove that the secularization of discipleship is not only unbiblical but also ineffective. Biblical counseling aims not to fix counselees but to lead them to live in obedience to God.

66. Miller, "How Addiction Hijacks the Brain."

67. Fletcher wrote, "Chemical dependency programs exaggerate their success rates. . . . Treatment has little scientific support." Elsewhere she stated, "For many clients [treatment is] a revolving door. . . . Even an elite treatment program has many failures. . . . As I found in researching this book, the current treatment system continues to suffer from many of these issues." Fletcher, *Inside Rehab*, 6.

68. Although a small sample size, the author completed treatment fifteen years ago. Of the twenty-eight addicts who completed treatment at the same time as the author, he is still in contact with fifteen of them; only two are still sober today. More people have died in the previous fifteen years than have remained sober. Additionally, the rehab center used for the example represents one of the premier drug and alcohol treatment facilities in the nation, as they consistently rate among the best Christian rehabs in the country. Due to confidentiality, the name of the treatment center cannot be disclosed.

Fingarette refuted the idea that addictions and mental illness have biological foundations. Peele wrote:

> Disease conceptions of misbehavior are bad science and are morally and intellectually sloppy. Biology is not behavior, even in those areas where a drug or alcohol is taken into the body. Alcoholism involves a host of personal and environmental considerations aside from how alcohol affects the bodies of drinkers. Furthermore, once we treat alcoholism and addiction as diseases, we cannot rule out that anything people do but shouldn't is a disease, from crime to excessive sexual activity to procrastination.[69]

The voices within the treatment field who argue against the disease model of addiction propose that addiction is purely a choice of the addict and any addiction diagnosed as a disease signifies poor science, ignorance, or financial profiteering from health care professionals.[70]

Research on the subject of addiction reveals a lack of biblical resources for SBC churches without heavy influences from culture or unbiblical organizations. Even in the broader Christian community, various biblical counseling journals rarely address addiction. The main avenue for churches to participate in helping addicts comes through CR or similar recovery ministries with a foundation in AA. Of the eighteen editions of *The Journal of Modern Ministry*, only one journal featured articles on addiction.[71] The remaining seventeen editions did not include a single article addressing addiction.

Compared to the numerous options available outside the church for dealing with addiction, Southern Baptist churches generally offer relatively little assistance. AA and those who propose the disease model influenced the SBC to view addiction as a medical problem rather than a sin issue. Despite boasting biblical counseling programs at most of their seminaries, the SBC has a relatively small number of churches willing to work with addicts without the use of programs influenced by AA.

---

69. Peele, *Diseasing of America*, 774, Kindle.

70. Peele, *Diseasing of America*, 774, Kindle; Davies, *Cracked*, 6; Whitaker, *Anatomy of an Epidemic*, 10; Fingarette, *Heavy Drinking*, 25. See also Bronowski, *The Ascent of Man*, 153.

71. Adams, "Sin and Counseling," Specifically, the journal featured four articles on the subject of addiction.

Introduction

Definitions of Terms

The following terms and definitions will aid the reader to understand and accurately interpret the research.

Addiction

Webster's Medical Dictionary defines addiction as "an uncontrollable craving, seeking, and use of a substance such as alcohol or another drug. Dependence is such an issue with addiction that stopping is very difficult and causes severe physical and mental reactions."[72]

Biblical Counseling

Biblical counseling is a theological discipline in which one ministers Scripture to another facing struggles in life or desires wisdom or God's direction.[73] Biblical counseling is a ministry of the local church, believing that the scripture is sufficient for all things, and lovingly confronts those living in sin.[74]

Diagnostic and Statistical Manual of Mental Disorders (*DSM*)

The *DSM* is the instruction manual used by health care professionals in the United States to guide the diagnosis of mental disorders.[75]

SBC Annual Meeting

A convention in each June where messengers from SBC churches gather for a two-day meeting. During this time the messengers elect trustees, approve the SBC budget, revise bylaws, and consider resolutions.

---

72. Stöppler and Shiel, *Webster's New World Medical Dictionary*, 8.
73. Lambert, *A Theology of Biblical Counseling*, 11.
74. Babler and Ellen, *Counseling by the Book*, 47.
75. *DSM-V-TR*, xli.

SBC Resolutions

While resolutions are not binding statements, they communicate the collaborative opinion of messengers on a particular subject at the SBC annual meeting. Covering a plethora of subjects encompassing social, practical, and theological issues, resolutions inform the SBC and its members about important ethical, moral, and cultural subjects. Resolutions empower SBC churches to speak with conviction in the public arena about the biblical implementation on cultural matters.

Soul Care

Soul care is the shepherding of the body of believers by teaching sound doctrine, nurturing one another by investing in the lives of others, and providing comfort and direction to those that are dealing with life's struggles.[76]

Research Methodology

A thematic analysis identified key themes which shaped how the SBC and its churches approach addiction. A historical timeline focusing on addictions and ascertaining the shifts within the church in the care of addicts clarify the scope of the dissertation. Rush and AA will be referenced as the primary contributors to the introduction of the disease model and the beginning of organizations apart from the church caring for the souls of alcoholics. From the outgrowth of AA's popularity and influence, the author will examine how the *DSM* solidified the disease concept of addictions. This study will demonstrate that SBC churches embraced and adopted AA teachings and the *DSM* as truth, which impacted the way the SBC and its pastors approached addictions. Additionally, the author will provide relevant information on the three perspectives of addiction: addiction as sin, addiction as disease, and addiction as not a disease.

---

76. The concept of soul care discussed in this study will amalgamate the thoughts and understandings of John Babler and Martin Bucer. See Babler and Ellen, *Counseling by the Book*, xiii–xiv; Bucer, *Concerning the True Care of Souls*, 33–121.

Chapter 2

Historical Shifts in Addiction Ideology and Treatment

Introduction

JESUS CHRIST CALLS HIS disciples to follow Him and to mimic Him, the mender of broken hearts. As the body of Christ, Christians have a mission to serve as care-givers of the members of the church and community of souls.[1] But regarding ministry to those who struggle with addiction, churches were largely uninvolved until the 1990s and relied on secular philosophies and methodologies to approach this section of society.[2] For the last two and a half centuries, culture, politics, and science acted as the primary influencers specifying the approaches to substance abuse in the United States of America.[3] Instead of representing the primary voice

---

1. 1 Corinthians 12:12–27 explains that the church body consists of many parts and that if one part suffers, all parts suffer. At the same time, if one part receives honor then they all rejoice together. "The accountability and role of the local church is vital in the transition of the counselee out of a structured residency program back to the environment of everyday life. In some ways, this kind of accountability and involvement are not extraordinary." Brown, "He's Coming Home: Are You Ready?" 66.

2. Powlison, *The Biblical Counseling Movement*, 101; Adams, *The Big Umbrella*, 109; Priolo, "Sin and Misery," 97; Shaw, *The Heart of Addiction*, 515–20, Kindle; Playfair and George Bryson, *The Useful Lie*, 26.

3. DiClemente, *Addiction and Change*, 3; Shaw, *The Heart of Addiction*, 515–20, Kindle; Playfair and Bryson, *The Useful Lie*, 33; Vaillant, *The Natural History of Alcoholism*, 20; National Institute on Drug Abuse, *Principles of Drug Addiction Treatment: A Research-Based Guide*; Towns and Lambert, *Habits that Handicap*, 177; Towns, *The Work of the Charles B. Towns Hospital*; Abadinsky, *Drug Use and Abuse*; McCarthy, "Early

on soul care for those who refuse to embrace sobriety, the SBC parroted and followed addiction treatment and ideology from the secular world.[4] In some cases, the SBC essentially deferred soul care to outside organizations without resistance.[5] This chapter presents a comprehensive look at ideological shifts, policy changes, attitudes, and approaches to addiction in the United States and the corresponding resolutions which the SBC passed during their annual meetings.

Ideological Shifts in the 1700s

Benjamin Rush predominated the debate for contemporary social or health issues which arose during the late 1700s and early 1800s.[6] Sometimes called the "father of American Psychiatry," he was one of the first medical doctors to speak about alcoholism.[7] In 1782, he wrote a newspaper article titled "Against Spirituous Liquors," which encouraged farmers to stop providing liquor to their day laborers.[8] A few years later, he wrote *An Enquiry into the Effects of Spirituous Liquors upon the Human Body and Their Influence upon the Happiness of Society*. Rush's work had thousands of reprints and represented the most significant early writing on the effects of alcoholism.[9] A mix of morality, science, and psychology influenced Rush's writings on the effects of treatment for those who struggled with alcohol.[10]

The writings of Rush contributed to the ideology behind current addiction treatments. He greatly influenced the early stages of American

Alcoholism Treatment: The Emmanuel Movement and Richard Peabody, 60; Dubiel, *The Road to Fellowship*.

4. *Annual of the 1968 Southern Baptist Convention*:78; Moore, "Is Alcoholism Really a Disease?";. Mersy, "Recognition of Alcohol and Substance Abuse,"1529.

5. *Annual of the 1946 Southern Baptist Convention*:127.

6. North, "Benjamin Rush, MD: Assassin or Beloved Healer?"45; Unger, *Dr. Benjamin Rush: The Founding Father Who Healed a Wounded Nation*; Switzer, "The Political, Philosophical, and Religious Thought of Dr. Benjamin Rush"; Veatch, *Disrupted Dialogue*: 85; Riedman and Green, *Benjamin Rush: Physician, Patriot, Founding Father*; Lassiter and Culbreth, *Theory and Practice of Addiction Counseling*, 28.

7. Unger, *Dr. Benjamin Rush*, 181; Barton, *The History and Influence of the American Psychiatric Association*, 301; Farr, "Benjamin Rush and American Psychiatry," 5; Solomon, *Alcoholism and Clinical Psychiatry*, 57.

8. Rorabaugh, *The Alcoholic Republic*, 40.

9. Katcher, "Benjamin Rush's Educational Campaign against Hard Drinking," 274; White and Crowley, *Slaying the Dragon*, 2.

10. Rush, *An Enquiry into the Effects of Spirituous Liquors*, 29-32.

medicine, and his enormous impact still manifests in society today.[11] While first known as one of the signers of the Declaration of Independence, Rush gained acclaim as one of the foremost teachers of physicians in the late 1700s and early 1800s.[12] Tracts he authored over the years were eventually published as the first American textbook on medicine.[13]

In Rush's *An Enquiry into the Effects of Spirituous Liquors*, he argued that drunkenness, as a disease, is a condition requiring treatment by physicians.[14] The disease concept of alcoholism did not appear as an acceptable medical condition until the 1870s, but Rush's publications signified the first time an American physician proposed a disease model for alcoholism.[15] He associated the consequences of over-consumption of alcohol and a drastic change in personality during inebriation as characteristics of alcoholism. Before its consideration as a biological disease, alcoholism was initially known as a "disease of the will."[16] This concept of "disease of the will" closely mirrors the current approach to substance abuse, the characteristics of which include an intense and uncontrollable desire that leads the addict to consume the mind-altering substance even though knowing the devastating consequences.[17]

While initially mocked by a society where alcohol consumption prevailed, Rush never wavered in his belief that abstinence cured the disease of alcoholism.[18] In the same era, Thomas Trotter agreed with Rush that over-consuming alcohol was truly a disease.[19] At the same time Rush and Trotter affirmed the disease model, the religious movements considered alcohol

11. Unger, *Dr. Benjamin Rush*, 184; Rush, *Medical Inquiries and Observations*; Katcher, "Benjamin Rush's Educational Campaign against Hard Drinking," 274; White and Crowley, *Slaying the Dragon*, 2.

12. King, "Receive the Olive Branch," 352; Strozier, "Benjamin Rush: Revolutionary Doctor," 415.

13. White and Crowley, *Slaying the Dragon*, 2.

14. "I am aware that the efforts of science and humanity, in applying their resources to the cure of a disease induced by an act of vice, will be met with cold reception from many people." Rush, *An Enquiry into the Effects of Spirituous Liquors*, 29.

15. "They seem as if constantly affected by a greater or less degree of stimulation from intoxicating liquors, while the expression of countenance furnishes an infallible proof of mental disease." Rush, *Medical Inquiries and Observations upon the Diseases of the Mind*.

16. Orcutt and Rudy, *Drugs, Alcohol, and Social Problems*, 21.

17. DiClemente, *Addiction and Change*, 3.

18. White and Crowley, *Slaying the Dragon*, 5.

19. Edwards, "Thomas Trotter's Essay on Drunkenness," 1565; White and Crowley, *Slaying the Dragon*, 6.

a problem and a tool of the devil. Together, their separate ideas united to form the foundation for the temperance movement.[20] What Rush proposed almost 200 years ago still echoes through both non-Christian and Christian approaches to combating alcoholism.[21] He believed the solution to alcoholism fell within three realms: medical, metaphysical, and religious.[22] These suggestions closely mirror the doctrine of Alcoholics Anonymous (AA).[23]

The influence of Rush appears in Twelve-step groups due to his emphasis on overcoming shame and guilt.[24] Another widely accepted concept in substance abuse treatment, as promoted by Cognitive Behavioral Therapy, substitutes an undesirable action with a more socially acceptable action.[25] Rush called this substitution process "exciting a counter passion in the mind."[26] He promoted another treatment belief called "going cold turkey," which suggested ceasing the use of substances immediately without weaning off. Rush stated, "Persons who have been addicted to [substances], should abstain from them suddenly and entirely. Taste not, handle not, touch not."[27] While not embraced by AA, substance abuse centers employ the idea of clean eating.[28] Rush wrote that those who maintain a vegan diet would be cured of their alcoholism.[29] While the terminology changed since the Rush's time, reading *An Enquiry into the Effects of Spirituous Liquors upon the Human Body and Their Influence upon the Happiness of Society* aligns with the proposals in AA's *The Big Book*. The suggestions Rush made to treat alcoholism in the 1700s closely compare to substance abuse treatments utilized today.

20. Porter, "The Drinking Man's Disease," 385; White and Crowley, *Slaying the Dragon*, 6.

21. As an interesting side note often left out, Rush did not see a problem with beer, wine, or even opium, as he recommended that these would be suitable replacements for distilled spirits. Katcher, "Benjamin Rush's Educational Campaign against Hard Drinking," 276.

22. Rush, *An Enquiry into the Effects of Spirituous Liquors*, 27.

23. Thombs and Osborn, *Introduction to Addictive Behaviors*, 9.

24. Bill W., *Alcoholics Anonymous*, 197.

25. Ellis, *Reason and Emotion in Psychotherapy*, 77.

26. Rush, *An Enquiry into the Effects of Spirituous Liquors*, 31.

27. Rush, *An Enquiry into the Effects of Spirituous Liquors*, 36.

28. "The reason that we had organic and clean eating options was due to the amount of damage that addicts did to their body." Tim P.

29. "A diet, consisting wholly of vegetables, cured a physician in Maryland of drunkenness probably by lessening that thirst, which is always more or less excited by animal food." Rush, *An Enquiry into the Effects of Spirituous Liquors*, 35.

Historical Shifts in Addiction Ideology and Treatment

The ideology behind alcoholism treatment shifted many times since Rush first proposed alcoholism was a disease.[30] As these shifts occurred, the main difference which emerged removed Rush's advocacy for religion and the need for the church's role in substance abuse treatment. The perspective on alcoholism transitioned from a vice or moral shortcoming to solely a disease. Over the last two centuries, both the church and society readily accepted the science behind the disease model, despite having few scientific studies to support the claim.[31] The acceptance of the disease model, despite the lack of scientific support, impacted the view that addiction should be seen as a disease, not a sin.

Ideological Shifts in the 1800s

Lyman Beecher preached a sermon series in 1825 titled "Six Sermons on Intemperance" in which he described those who struggle with alcohol consumption as "addicted to sin."[32] He commented on those with an "insatiable desire to drink" and warned of signs characterizing individuals addicted to distilled spirits.[33] Beecher's sermon represents one of the first documented occasions of a minister speaking about the dangers of "addiction." A few years later in 1840, Samuel Woodward, the first doctor to suggest asylums for drunkards, called for the creation of what he termed "inebriate asylums."[34] One of the first inebriate homes was the New York

---

30. "I am aware that the efforts of science and humanity, in applying their resources to the cure of a disease induced by a vice, will be met with a cold reception from many people." Rush, *An Enquiry into the Effects of Spirituous Liquors*, 29.

31. Peele, *Diseasing of America: How*, 774, Kindle; Heather, "Challenging the Brain Disease Model of Addiction," 249; Tekin, "Brain Mechanisms and the Disease Model of Addiction," 401; Lewis, "Brain Change in Addiction as Learning, Not Disease," 1552; Schaler, Addiction Is a Choice, 16; Heather, "Q: Is Addiction a Brain Disease or a Moral Failing? A: Neither," 115–117; Pickard, Ahmed, and Foddy, "Alternative Models of Addiction,"; Satel and Lilienfeld, "Addiction and the Brain-Disease Fallacy."

32. Beecher, *Six Sermons on Intemperance*, 25. Beecher was a Presbyterian minister who co-founded of the American Temperance Society. He began his ministry in Long Island and retired in Brooklyn.

33. Beecher, *Six Sermons on Intemperance*, 26.

34. Meil and Ruby, *Recent Advances in Drug Addiction Research*, 145; White and Crowley, *Slaying the Dragon*, 32; Galanter, *Recent Developments in Alcoholism*, 145;. Diehl, *Wasted*, 49; Warsh, *Drink in Canada*, 92; White and Crowley, *Drunkard's Refuge*, 107; Hall and Applebaum, "The Origins of Commitment for Substance Abuse in the United States," 33.

Christian Home for Intemperate Men, and religious organizations financially supported similar facilities.[35] With the establishment of inebriate homes, the thought behind the early forms of treatment still split between seeing addiction as a medical issue or a moral issue.[36]

In the 1840s, a group called the Washingtonians, America's first society of recovered alcoholics, spoke not of alcoholism but of drunkenness and referred to themselves as confirmed drinkers, drunkards, hard cases, inveterate cases, sots, tipplers, and inebriates.[37] The formation of The Washingtonian Society was organized by and for those considered as the "hard cases."[38] The Washingtonian Society grew to a membership of more than 600,000 individuals before declining in the mid-1840s.[39] A new organization called the Fraternal Temperance Society, whose primary goal was to help reform men, contributed to The Washingtonian Society's decline.[40]

Swedish doctor Magnus Huss first used the word "alcoholism" in 1849 in his work *Alcoholismus Chronicus* to describe those who struggled with "chronic alcohol intoxication."[41] Huss distinguished alcoholics as those with severe physical ailments and disrupted social functioning.[42] Others coined various terms to describe alcoholism: barrel fever, intemperance, habitual drunkenness, dipsomania, liquor habit, and inebriety.[43]

In the late 1800s, Jerry McAuley's Water Street Mission located in New York City operated as one of the first faith-based organizations seeking to

---

35. White and Crowley, *Slaying the Dragon*, 35; Bunting, *Hope for the Victims*, 7.

36. White and Crowley, *Slaying the Dragon*, 52.

37. Acker and Tracy, *Altering American Consciousness*, 34; White and Crowley, *Slaying the Dragon*, xvii.

38. White and Crowley, *Slaying the Dragon*, 12.

39. *Proceedings and Address of the Washingtonian Mass Convention: Held in the City of Boston, at Tremont Temple, Thursday May 29, 1845*; Meil and Ruby, *Recent Advances in Drug Addiction Research and Clinical Applications*; Galanter, *Recent Developments in Alcoholism*, 145; Diehl, *Wasted*, 49; Warsh, *Drink in Canada*, 92; White and Crowley, *Drunkard's Refuge*, 107; Hall and Applebaum, "The Origins of Commitment for Substance Abuse in the United States," 33.

40. Woolley, *Temperance Progress of the Century*, 99; Meil and Ruby, *Recent Advances in Drug Addiction Research and Clinical Applications*; Galanter, *Recent Developments in Alcoholism*, 145.

41. Huss and von dem Busch, *Chronische Alkoholskrankheit*, 11; Winslow, *Journal of Psychological Medicine and Mental Pathology*, 128.

42. Lesch, "Diagnosis of Chronic Alcoholism: Classificatory Problems," 88.

43. Levine, "The Vocabulary of Drunkenness," 1039.

Historical Shifts in Addiction Ideology and Treatment

help addicts and alcoholics.[44] McAuley's approach occurred during a rare and short-lived time when secular ideologies were not at the forefront of treatment and faith-based organizations were the primary helpers for those who struggled with alcoholism. In the mid-to-late 1800s, various religious organizations rose to the forefront to treat those who struggled with alcoholism:

> The image of former drunkards standing at religious revivals of the 1850s and 1860s proclaiming that God had taken away their appetite for alcohol was a common one. These religious movements were also part of a broader network of lodges, conventions, tent meetings, missions and informal helping services within which the newly reformed drunkard could become enmeshed.[45]

While Rush proposed that the rehabilitation process required religious influence, individuals such as Jerry McAuley believed that Christianity itself was sufficient on its own to treat alcoholism without medical intervention.[46]

Using his own testimony and pleas for people to donate to his Water Street Mission, McAuley housed 5,144 men and served 26,262 meals in the first year of the mission's opening.[47] The small staff included McAuley, his wife Maria, and a janitor, and each decided to treat those who sought help with respect instead of despising them as derelicts and prostitutes.[48] During this time, Evangelical Protestantism and their missionary societies established most of the urban missions.[49] The Water Street Mission focused on meeting the primary physical needs of those who needed help by first providing shelter and food.[50] The Sunday newspaper featured an advertisement stating, "Everyone welcome, especially drunkards."[51] While other religious organizations aided drunks, thieves, and prostitutes in some

---

44. White and Crowley, *Slaying the Dragon*, 98–101.
45. White and Crowley, *Slaying the Dragon*, 97.
46. Offord, *Jerry McCauley*, 28.
47. Offord, *Jerry McCauley*, 52; White and Crowley, *Slaying the Dragon*, 99.
48. White and Crowley, *Slaying the Dragon*, 99.
49. Boyer, *Urban Masses and Moral Order in America*, 1808.
50. McAuley said, "I felt for those poor hungry men. Some of them had probably not tasted a bit of food for two and three days; they had no money to help themselves, and when they came on Saturday night we usually kept them over Sunday, but on this night we were broke." Offord, *Jerry McAuley*, 52.
51. White and Crowley, *Drunkard's Refuge*, 11; Bonner, *Jerry McAuley and His Mission Front Cover*, 87.

manner, the Water Street Mission received widespread recognition for their intentional outreach to social misfits.[52]

Jerry McAuley's approach to his Mission reflects one of the outliers to how the church addressed substance abuse. He focused his ministry on God and the Scripture, not psychology or other unbiblical influences. The organization provided for basic needs, evangelized, led alcoholics to the Lord, and taught addicts how to live a life pleasing to God. McAuley declared, "Multitudes of poor sinful ones come in during the day for help and counsel. We point them to Jesus, the great physician and helper of body and soul, and many a one has it been our pleasure to lead to the foundation open for sin and uncleanness."[53] The meetings at Water Street typified prayer gatherings mirroring a church revival. Signs for the meetings advertised, "Prayer meeting here this afternoon at three o'clock."[54] The format of these meetings comprised testimonies of God's grace, a message by a pastor, and then a time for pastors to pray over those seeking payer. Unfortunately, McAuley died a few years after he started the Water Street Mission, causing the Mission's demise. The Mission's vacancy led to a rise in for-profit institutions, exemplifying a normative pattern for other for-profit organizations to replace non-profit organization.[55]

In the mid-to-late 1870s, inebriate asylums and homes began to close and were replaced with drunk tanks, foul wards and cells of police stations and public hospitals, and insane asylums wards.[56] Private institutions called "jag farms," "jitter joints," or "dip shops" received the wealthy sent to them.[57] A progression occurred in 1880 with one of the first business-oriented treatment options, the Keeley Institute. From 1880–1920, the Keeley Institute launched more than 200 facilities that helped addicts and alcoholics.[58] Leslie E. Keeley worked as a medical doctor who approached substance abuse treatment as a biological disease.[59] The Keeley Institute

---

52. Bonner, *Jerry McAuley and His Mission Front Cover*, 98.

53. Hatch, *Jerry McCauley*, 46.

54. Hatch, *Jerry McCauley*, 86.

55. Offord, *Jerry McCauley*, xiii.

56. Kisacky, *Rise of the Modern Hospital*, 76; Turner, *History of the First Inebriate Asylum*, 304; Galanter, *Recent Developments in Alcoholism*, 162.

57. Hidalgo, *What the Hell Is Behavioral Health*, 35.

58. Hidalgo, *What the Hell Is Behavioral Health*, 31.

59. White and Crowley, *Slaying the Dragon*, 71; Keeley, *The Non-Heredity of Inebriety*, 192;. Hickman, "Keeping Secrets: Leslie E. Keeley," 1739.

served as the precursor to Drug and Alcohol Treatment Centers known today.

Keeley treatment teams consisted of medical doctors who supervised the alcoholic and administered what Keeley called the "Double Chloride of Gold" or "The Keeley Gold Cure injections." The concoction's exact ingredients included alcohol, strychnine, ginger, willow bark, aloe, opium, coca (cocaine), morphine, ammonia, atropine, belladonna, and hyoscine.[60] Despite his reputation as a fraud in most medical circles, Keeley's detailed patient records and emphasis for his staff to perform diligent clinical examinations provided an air of legitimacy.[61] At the time of his death, the Keeley Institute profited $1.6 million between 1892 and 1894.[62]

Up until this point, the SBC neglected to address the subject of addictions. Finally, in 1886, the SBC passed a resolution at its annual convention protesting the sale and manufacturing of alcohol. This resolution demonstrates the first time the SBC addressed substance abuse addictions.[63] In 1896, the SBC took its firmest stance against addiction. The convention not only viewed the sale and manufacture of alcohol as unacceptable, the SBC now saw participation in these activities as grounds for removal from church membership.[64] This position marked the beginning of the SBC's

---

60. "The Keeley 'Gold Cure' For Inebriety," 85; Lender and Martin, *Drinking in America*, 122–23.

61. Warsh, "Adventures in Maritime Quackery," 109.

62. Blocker, Fahey, and Tyrrell, *Alcohol and Temperance in Modern History*, 347. In today's economy, this amount equates to $46 million.

63. "WHEREAS, The manufacture and sale of intoxicating liquors as a beverage, in the opinion of this Convention, are opposed to the best interests of society and government, and the progress of our holy religion, and believing that all honorable means should be employed for their suppression, therefore be it
RESOLVED, That we, as members of the Southern Baptist Convention, do most solemnly protest against its manufacture and sale, and pledge our influence in the exercise of our rights as citizens of this free country, socially, morally, religiously and in all other proper ways, to work for its speedy overthrow, and to this end we invoke the aid and blessing of Almighty God." *Annual of the 1886 Southern Baptist Convention*, 33.

64. "Furthermore, we announce it as the sense of this body that no person should be retained in the fellowship of a Baptist church who engages in the manufacture or sale of alcoholic liquors, either at wholesale or retail, who invests his money in the manufacture or sale of alcoholic liquors, or who rents his property to be used for distilleries, wholesale liquor houses, or saloons. Nor do we believe that any church should retain in its fellowship any member who drinks intoxicating liquors as a beverage, or visits saloons or drinking places for the purpose of such indulgence." *Annual of the 1896 Southern Baptist Convention*, 45.

approach to substance abuse, forming the basis for seventy future resolutions, sixty-seven of which stood against the advertisement, distribution, and sale of alcohol.

Ideological Shifts in the 1900s

In 1906, the Emmanuel Clinic featured lay therapy as a treatment option for alcoholism. Some of the most well-known lay therapists of the time originated from the clinic.[65] Courtenay Baylor influenced Richard Peabody, who in turn impacted Francis T. Chambers Jr., each a prominent lay therapist at the time.[66] Their influence on alcohol treatment lasted for decades, as they introduced the concept that alcoholics could stop drinking with therapy.[67]

Psychoanalysis also played a role in shaping addiction treatment. In 1908, Karl Abraham, who was a student of Sigmund Freud, proposed that drinking was the sexual activity of those who struggled with homosexuality.[68] He argued that "every drinking bout is tinged with homosexuality" and that men drink to replace "vanishing procreative power."[69] While Abraham wrote on the subject as one of the first psychoanalysts, Sigmund Freud also eventually described alcoholism as a manifestation of repressed homosexuality.[70] Considering Freud proposed using cocaine to help those suffering from alcoholism, this treatment option for alcoholism severely damaged his credibility.[71] The psychoanalytic views substance abuse as a symptom of a personality disorder, psychosis, or neurotic conflict, rather than a primary disease.[72] Treatment for substance abuse varied between

---

65. Coombs, *Addiction Counseling Review*, 88; Sanford Gifford, *The Emmanuel Movement*, 142.

66. Baylor, *Remaking a Man: One Successful Method of Mental Refitting*; Peabody, *The Common Sense of Drinking*; Strecker and Chambers, *Alcohol: One Man's Meat*.

67. McCarthy, "Early Alcoholism Treatment," 60; Dubiel, *The Road to Fellowship*.

68.. Levin, *Introduction to Alcoholism Counseling: A Bio-Psycho-Social Approach*, 185.

69. Abraham, "The Psychological Relations between Alcoholism and Sexuality," 233.

70. Israelstam and Lambert, "Homosexuality as a Cause of Alcoholism: A Historical Review," 1087.

71. Dasgupta and Langman, *Pharmacogenomics of Alcohol*, 137; Loose, *The Subject of Addiction*, 7.

72. Bratter and Forrest, *Alcoholism and Substance Abuse*, 307; White and Crowley,

therapists, but the foundation for treatment usually involved psychotherapy to bring out unconscious motivations to the individuals' conscious level.[73]

After the passage of The Harrison Tax Act, which brought cocaine and opiates under the control of the federal government in 1914, physicians became gatekeepers for accessing these narcotics.[74] Additionally, the United States government enacted the Eighteenth Amendment in 1919, which prohibited the sale, manufacture, and transportation of intoxicating liquors.[75] A crackdown on all mind-altering substances started to take place nationwide.

Another significant change occurred in 1919 when Webb vs. the United States, a decision rendered by the Supreme Court, declared physicians subject to indictment if they kept their patients on opiates or cocaine.[76] Between 1919 and 1935, the Drug Enforcement Administration cited 25,000 doctors for violations of the Harrison Act.[77]

With so many new laws prohibiting drugs and alcohol, the 1920s mostly saw an increase in the closings of private addiction cure institutes, inebriate asylums, and inebriate homes between 1920 and 1925.[78] With Prohibition in place, the SBC passed a resolution in 1921 advocating for harsher prison sentences for individuals convicted of bootlegging moonshine.[79] Despite the changes in laws, the use of drugs and alcohol remained a staple of life in the United States. In 1933, the Twenty-First Amendment

---

Slaying the Dragon, 132.

73. Lobdell, *This Strange Illness*, 159.

74. Known as Harrison Narcotic Law.

75. Levy, Karst, and Winkler, *Encyclopedia of the American Constitution*; Olson and Gerstein, *Alcohol in America: Taking Action to Prevent Abuse*, 1–2.

76. Webb v. United States.

77. Libby, "Treating Doctors as Drug Dealers," 515.

78. Baumohl, "Inebriate Institutions in North America, 1840–1920," 1198; Corwin, "Institutional Facilities for the Treatment of Alcoholism," 19.

79. "The Southern Baptist Convention composed of over five thousand messengers representing a constituency of more than three million white Baptists in Convention assembled at Chattanooga, Tenn., May 16, 1921, memorialize the United States Government to wipe out 'moonshining' and 'bootlegging' in the United States of America. The illegal manufacture of 'whitelightning' decreases the efficiency and available supply of labor, impairs health and even kills, lowers morals, leads to violation of law and to destruction of life and property. We doubt whether this can be done unless the penalty is made more drastic and prison sentence made mandatory instead of being left optional with the judges." *Annual of the 1921 Southern Baptist Convention*, 86.

repealed Prohibition.[80] With the repeal of Prohibition in effect, the SBC in 1935 encouraged its Sunday School teachers, pastors, and other leaders to continue educating the congregations about the dangers of alcohol. The SBC continued to advocate for the government to legislate alcohol.[81]

Two significant events happened in 1935 with regard to addiction treatment. First, the US Public Health Prison Hospital (narcotics farm) opened in Lexington, Kentucky.[82] The narcotics farm initiative represented the start of the federal government taking an active role in addiction treatment and research.[83] As for the second and most important event, Bill W. and Dr. Bob founded AA.[84] The medicalization of addiction treatment and pushing of the disease model started to see increased effort.

A few years later, in 1943, the Yale Center of Alcohol created an important research program called the Summer School of Alcohol Studies and the Yale Plan Outpatient Clinics. One of the major influencers involved with the program was E. M. Jellinek, who later wrote *The Disease Concept of Alcoholism*.[85]

A few significant events shaped addiction ideology in the 1950s. In 1952, the American Medical Association (AMA) first defined alcoholism.[86] Alcoholism fell under the classification of a Sociopathic Personality Disturbance with the release of the *Diagnostic and Statistical Manual of*

---

80. US Constitution, amend. 21.

81. "2. That we urge upon our pastors, churches, our schools and colleges, our Sunday School Board and all other teaching and educational agencies connected with our denominational life, that they be constant and diligent in setting forth the facts as to the evil effects of alcohol in all forms and urging upon our people the necessity for total abstinence from all alcoholic drinks as the wise and proper course for the individual.

That we reiterate our condemnation of the liquor license policy of governments, county, state and federal, as an utterly unjustifiable prevision and prostitution of governmental power by which the government enters into partnership with vice and crime through the short-sighted hope of financial gain only in the end to suffer great financial loss and to degrade the morals of its citizens and to produce an increasing caravan of crime." *Annual of the 1935 Southern Baptist Convention*, 71.

82. Campbell, Olsen, and Walden, *The Narcotic Farm*, 15.

83. Campbell, Olsen, and Walden, *The Narcotic Farm*, 15; Campbell, *Discovering Addiction*, 54.

84. Bill W., *Alcoholics Anonymous*. An extensive review of AA will take place in the following chapter.

85. Ward, "Re-Introducing Bunky at 125," 376.

86. Smith, "The Evolution of Addiction Medicine as a Medical Specialty," 900.

Mental Disorders (DSM).[87] The biggest ideological shift in regard to addiction occurred in 1956 when the AMA declared alcoholism a disease.[88] They asserted, "Hospitals should be urged to consider admission of such patients with a diagnosis of alcoholism based upon the condition of the individual patient, rather than a general objection to all such patients."[89] Finally, the American Hospital Association passed a 1957 resolution preventing discrimination against addicts and alcoholics.[90]

After the redefinition of addictions in the 1950s, the 1960s saw corresponding changes in how to treat addiction as a disease. In 1961, the AMA and American Bar Association (ABA) released the book *Drug Addiction: Crime or Disease*. The findings called for community-based programs to help with addictions.[91] In response, funding for addiction and alcohol counseling became part of federal legislation between 1963 and 1966. This counseling program received funding in conjunction with anti-poverty programs, mental health centers, and criminal justice diversion programs. As more funds became available, psychiatrists, paraprofessionals, and psychologists battled over who should receive the monies to combat alcoholism.[92]

As one of the most wide-reaching changes which occurred with redefining addiction as a disease, insurance companies began paying insurance claims on alcohol treatments at the same level as other diseases. The influx of money into the treatment industry led to a large expansion of hospital-based and private treatment programs.[93] In 1966, President Lyndon Johnson even went so far as to appoint the first National Advisory Committee on Alcoholism, stating, "The alcoholic suffers from a disease which will

---

87. *Diagnostic and Statistical Manual of Mental Disorders: DSM-I*, 7. Chapter four will examine the *DSM* and its influence on the medicalization of addictions.

88. Mersy, "Recognition of Alcohol and Substance Abuse," 1529. Moore wrote, "In l956, the American Medical Association officially said alcoholism met three standard criteria for being declared a disease. First, it had an identifiable set of symptoms. Second, it followed a predictable and malignant progression if not treated, and third, it did respond to treatment. What this meant was that the insurance industry agreed to pay for treatment, just as if you came down with diabetes." Moore, "Is Alcoholism Really a Disease?"

89. Smith, "The Evolution of Addiction Medicine as a Medical Specialty," 900.

90. Metlay, "Federalizing Medical Campaigns against Alcoholism and Drug Abuse," 155.

91. Anonymous, *Drug Addiction: Crime or Disease? Interim and Final Reports*.

92. Harwood and Gerstein, *Treating Drug Problems*, 64.

93. Barry, Huskamp, and Goldman, "A Political History of Federal Mental Health and Addiction Insurance Parity," 404.

yield eventually to scientific research and adequate treatment."[94] The formation of the advisory committee initiated the increase of federal funding to support local addiction services with the creation of the Narcotic Addict Rehabilitation Act (NARA).[95]

Several interesting occurrences began in the late 1960s, the first of which occurred in 1967 when the AMA released a resolution that identified alcoholism as a "complex disease that merits the serious concern of all members of the health professions."[96] The following year, the SBC passed a resolution labeling alcoholism as a mental health issue.[97] Additionally, in 1968, the Federal Appeals Court made the decision in Powel vs. Texas supporting the disease concept of alcoholism.[98]

With more money diverted to address addiction, the Hughes Act, also known as the "Comprehensive Alcohol Abuse and Alcoholism Prevention Treatment and Rehabilitation Act," passed in 1970. This Act signified the "single piece of legislation that birthed today's system of addiction treatment."[99] The Hughes Act created the National Institute on Alcohol Abuse and Alcoholism (NIAAA).[100] Prominent supporters who testified before Congress included Bill W. and Marty Mann of AA[101]

A few months later, *The Annals of Internal Medicine* and *The American Journal of Psychiatry* published the "Criteria for the Diagnosis of

94. Travis, *The Language of the Heart*, 45.

95. Travis, *The Language of the Heart*, 45; Stolberg, "Narcotic Addict Rehabilitation Act."

96. Coombs, *Addiction Counseling Review*, 96.

97. "WHEREAS, The federal government has spent vast sums of money for the study of the effects of smoking on health, and
WHEREAS, Legislation has been passed requiring cigarette manufacturers to warn of the health hazards of their product,
Therefore be it RESOLVED, That we express gratitude to our government for its actions attempting to protect the health of American citizens, and
Be it further RESOLVED, That we request the Surgeon General of the United States to undertake a similar effort on the effect of alcoholic beverages on physical and mental health." *Annual of the 1968 Southern Baptist Convention*, 78.

98. Barry, Huskamp, and Goldman, "A Political History of Federal Mental Health," 404. Powell, previously convicted of public intoxication, should not have been pronounced guilty due to his chronic alcoholism. The Supreme Court ruled against Texas for criminalizing his alcoholism since it was considered a disease.

99. White and Crowley, *Slaying the Dragon*, 377.

100. *Broadening the Base of Treatment for Alcohol Problems*, 406.

101. Kurtz, "Alcoholics Anonymous and the Disease Concept of Alcoholism," 14; White and Crowley, *Slaying the Dragon*, 377.

Alcoholism."[102] The National States Conference of Commissioners on Uniform State Laws introduced the Uniform Alcoholism and Intoxication Act.[103] The act led to the decriminalization of public drunkenness but mandated treatment for skid row alcoholics.[104] The act also prompted the beginning of detoxification centers across the United States.[105] The American Public Health Association adopted Policy 7121 which described alcoholism a treatable illness.[106] Continuing to follow the public model rather than lead in the ministry to addicts, the SBC passed a resolution in 1972 urging politicians to stop providing "simplistic solutions" for the complex issues surrounding alcoholism and drug addiction.[107]

Another shift in how to treat addiction occurred in the 1980s. President Ronald Reagan's Zero Tolerance Policy significantly reduced the federal government's support for drug rehabilitation treatment.[108] This missing support led to a corresponding rise in incarcerations for drug offenses. The massive influx of drug-addicted offenders in the 1980s introduced the concept of a drug court and the need for prison facilities to offer treatment in the 1990s.[109] Due to less government options for treatment, the California Society of Addiction Medicine offered the first certification specializing in

---

102. Seixas, "The NCA Criteria for the Diagnosis of Alcoholism—Intent, Use, and Practicality," 71.

103. . Kurtz and Regier, "The Uniform Alcoholism and Intoxication Treatment Act," 1428.

104. Pratt, "A Mandatory Treatment Program for Skid Row Alcoholics," 167; s McCarty, "Alcoholism, Drug Abuse, and the Homeless," 1141; Kurtz and Regier, "Policy Lessons of the Uniform Act: A Response to Comments," 382–83.

105. McCarty, "Detoxification Centers: Who's in the Revolving Door?" 245; Kurtz and Regier, "The Uniform Alcoholism and Intoxication Treatment Act," 1428.

106. American Public Health Association, "Substance Abuse as a Public Health Problem,"

107. "WHEREAS, Grave moral issues of our time, such as family breakdown, racism, war, poverty, pollution, violence, injustice, crime, gambling, taxation, consumer exploitation, political corruption, welfare reform, and addiction to alcohol and other drugs are all complex issues, the proper facing of which demand personal evangelism, political involvement, and the best judgment of all. . . . BE IT FURTHER RESOLVED, That we plead with politicians to refrain from offering simplistic solutions for complex problems." *Annual of the 1972 Southern Baptist Convention*, 86.

108. Marion and Oliver, *Drugs in American Society*, 336; Fisher and Roget, *Encyclopedia of Substance Abuse Prevention*, 998.

109. Clinton, *The Early Drug Courts Case Studies in Judicial Innovation*, ix–x.

addiction treatment in California in 1983.[110] The private sector of addiction treatment now had its first licensed counselors to help combat addiction.

By the mid-1980s, the emergence of so-called "crack babies pushed crack cocaine to the forefront of the American consciousness."[111] The crack baby tragedy led to an increase of drug treatment options for women, especially those whose children entered Child Protective Services (CPS).[112] With the prominence of crack and powder cocaine, G. A. Marlatt introduced the need for relapse prevention, which became a new innovation to addiction treatment.[113] Drug Treatment Centers started to focus on "special populations:" homosexuals, the elderly, women, and adolescents.[114] The centers coined the new term "dual diagnosis," or co-occurring disorders, for those with addictions.[115] The disorders under this classification included: anxiety, depression, bi-polar disorder, ADHD, borderline personality disorder, eating disorders, schizophrenia, post-traumatic stress disorder, and obsessive compulsive disorder.[116] This shift culminated from the medicalization of addiction and the disease model and still impacts addiction treatment today.

President Reagan declared a "War on Drugs" in 1987. Instead of rehabilitation or institutionalization, a push toward incarceration took place.[117] While the federal government pushed policy shifts against treating addicts, the AMA presented a medical model calling substance abuse a disease in

---

110. El-Guebaly and Violato, "The International Certification of Addiction Medicine," 78.

111. Humphries, *Crack Mothers*, 1; Kusserow, *Crack Babies*, 9.

112. Logan, "The Wrong Race, Committing Crime, Doing Drugs," 115; Schatz and Mallea, *Fetal Alcohol Syndrome*.

113. Cooper, *The Emergence of Crack Cocaine*, 48; Marlatt and George, "Relapse Prevention," 261; *Prevention and Treatment of Alcohol Problems: Research Opportunities*, 184; Washton, *Cocaine Addiction*. Mackay and Marlatt proposed, "Within this model, relapse is not automatically defined as a treatment failure but as an opportunity for intervention and the interruption of the relapse process. Determinants and predictors of relapse are discussed, and assessment and intervention strategies provided." Mackay and Marlatt, "Maintaining Sobriety: Stopping Is Starting," 1257.

114. De Leon, *Community as Method*, 3.

115. "The co-occurrence of one or more psychiatric disorders related to substance abuse or dependence." Stohler and Wulf, *Dual Diagnosis*, 105.

116. Doweiko and Evans, *Concepts of Chemical Dependency*, 316.

117. Mallea, *War on Drugs: A Failed Experiment*, 35.

the *DSM-III-R*, arguing for this model as the best form of treatment for addicts.[118]

In the 1990s, the Americans with Disabilities Act (ADA) passed in Congress, classifying addiction as a disability and thus providing job protection for drug addicts and alcoholics in the private sector.[119] The new law prevented employers from discriminating against employees with substance abuse problems. The ADA protects addicts as long as they are not currently under the influence of illegal drugs.[120] The U.S. Food and Drug Administration (FDA) approved naltrexone, otherwise known as Antabuse, as a prescription treatment for alcoholism.[121] The use of pharmaceutical drugs as part of the solution for addiction solidified the ideology that substance abuse is a disease. In 1997, the SBC passed a resolution specifically addressing drug abuse for the first time. The resolution encouraged church leaders and other SBC ministries to minister specifically to those with drugs problems.[122]

Ideological Shifts in the 2000s

A significant shift in addiction as a medical issue occurred when the FDA approved buprenorphine (Suboxone) as a pharmacotherapy option for opiate addiction in 2002.[123] The medical realm now operated with the ability to fully treat addictions. Medication could now replace personal care for addicts.[124] As of 2022, the SBC's 2006 resolution remains the last time the SBC addressed alcohol in any resolutions.[125]

---

118. Robinson and Adinoff, "The Classification of Substance Use Disorders," 12.

119. Harrison and Gilbert, *The Americans with Disabilities Act Handbook*.

120. Perritt, *Americans with Disabilities Act Handbook* 288.

121. Cummings, *Progress in Neurotherapeutics and Neuropsychopharmacology*, 260.

122. "RESOLVED, That we commend organizations which treat alcohol related problems as well as those organizations which promote prevention, using scripturally based principles." *Annual of the 1997 Southern Baptist Convention*, 98.

123. Jones, "Practical Consideration for the Clinical Use of Buprenorphine," 4.

124. Badgaiyan, "Correction: Do We Really Need to Continue Pharmacotherapy for Opioid Use Disorder (OUD) Indefinitely?"

125. "That we commend organizations and ministries that treat alcohol-related problems from a biblical perspective and promote abstinence and encourage local churches to begin and/or support such biblically-based ministries." *Annual of the 2006 Southern Baptist Convention*, 108–09.

From Sin to Disease

The Mental Health Parity and Addiction Equity Act (MHPAEA) was signed into law in 2008. The Act requires health plans and insurance companies to offer benefits for addicts seeking medical care.[126] Two years later, President Barak Obama's signed his signature legislation: The Affordable Care Act (ACA).[127] The ACA, otherwise known as Obamacare, radically expanded and changed how to treat addiction. An expansion of coverage criteria forced all insurance plans offered through state insurance marketplaces to include mental health services, including substance abuse treatment.[128]

One of the negative consequences of Obamacare manifested as an increase in the use of painkillers.[129] In a shift away from always using medication to combat problems, the AMA petitioned that pain be dropped as the fifth vital sign.[130] This change freed doctors from requiring a narcotic to treat patients who complained about experiencing pain. With the opiate epidemic killing tens of thousands every year, President Donald Trump signed the Support for Patients and Communities Act in 2018.[131] The Act provided provisions to improve pain management options and to eliminate fraud occurring via kickbacks given to those referring clients to treatment centers and sober livings.[132] The most essential provisions increased access to evidence-based programs and aftercare, especially for children, pregnant women, and those in rural areas.[133]

---

126. Centers for Medicare & Medicaid Services, "The Mental Health Parity and Addiction Equity Act (MHPAEA)."

127. Healthcare.gov, "Affordable Care Act (ACA)."

128. Barry and Huskamp, "Moving beyond Parity," 973.

129. Saloner, "The Affordable Care Act in the Heart of the Opioid Crisis," 633.

130. Bonnie, Ford, and Phillips, *Pain Management and the Opioid Epidemic*.

131. US Congress, SUPPORT for Patients and Communities Act, 115–78.

132. SUPPORT for Patients and Communities Act: Sec. 8122. The bill amends the federal criminal code to make it a crime to knowingly and willfully solicit, receive pay, or offer payment for referrals to a recovery home, clinical treatment facility, or laboratory, subject to limitations.

133. SUPPORT for Patients and Communities Act: Sec. 7121. The bill also requires SAMHSA to award grants to establish or operate at least 10 comprehensive opioid recovery centers across the country. Such centers must conduct outreach and provide specified treatment and recovery services, including approved drug treatments (e.g., methadone), counseling, residential rehabilitation, and job-placement assistance (Sec. 7151). SAMHSA must award grants to support recovery community organizations (nonprofit organizations that are wholly or principally governed by individuals in recovery for substance-use disorders) (Sec. 8062). The bill allows the Appalachian Regional

Conclusion

Since its inception, the SBC passed seventy resolutions in regard to mind-altering substances (alcohol or drugs), sixty-five of which primarily concerned the manufacture, distribution, and advertisement of these substances. Upon examining these resolutions, a clear pattern emerged: Anytime a policy shift occurred within the government or medical field, the SBC issued a response mimicking the current culture. At no time did a resolution pass within the SBC as a leader in the fight against the abuse of mind-altering substances. In fact, since 2006, the SBC remained silent and neglected to warn of the dangers of alcohol.

A timeline detailing all the shifts in the definition and treatment of substance abuse highlights how the SBC, through its resolutions, took its lead from the culture. Instead of engaging the culture to influence how to address and treat addiction, the SBC played a negligible role.

Commission to support projects and activities addressing drug abuse, such as infrastructure development for telemedicine (Sec. 8081). HHS must develop guidance for states on ways to support family-focused residential treatment programs (substance-use disorder treatment programs for pregnant and postpartum women, as well as parents and guardians, which allow their children to remain with them during treatment).

Chapter 3

Alcoholics Anonymous and Its Influence on the Church

Introduction

THE HISTORICAL SURVEY OF the ideological shifts toward addiction revealed that the SBC and its churches failed to lead in combating substance abuse. One of the primary driving forces which influenced the church to support the disease model came from Alcoholics Anonymous (AA).[1] AA actively recruited and influenced pastors and church leaders to support their model of helping those with addiction problems. Part of the literature AA published specifically encouraged the clergy to familiarize themselves with the AA program.[2] The suggestions AA made since its inception caused churches to embrace the Twelve Steps as a foundational part of their

---

1. Jellinek, *The Disease Concept of Alcoholism*, 160; Playfair and Bryson, *The Useful Lie*, 28.

In a recent phone conversation with a recovery pastor after a mutual friend committed suicide, the pastor said, "It's too bad his disease took his life." Adherents of the disease model firmly believe that the alcoholics or addicts suffer from a disease that will be with them for the rest of their lives.

2. "There are several things that members of the clergy can do to familiarize themselves with the AA program—1: Attend some open AA meetings. 2: Become acquainted with AA literature—such as the books *Alcoholics Anonymous*, *Twelve STEPS and Twelve Traditions*, and *AA Comes of Age*; the booklets *Living Sober* and *Came to Believe*; and some of the pamphlets listed on the inside back cover. 3: Recognize the spiritual (though nondenominational) aspects of the AA program. 4: Call upon AA for help when the situation warrants it. 5: Open their doors to AA meetings." Anonymous, *Members of the Clergy Ask*, 18.

ministries.³ Apparently, some of the SBC churches' naivete regarding the foundations of AA resulted in an unbiblical organization influencing church members on the topic of addiction.⁴

Intentionally reaching out to the clergy remained at the forefront of AA since its inception.⁵ Even AA publications discussed the prevalence of the infiltration of the disease model into the church: "After centuries of treating alcoholism as a moral weakness, most present-day medical opinion considers alcoholism a disease which, like diabetes, can be arrested but not cured. Many of the clergy, too, now accept alcoholism as sickness and not sin."⁶ What was once traditionally accepted as a spiritual and moral issue transformed into what the recovery field deemed a medical issue.⁷ Since the shift of redefining the underlying cause of addiction, churches have been less likely to address the problem and have deferred to those in the medical realm.⁸ The information in this chapter will provide a historical purview of AA. Importantly, AA made an unmistakable impact on how the SBC and its churches help addicts, rendering significant damage.

---

3. A look at a faith-based organization that combine the Bible and the 12 Steps will take place later in the chapter.

4. *Annual of the 2006 Southern Baptist Convention,* 108–09.

5. "The contacts of the clergymen with Alcoholics Anonymous groups, and their acquaintances with the spiritual outlook and the striking success of that fellowship, have contributed to the changes in denominational attitudes." Jellinek, *The Disease Concept of Alcoholism,* 171.

6. Anonymous, *Al-Anon Family Groups,*8.

7. Dr. W. W. Bauer held a high position within the AMA. He said the following in July 1955 at the annual AA Convention in St. Louis about alcoholism: "Today we know that cancer is a misfortune, and we are beginning now to realize that we must adopt the same attitude toward mental and emotional illness that we have slowly and painfully adopted toward tuberculosis and cancer. Illness of the emotions is no more something to be ashamed of than is illness of the body." Bauer went on to quote Sir William Osler about how addictions should be seen as a disease: "It isn't so important what disease the patient has, as what kind of patient has the disease." Bill W., *Alcoholics Anonymous Comes of Age,* 244.

8. Powlison, *The Biblical Counseling Movement,* 101; Adams, *The Big Umbrella,* 109; Priolo, "Sin and Misery," 97; Shaw, *The Heart of Addiction,* 515–20, Kindle; Playfair and Bryson, *The Useful Lie,* 26.

From Sin to Disease

History of Alcoholics Anonymous

Bill W. and Dr. Bob

AA was founded in 1935 in Akron, Ohio, by a New York stockbroker, Bill W., and an Akron surgeon known as Dr. Bob.[9] Both were alcoholics who first met through The Oxford Group.[10] Through this group, Bill W. attained sobriety and determined that helping fellow alcoholics work through their struggles maintained his recovery. At the same time, Dr. Bob's membership of The Oxford Group failed to effectively lead him to sobriety. When the two finally connected, Bill W. so profoundly influenced Dr. Bob that the two decided to form AA.[11]

Bill W. proposed to Dr. Bob that alcoholism was a malady of mind, body, and spirit.[12] He reached this conclusion through his time as a patient under William D. Silkworth of Towns Hospital in New York.[13] Even though a physician himself, Dr. Bob did not view alcoholism as a disease. Convinced by Bill W. and Silkworth's proposal that alcoholism was a disease, Dr. Bob got sober and remained so for the rest of his life.[14]

After their immediate connection, both men started to work with fellow alcoholics at Akron City Hospital, where Dr. Bob already worked. In a short period of time, they helped another alcoholic achieve sobriety, and this event provided the humble beginnings of AA.[15] By the fall of 1935, another group of alcoholics formed the second gathering of AA in New

---

9. The AA culture rarely uses last names. Even Bill Wilson, co-founder of AA, was commonly known as Bill W. Throughout this chapter, authors and contributors may identify themselves by a pseudonym or with only the initial of their last name.

10. Bill W., *Alcoholics Anonymous Comes of Age*, 67. Hartigan commented, "The Oxford Group, originally known as a First Century Christian Fellowship and later as Moral Rearmament, was an evangelical sect that was founded by Frank Buchman, a Lutheran minister." Hartigan, *Bill W.: A Biography*, 82.

11. Cheever, *My Name Is Bill*, 151.

12. "I told Dr. Bob about alcoholism, the malady of my own experience of drinking, of my release, and, frankly, of my present peril. I told him how much I needed him and I think we had begun to get the essentials of it, for something passed between us." Bill W., "The Power of One Alcoholic Talking to Another."

13. Fitzpatrick, *Dr. Bob and Bill W. Speak*, 61.

14. Alcoholics Anonymous, *"Pass It On,"* 43.

15. In a lecture Bill W. gave at AA's 20th Anniversary Dinner, he stated that AA started with just three people—himself, Dr. Bob, and Bill D.: "Presently, Doctor Bob and I looked at the first man on the bed, and that was Bill D. who passed out the city on the hill, three candles were lit that stayed lit." Bill W., "Transformation."

York. The third group started in 1939 in Cleveland, with over 100 sober alcoholics forming the three inaugural groups within four years.[16]

In 1939, AA published its seminal textbook, now called *The Big Book of Alcoholics Anonymous*.[17] Bill W. authored the book and included the Twelve Steps in addition to the methods and philosophy of AA—designated as the teaching portion of *The Big Book*. The second half of this text included stories of thirty members who achieved sobriety through attending AA meetings—the section designated as the testimonial portion. The current version, *Alcoholics Anonymous Big Book*, 4th edition, contains forty-one stories of its members divided into three sections:

> Part One: Pioneers of AA
>
> Dr. Bob and the nine men and women who tell their stories were among the early members of AA's first groups. All ten have now passed away of natural causes, having maintained complete sobriety. Today, hundreds of additional AA members can be found who have had no relapse for more than fifty years. All of these, then, are the pioneers of AA They bear witness that release from alcoholism can really be permanent.[18]
>
> Part Two: They Stopped in Time.
>
> Among today's incoming AA members, many have never reached the advanced stages of alcoholism, though given time all might have. Most of these fortunate ones have had little or no acquaintance with delirium, with hospitals, asylums, and jails. Some were drinking heavily, and there had been occasional serious episodes. But with many, drinking had been little more than a sometimes uncontrollable nuisance. Seldom had any of these lost either health, business, family, or friends. Why do men and women like these join AA? The seventeen who now tell their experiences answer that question. They saw that they had become actual or potential alcoholics, even though no serious harm had yet been done.[19]

---

16. Bill W., *Alcoholics Anonymous Comes of Age*, 180.

17. Four editions with many revisions of *The Big Book* have been published, with over 30 million books sold. In 2007, *Time* magazine listed *The Big Book* in the top 100 most influential books written since 1923. The Library of Congress distinguished it as one of the 88 "Books that Shaped America" in 2012. Various editions will be used in this chapter due to differences among the revisions.

18. *Alcoholics Anonymous Big Book*, 4th ed, 88.

19. *Alcoholics Anonymous Big Book*, 147.

Part Three: They Nearly Lost It All.

The fifteen stories in this group tell of alcoholism at its miserable worst. Many tried everything—hospitals, special treatments, sanitariums, asylums, and jails. Nothing worked. Loneliness, great physical and mental agony—these were the common lot. Most had taken shattering losses on nearly every front of life. Some went on trying to live with alcohol. Others wanted to die. Alcoholism had respected nobody, neither rich nor poor, learned nor unlettered. All found themselves headed for the same destruction, and it seemed they could do nothing whatever to stop it. Now sober for years, they tell us how they got well. They prove to almost anyone's satisfaction that it's never too late to try Alcoholics Anonymous.[20]

While Bill W. wrote *The Big Book*, Dr. Bob's contribution as the co-founder came from his medical work with those who struggled with addiction.[21]

The Cleveland Plain Dealer newspaper ran a series of articles in 1939 supporting the rise of AA, even though only twenty members participated in the Cleveland group.[22] For the first time, this group showed that sobriety could be duplicated on a massive scale.[23] At the same time, AA grew more organized in New York through its connection with friends of John D. Rockefeller Jr., who came along as board members. While Rockefeller did not personally finance the organization, he held dinners with his wealthy and influential friends to publicize the importance of AA.[24]

The Twelve Steps

The Twelve Steps are divided into three categories: decision (One–Three), action (Four–Nine), and maintenance (Ten–Twelve).[25] The Twelve Steps include:

---

20. *Alcoholics Anonymous Big Book*, 34.

21. When the editor of the AA newsletter was asked what role Dr. Bob played, he replied, "One was, 'He provided medical care to thousands of alcoholics for no charge.' The second was, 'He was the steady figure in Bill W.'s life that helped keep Bill from getting too far off course.'" Fitzpatrick, *Dr. Bob and Bill W. Speak*, 68.

22. Bill W., *Alcoholics Anonymous Comes of Age*, 19. AA did, however, see its membership grow to over 500 within a few months.

23. Bill W., *Alcoholics Anonymous Comes of Age*, 20.

24. Fitzpatrick, *Dr. Bob and Bill W. Speak*, 123; Bill W., *Alcoholics Anonymous Comes of Age*, 147.

25. Siluk, *A Path to Relapse Prevention*, 44l; Paul H. and Scott N., *Simple but Not Easy*,

1. We admitted we were powerless over alcohol—that our lives had become unmanageable.

2. Came to believe that a Power greater than ourselves could restore us to sanity.

3. Made a decision to turn our will and our lives over to the care of God as we understood Him.

4. Made a searching and fearless moral inventory of ourselves.

5. Admitted to God, to ourselves, and to another human being the exact nature of our wrongs.

6. Were entirely ready to have God remove all these defects of character.

7. Humbly asked Him to remove our shortcomings.

8. Made a list of all persons we had harmed, and became willing to make amends to them all.

9. Made direct amends to such people wherever possible, except when to do so would injure them or others.

10. Continued to take personal inventory and when we were wrong promptly admitted it.

11. Sought through prayer and meditation to improve our conscious contact with God, as we understood Him, praying only for knowledge of His will for us and the power to carry that out.

12. Having had a spiritual awakening as the result of these STEPS, we tried to carry this message to alcoholics, and to practice these principles in all our affairs.[26]

The decision category informed alcoholics of their powerlessness over alcohol, their need for a higher power, and their need to submit to the higher power.[27] Upon deciding to try to live a sober life, the action steps intended

---

4; Ness, *Encyclopedia of American Social Movements*, 913.

26. Bill W., *The Big Book: The Original 1939 Edition*, 90–92.

27. "No matter how grievous the alcohol obsession, we happily find that other vital choices can still be made. For example, we can choose to admit that we are personally powerless over alcohol; that dependence upon a 'Higher Power' is a necessity, even if this be simply dependence upon an AA group. Then we can choose to try for a life of honesty and humility, of selfless service to our fellows and to 'God as we understand him.'" Anonymous, *Members of the Clergy*, 5.

to change the alcoholics' attitudes, beliefs, and practices regarding how to interact with others.[28] In the third division of maintenance, the removal of self-reliance and self-will helped alcoholics overcome poor decision-making and achieve greater relationships with others.[29]

Evaluation of Alcoholics Anonymous

Evaluating AA's influencers, their concept of God, perception of sin, and solutions will shed light on the underlying convictions of Bill W. and, consequently, the program he created.[30] Analyzing AA texts, journals, books written by influencers, and correspondence between key individuals reveals that the content in *The Big Book of Alcoholics Anonymous* is incompatible with the Bible. At its core, AA builds upon unbiblical theories and assumptions popular during the early 1900s.

In the 1953 article "12 in 30 Minutes," which appeared in the *AA Grapevine: The International Journal of Alcoholics Anonymous*, Bill W. was asked where the Twelve Steps came from. He answered, "So far as people were concerned, the main channels of inspiration for our Steps were three in number—the Oxford Groups, Dr. William D. Silkworth of Towns Hospital, and the famed psychologist, William James, called by some the father of modern psychology."[31] AA historians from the Hazelden/Betty Ford Foundation assessed that Bill W. borrowed the spiritual foundations of AA from The Oxford Group, the conversion to a higher power from James, and the biological cause of addiction as a disease from Silkworth.[32] A content analysis of how The Oxford Group, Silkworth, and James understood addiction and God will reveal that their stances, found throughout *The Big Book*, contradict the Word of God.[33]

28. Paul H. and Scott N., *Simple but Not Easy*, 4.

29. Siluk, *A Path to Relapse Prevention*, 441.

30. Bill W. used the term "influencers" instead of "founders." See Bill W., "12 STEPS in 30 Minutes," The *AA Grapevine* does not undergo peer review. The AA home office handles all writing, edits, illustrations, and publishing.

31. Bill W., "12 STEPS in 30 Minutes."

32. The Hazelden/Betty Ford Foundation appears at the forefront of all inpatient 12-Step treatment programs for drugs and alcohol. Kurtz, *Not-God*, 21. Kurtz published *Not-God* from his dissertation at Harvard for his Ph.D. in History of American Civilization. See also Mitchel, *Silkworth: The Little Doctor*, 1.

33. Content analysis is an "approach to analysis that focusses on interpreting and describing, meaningfully, the topics and themes that are evident in the contents of

The Oxford Group and Foundations of AA

Originally formed in 1908 under the name "The First Century Christian Fellowship," The Oxford Group was a non-denominational, evangelistically focused, and theologically conservative group.[34] The Group aimed to recapture a primitive and fundamental form of Christianity.[35] Protestant evangelist Frank Buchman re-organized the group in 1919 and changed the new name to The Oxford Group in 1931.[36] These changes were partially done to differentiate itself from The Oxford Movement.[37] With a clearly defined vision, they wanted the world to realize the power of the Holy Spirit and for the Spirit to awaken within individuals God's plan for mankind: "[the vision] means we surrender to God everything that stands between Him and us."[38] At the same time, however, the group desired compatibility with Islam, Hinduism, and Buddhism in order to evangelize across the world—a very odd combination of conservatism and New Age thinking.[39]

Bill W. credited Steps Three–Twelve to The Oxford Group's Four Practical Spiritual Activities.[40] According to The Oxford Group:

communications when framed against the research objectives of the study." Williamson and Johanson, *Research Methods*, 453.

34. Hegstad, *The Real Church*, 65; Randall, *Evangelical Experiences*, 239; Miller, *Treating Addictive Behaviors*, 38; Kurtz, *Not-God*, 39.

35. Kurtz, referring to the foundation of The Oxford Group, wrote, "The briefest statement of fundamental primitive Christian message runs: 'Jesus saves.'" Kurtz, *Not-God*, 51.

36. Driberg, *The Mystery of Moral Re-Armament*, 52.

37. Kurtz, *Not-God*, 39.

38. The Layman with a Notebook, *What Is The Oxford Group?* 6.

39. Moral Re-Armament (MRA) was another name for the Oxford Group. "MRA must, therefore, be so projected in India that it would not seem to the most devote Hindu or Muslim to be just another Christian mission. So we find that in MRA propaganda designed for the oriental market, there is practically no mention of Christianity: Christ, if named at all, is sandwiched unobtrusively between Gautama the Buddha and Mahatma Gandhi; the suggestion is that, whatever your faith, you will be the better—a better Hindu or Buddhist or Muslim—for accepting MRA rule of life; and this rule of life, so far as it is theistic at all, is consistent . . . with a relatively undogmatic pantheism." Driberg, *The Mystery of Moral Re-Armament*, 163. This technique of presenting beliefs in a compatible way with other belief systems appears in *The Big Book* as well: "When dealing with such a person, you had better use everyday language to describe spiritual principles. There is no use arousing any prejudice he may have against certain theological terms and conceptions about which he may already be confused. Don't raise such issues, no matter what your own convictions are." *Alcoholics Anonymous Big Book*, 49.

40. Bill W., *Alcoholics Anonymous Comes of Age*, 39.

To be spiritually reborn, and to live in the state in which these four points are the guides to our life in God, the Oxford Group advocates four practical spiritual activities:

1. The sharing of our sins and temptations with another Christian life given to God, and to use Sharing as Witness to help others, still unchanged, to recognize and acknowledge their sins.

2. Surrender of our life, past, present, and future, into God's keeping and direction.

3. Restitution to all whom we have wronged directly or indirectly.

4. Listening to, accepting, relying on God's Guidance and carrying it out in everything we do or say, great or small.[41]

Before Bill W. wrote all Twelve steps, he started with only 6 Steps in the fall of 1934:

1. We admitted that we were licked, that we were powerless over alcohol.

2. We made a moral inventory of our defects.

3. We confessed or shared our shortcomings with another person in confidence.

4. We made restitution to all those we had harmed by our drinking.

5. We tried to help other alcoholics, with no thought of reward in money or prestige.

6. We prayed to whatever God we thought there was for power to practice these precepts.[42]

Similarities clearly appear between the Four Practical Spiritual Activities of The Oxford Group and the initial 6 Steps which later formed the foundation of the Twelve Steps. These similarities show The Oxford Group's effect on AA.

Out of all the individuals from the Oxford Group, Ebby Thatcher most significantly influenced Bill W.[43] Ebby T. participated as an original member of both AA and The Oxford Group and was the first sponsor of

---

41. The Layman with a Notebook, *What Is The Oxford Group?* 9.
42. Bill W., "How the Twelve Steps Were Born."
43. Without Ebby, Bill W. probably would have never accepted a God of his own conception. Cheever, *My Name Is Bill*, 124; Kurtz, *Not-God*, 10; Hartigan, *Bill W.*, 81.

Bill W. He introduced Bill W. to The Oxford Group and Frank Buchman in November of 1934.[44] In addition, Thatcher helped Bill W. overcome his struggle with submitting to God. Bill W. recalled: "My friend suggested what then seemed a novel idea. He said, 'Why don't you choose your own conception of God?' That statement hit me hard. It melted the icy intellectual mountain in whose shadow I had lived and shivered many years. I stood in the sunlight at last."[45] Ebby T. was the first person to mention the concept of choosing a God of his own understanding to Bill W.[46]

While the teachings of The Oxford Group significantly influenced the formation of AA in its earliest stages, the broader AA community did not embrace everything the group taught.[47] If a distinctly Christian component existed within The Oxford Group, then their "absolutes" fit the description.[48] Several of The Oxford Group's absolutes became part of the Twelve Steps in AA The first of the absolutes emphasized purity of body and mind. The Group believed: "There can be no outward purity unless we are clean at the heart's core. The carnally impure cannot see God, nor can they see others right." [49] The 6th Step says, "We're entirely ready to have God remove all these defects of character." [50] The second absolute was honesty: "This is why we must regularly scrutinize our motives, desires, fears, and ambitions lest we come within the circle of moral disaster."[51] The 10th Step encouraged individuals to "continue to take personal inventory and when we [are] wrong promptly admit it."[52] The third absolute was unselfishness: "We can only keep that which we give."[53] The Twelfth Step says, "Having had a spiritual awakening as the result of these steps, we tried to carry this

---

44. Cheever, *My Name Is Bill*, 124; Kurtz, *Not-God*, 10; Hartigan, *Bill W.*, 81.

45. *Alcoholics Anonymous Big Book*, 7.

46. Fichter, *The Rehabilitation of Clergy Alcoholics*; Kurtz, *Not-God*, 17.

47. A split occurred between the Akron group and New York groups on regarding what to use from the Oxford Group. Kurtz, *Not-God*, 205.

48. "Are absolute love, purity, honesty, and unselfishness possible? The answer is that they are the standard which Jesus Christ set for those who follow Him. 'Be ye therefore perfect even as your Father who is in heaven is perfect.' No authority, however great, has any right to demand the impossible of us." Benson, *The Eight Points of the Oxford Group*, 45.

49. Benson, *The Eight Points of the Oxford Group*, 52.

50. *Alcoholics Anonymous Big Book*, 31.

51. Benson, *The Eight Points of the Oxford Group*, 53.

52. *Alcoholics Anonymous Big Book*, 31.

53. Benson, *The Eight Points of the Oxford Group*, 54.

message to alcoholics and to practice these principles in all our affairs."[54] The last of the absolutes was love, which was accomplished by "receiving Christ into our hearts by faith."[55] Ultimately, the fourth of the absolutes never became part of the Twelve Steps.[56]

Despite Bill W. writing about the importance of The Oxford Group in 1953, by 1955 another shift took place. While he still appreciated what the group had done for him in the early stages of AA, he started to distance himself from The Oxford Group. At AA's 1955 twentieth anniversary celebration called the "Coming of Age" convention, Bill W. brought clarification to the relationship between AA and The Oxford Group.[57] He identified four negative contributions of The Oxford Group that he wanted to distance from AA, saying that, first, AA unswervingly and persistently rejects absolutes; second, AA embraces anonymity; third, AA avoids any sort of evangelism; and fourth, AA seeks not to offend any person of any faith who might need help getting sober.[58] While The Oxford Group had some theological problems (such as a willingness to co-exist with other religions in their home countries), the Group attempted to impact the world with the teachings found in the Bible. Bill W.'s decision to sever ties with the group in the mid-1950s marked the last time a biblical entity overtly connected to AA.[59]

---

54. *Alcoholics Anonymous Big Book*, 31.

55. Benson, *The Eight Points of the Oxford Group*, 56.

56. "Several of the Oxford Group's other ideas and attitudes had been definitely rejected, including any which could involve us in theological controversy. In important matters, there was still considerable disagreement between the Eastern and the Midwestern viewpoints. Our people out there were still active Oxford Group members, while we in New York had withdrawn a year before. In Akron and vicinity, they still talked about the Oxford Group's absolutes: absolute honesty, absolute purity, absolute unselfishness, and absolute love. This dose was found to be too rich for New Yorkers and we had abandoned the expressions." Bill W., "How the Twelve Steps Were Born."

57. Bill W., "Coming of Age."

58. "The Oxford Groupers had clearly shown us what to do. And just as importantly, we had learned from them what not to do as far as alcoholics were concerned. . . . They would not stand for the rather aggressive evangelism of The Oxford Group. . . . They simply did not want to get 'too good too soon.' The Oxford Group's absolute concepts were frequently too much for the drunks. . . . Our debt to them, nevertheless, was and is immense, and so the final breakaway was very painful." Bill W., *Alcoholics Anonymous Comes of Age*, 74–75.

59. While looking over the various of editions of *The Big Book*, the author identified no clear biblical resources which influenced AA.

William James and the God of One's Own Understanding

At the second AA General Service Conference in 1952, Bill W. told attendees that James, whom he called the "father of modern psychology," "lit a candle for Alcoholics Anonymous."[60] In a letter to Carl Jung, Bill W. expressed whom he believed was important to the foundation of AA: "So to you, to Dr. Shoemaker of the Oxford Group, to William James, and to my own physician, Dr. Silkworth, we of AA owe this tremendous benefaction."[61] While Bill W. often wrote that no one person could be credited as the founder of AA, he always mentioned James as one of the foundational influences of the fellowship.[62]

James was a leader of the New Age thought sweeping the nation in the early 1900s and one of the first psychological theorists who "recognized altered states of consciousness."[63] He emphasized "self" and the idea that the tools needed to unlock the mysteries of religion and reality were "in ourselves."[64] He was enamored with the idea of mysticism and experiences, and while not a mystic himself, he was influenced by his mystically inclined father, Henry James Sr.[65] Bill W. avidly read anything James wrote and was especially captivated with *The Varieties of Religious Experience*:[66]

> At this point a third stream of influence entered my life through the pages of William James' book, *Varieties of Religious Experience*. Somebody had brought it to my hospital room. Following my sudden experience, Dr. Silkworth had taken great pains to convince me that I was not hallucinating. But William James did even more. Not only, he said, could spiritual experiences make people saner, they could transform men and women so that they could do, feel, and believe what had hitherto been impossible to them. It mattered little whether these awakenings were sudden or gradual; their variety could be almost infinite. But the biggest payoff of that noted book was this: In most of the cases described, those who had been transformed were hopeless people. In some controlling

---

60. Bill W., "A Benediction from Bill . . . Memo to the Folks Back Home."
61. Silkworth.net, "Dr. Carl Jung's Letter to Bill W."
62. Cheever, *My Name Is Bill*, 251.
63. Sire, *The Universe Next Door*, 173.
64. Holifield, *A History of Pastoral Care in America*, 198.
65. Barnard, *Exploring Unseen Worlds*, 5; Nelstrop and Magill, *Christian Mysticism*, 48; Harmless, *Mystics*, 57.
66. Kurtz, *Not-God*, 28.

> area of their lives they had met absolute defeat. Well, that was me all right. In complete defeat, with no hope or faith whatever, I had made an appeal to a Higher Power.[67]

The impact of James's writing also became evident in *The Big Book*, particularly in the section called "Bill's Story:"

> The great fact is just this, and nothing less: That we have had deep and *effective spiritual experiences* which have revolutionized our whole attitude toward life, toward our fellows and toward God's universe. The central fact of our lives today is the absolute certainty that our Creator has entered into our hearts and lives in a way which is indeed miraculous. He has commenced to accomplish those things for us which we could never do by ourselves.[68]

The New Age language and the ambiguous way to view God reflects James's impact on Bill W.[69]

James' idea that many ways lead to God strengthened Bill W.'s conviction that one may acquire faith through a variety of ways rather than through a single particular way.[70] Bill W. elaborated further in *The Big Book*:

> We found that as soon as we were able to lay aside prejudice and express even a willingness to believe in a Power greater than ourselves, we commenced to get results, even though it was impossible for any of us to fully define or comprehend that Power, which is God. Much to our relief, we discovered we did not need to consider another's conception of God. Our own conception, however inadequate, was sufficient to make the approach and to effect a contact with Him. As soon as we admitted the possible existence of a Creative Intelligence, a Spirit of the Universe underlying the totality of things, we began to be possessed of a new sense of power and direction, provided we took other simple steps.[71]

---

67. The "sudden experience" was the spiritual awakening that Bill W. often wrote about in AA literature. See Bill W., "12 STEPS in 30 Minutes."

68. *Alcoholics Anonymous Big Book*, 14; emphasis original. While Bill W. called his experiences spiritual, William James called them religious experiences. AA determined to avoid anything religious in nature and instead used spiritualism to replace it.

69. Kurtz, *The Collected Ernie Kurtz*, 65.

70. Bill W., "Thirty-Third AA Anniversary Party."

71. *Alcoholics Anonymous Big Book*, 25.

James instrumentally influenced AA's notion of God representing whatever concept the individual needed in order to associate with his or her Higher Power.[72]

James's concept of a higher power may be considered his most significant influence to AA. He wrote: "Believing that a higher power will take care of us in certain ways better than we can take care of ourselves, if we only genuinely throw ourselves upon it and consent to use it, it finds the belief, not only not impugned, but corroborated by its observation."[73] This quote resonates with AA's second and third steps—"Came to believe that a Power greater than ourselves could restore us to sanity," and, "Made a decision to turn our will and our lives over to the care of God as we understood Him."[74] Investigating what James classified as a higher power is telling:

> The great field for this sense of being the instrument of a higher power is of course "inspiration." It is easy to discriminate between the religious leaders who have been habitually subject to inspiration and those who have not. In the teachings of Buddha, of Jesus, of Saint Paul (apart from his gift of tongues), of Saint Augustine, of Huss, of Luther, of Wesley, automatic and semi-automatic composition appears to have been only occasional. In the Hebrew prophets, on the contrary, in Mohammed, in some of the Alexandrians, in many minor Catholic saints, in Fox, in Joseph Smith, something like it appears to have been frequent, sometimes habitual. We have distinct professions of being under the direction of a foreign power and serving as its mouthpiece.[75]

James clearly believed the teachings of Jesus, Buddha, Mohammed, and Joseph Smith all fell under the same conception of a higher power. The introduction of the idea of a higher power impacted how those in AA viewed God. Individuals could choose a higher power in the form of a leader or of a different faith, but they could also choose a doorknob, the universe, or a moon goddess from Venus.[76]

---

72. Bill W., "After Twenty-Five Years."
73. James, *The Varieties of Religious Experience*, 118.
74. *Alcoholics Anonymous Big Book*, 31.
75. James, *The Varieties of Religious Experience*, 475–76.
76. The key to AA's attractiveness to all religions relied on the ambiguity and the ability granted to members to choose whatever "god" they desire. One may commonly hear about individuals selecting a god as a doorknob, the universe, or a moon goddess from Venus.

AA's Conceptions of God

After conducting a content analysis of AA's *The Big Book*, identifiable themes associated with the word "God" emerged. AA's lack of a biblical view of God indicates an important area to examine. *The Big Book of Alcoholics Anonymous* includes 329 mentions of God which show an inconsistency with AA's definition of God. As presented earlier in this chapter, unbiblical influences partly formed *The Big Book*, so categorizing each instance the term "God" becomes essential. Establishing AA's incorrect view of God reveals why faith-based approaches to addiction should avoid unwisely adopting foundational aspects of AA.

In order to accomplish a content analysis of *The Big Book*'s teachings about God, the author chose eight descriptive categories. The methodology used to determine the eight categories for each mention of God was as follows: "Ambiguous concept of God" refers to a usage of the term absent of any mention of the writer's time spent in church or raised in a Christian home; "New Age concept of God" refers to usages in the context of a "God of one's own understanding;" the "Incorrect view of God" designation signifies that the writer held a theologically incorrect interpretation of God; "Possible Evangelical concept" indicates that the writer mentioned growing up in a Christian home or used any sort of terminology that could indicate a salvation experience; "Taking God's name in vain" and "Questioning God" are self-explanatory; finally, the one instance in which there was no doubt the writer specifically referenced the God of the Bible ("From the Bible") was when the writer used Scripture. The results of this analysis are as follows:

TABLE ONE: DISTRIBUTION OF CATEGORIES IN ENTIRE BOOK BY NUMBER AND FREQUENCY

Rank	Category	Number	Frequency
1	Ambiguous Concept of God	188	57.1%
2	New Age Concept of God	56	17%
3	Incorrect View of God	38	11.5%
4	Possible Evangelical Concept	18	5.5%
5	Common Sayings	17	5.1%
6	Taking God's Name in Vain	7	2.1%
7	Questioning God	4	1.2%
8	From the Bible	1	.3%

A detailed breakdown can be accomplished by separating the first half of *The Big Book*, essentially comprising the teaching section, and the second half, called the testimonial section, which starts on page 94 with the testimony of Alcoholics Anonymous Number Three.[77]

TABLE TWO: DISTRIBUTION OF CATEGORIES IN TEACHING SECTION BY NUMBER AND FREQUENCY

Rank	Category	Number	Frequency
1	Ambiguous Concept of God	94	68.1%
2	New Age Concept of God	20	20.2%
3	Incorrect View of God	9	6.5%
4	Common Sayings	4	2.8%
5	Taking God's Name in Vain	2	1.4%
6	Questioning God	1	.07%
7	Possible Evangelical Concept	0	0%
8	From the Bible	0	0%

TABLE THREE: DISTRIBUTION OF CATEGORIES IN TESTIMONIAL SECTION BY NUMBER AND FREQUENCY

Rank	Category	Number	Frequency
1	Ambiguous Concept of God	94	49.2%
2	Incorrect View of God	29	15.1%
3	New Age Concept of God	28	14.6%
4	Possible Evangelical Concept	18	9.4%
5	Common Sayings	13	6.8%
6	Taking God's Name in Vain	5	2.6%
7	Questioning God	3	1.6%
8	From the Bible	1	.5%

One of the most critical questions asks: What "god" are those in AA serving and asking for help? Bill W. himself gave a vague description of God:

---

77. "Pioneer member of Akron's Group No. 1, the first AA group in the world. He kept the faith; therefore, he and countless others found a new life." *Alcoholics Anonymous Big Book*, 94.

From Sin to Disease

> The word *God* still aroused a certain antipathy. When the thought was expressed that there might be a God personal to me, this feeling was intensified. I didn't like the idea. I could go for such conceptions as Creative Intelligence, Universal Mind, or Spirit of Nature, but I resisted the thought of a Czar of the Heavens, however loving His sway might be.
>
> ... I have since talked with scores of men who felt the same way.[78]

Bill W.'s dalliances with the occult and mysticism may partially explain his New Age perspective of God.[79] While not discussed in *The Big Book*, his authorized biographies provide several examples of these practices.[80] Ultimately, the New Age ideas found in *The Big Book* resulted from the inspiration of James.[81]

In *"Pass It On"*, one of Bill W.'s official biographies, a section describes the co-founder of AA communicating with demonic spirits while practicing séances during the time that he wrote *Alcoholics Anonymous and the Twelve Steps*.[82] Interestingly, Bill W. detailed one of the experiences he had with a Ouija board:

> The Ouija board began moving in earnest. What followed was the reasonably usual experience—it was a strange mélange of

---

78. *Alcoholics Anonymous Big Book*, 6–7; emphasis original.

79. "Bill W. believed that the cumulative weight of these phenomena validated his belief in humanity's divine and therefore immortal nature, and he wanted all alcoholics to be able to say, as he could, that their belief in god was 'no longer a question of faith' but 'the certainty of knowledge gained through evidence.'" Hartigan, *Bill W.*, 241.

80. "There is a 'spook' room downstairs in Stepping Stones where he, Lois, and other likeminded recovering alcoholics tried to visit the spirit world and communicate with the dead. The archives have folders of the automatic writing he did when he and Lois would use their Ouija board to invite the spirits to join them." Cheever, *My Name Is Bill*, 157.

81. William James wrote, "We have now seen enough of this cosmic or mystic consciousness, as it comes sporadically. ... That the mind itself has a higher state of existence, beyond reason, a superconscious state, and that when the mind gets that higher state, then this knowledge beyond reasoning comes." James, *The Varieties of Religious Experience*, 391. Schalow stated, "Bill Wilson turned to one of the fathers of American pragmatism, William James, to find a detailed account of the phenomenon of religious conversion. Wilson carefully read James' pivotal work *Varieties of Religious Experience*. However, while neither fell under the 'pragmatist' label, Wilson and Jung both epitomized the therapeutic value of religion." Schalow, *Toward a Phenomenology of Addiction*, 123.

82. Alcoholics Anonymous, *"Pass It On"*, 278.

> Aristotle, St. Francis, diverse archangels with odd names, deceased friends—some in purgatory and others doing nicely, thank you! There were malign and mischievous ones of all descriptions telling of vices quite beyond my ken [sic] as former alcoholics. Then, the seemingly virtuous entities would elbow them out with messages of comfort, information, advice—and sometimes just sheer nonsense.[83]

As indicated from the official biography of the co-founder of AA, other psychic undertakings and the occult influenced Bill W.'s writing while coming up with the Twelve Steps.

The influence of the occult on AA also appears within its symbol. The AA symbol combines a triangle in a circle. On the three sides of the triangle are the words "unity," "recovery," and "service," the proposed solutions of the three disease components of alcohol: mental, physical, and spiritual. When asked about the emblem, Bill W. stated: "That we have chosen this symbol [for AA] is perhaps no mere accident. The priests and seers of antiquity regarded the circle enclosing the triangle as a means of warding off spirits of evil, and AA's circle of Recovery, Unity, and Service has certainly meant all that to us and much more." [84]

Another voice that influenced AA's incorrect view of God came from Harry Emerson Fosdick.[85] His books *On Being a Real Person* and *Great Time to Be Alive* were two of the first recommendations added to the bookshelf of those in AA.[86] Fosdick reflected, "If to be a Christian means to be Christlike, such persons have missed its deepest secrets."[87] In his sermon titled "Shall the Fundamentalists Win?" Fosdick rejected the sufficiency of Scripture, the virgin birth of Christ, and Jesus's second coming.[88] Fosdick

83. Alcoholics Anonymous, *"Pass It On"*, 278.

84. Bill W., *Alcoholics Anonymous Comes of Age*, 139.

85. "When Bill Wilson in 1939 sent Fosdick a copy of Alcoholics Anonymous, he grasped it in gratitude, and his praiseful review appeared in three religious journals. In 1940, Fosdick represented the world of religion when Rockefeller arranged with Wilson's struggling group a dinner to inform New York's financial and civic leadership of AA's purpose, and though Rockefeller's ultimate financial support was parsimonious, doors were opened, publicity given, and funds raised." Miller, *Harry Emerson Fosdick*, 281.

86. Bill W., "Good Reading,"; Fosdick, *On Being a Real Person*; Fosdick, *A Great Time to Be Alive*.

87. Fosdick, *On Being a Real Person*, 238.

88. "They insist that we must all believe in the historicity of certain special miracles, preeminently the virgin birth of our Lord; that we must believe in a special theory of inspiration—that the original documents of the Scripture, which of course we no longer

wrote on the concept of a "God as we understood him" in a 1960 article, saying, "I can imagine a certain type of theological thinker who lifts his eyebrows at that italicized phrase twice used, 'God as we understood Him.' I applaud it."[89] He went on to describe Bill W. as just a man who used his previous experience battling addictions to come up with the Twelve Steps, not a theologian presenting a correct theology of God.[90]

Bill W.'s openness to allow AA members to have whatever understanding of God they desired impacted the lives of those who embraced AA doctrine. The teaching portion of *The Big Book* encourages the agnostic to reject the traditional definition of God and openly accept whatever expression of God fits his or her understanding:

> We found that God does not make too hard terms with those who seek Him. To us, the Realm of Spirit is broad, roomy, all inclusive; never exclusive or forbidding to those who earnestly seek. It is open, we believe, to all men. When, therefore, we speak to you of God, we mean your own conception of God. This applies, too, to other spiritual expressions which you find in this book.[91]

Many of his followers embraced and lived out the notion that they can follow a god of their own conception. Some of these followers' testimonies include:

> This is the Great Fact for us. Abandon yourself to God as you understand God. Admit your faults to Him and to your fellows. Clear away the wreckage of your past. Give freely of what you find and join us. We shall be with you in the Fellowship of the Spirit, and you will surely meet some of us as you trudge the Road of Happy Destiny. . . .[92]

possess, were inerrantly dictated to men a good deal as a man might dictate to a stenographer; that we must believe in a special theory of the Atonement—that the blood of our Lord, shed in a substitutionary death, placates an alienated Deity and makes possible welcome for the returning sinner; and that we must believe in the second coming of our Lord upon the clouds of heaven to set up a millennium here, as the only way in which God can bring history to a worthy denouement. Such are some of the stakes which are being driven to mark a deadline of doctrine around the church. If a man is a genuine liberal, his primary protest is not against holding these opinions, although he may well protest against their being considered the fundamentals of Christianity." Fosdick, "Shall the Fundamentalists Win?"

89. Fosdick, "Those Marvelous 12 Steps."
90. Fosdick, "Those Marvelous 12 Steps."
91. *Alcoholics Anonymous Big Book*, 25.
92. *Alcoholics Anonymous Big Book*, 85.

I don't think the boys were completely convinced of my personality change, for they fought shy of including my story in the book, so my only contribution to their literary efforts was my firm conviction—since I was still a theological rebel—that the word God should be qualified with the phrase "as we understand Him"—for that was the only way I could accept spirituality. . . .[93]

Then I came to believe that a Power greater than myself could restore me to sanity. And eventually, I made a decision to turn my will and my life over to the care of God as I understood God. Years before, in my search, I had explored numerous religions and dropped them because they preached a patriarchal God, which I felt never included me. Alcoholics Anonymous, I was told, is a spiritual program, not a religious one.[94]

The importance of having a proper understanding of God cannot be understated. AA pushed a narrative where its members' view of God did not matter.[95] The only thing that mattered was for those in the AA fellowship to have a God of their own understanding.[96]

The concept of a Higher Power is found throughout the AA organization and its literature. Some argue that the term "Higher Power" always referred to God when used in AA resources.[97] In addition to James, Emmet Fox acted as another influential figure who advocated for using the term "Higher Power." Fox's effect on AA partially came through his secretary, whose son was one of the first alcoholics Bill W. helped. Early AA members listened to Fox's lectures after they adjourned from their AA meetings in Steinway Hall.[98] He encouraged those who attended AA to find whatever path to God they take. One AA member recalled:

---

93. *Alcoholics Anonymous Big Book*, 121.

94. *Alcoholics Anonymous Big Book*, 183.

95. "The fundamental first message of Alcoholics Anonymous, proclaimed by the very presence of a former compulsive standing sober, ran: 'Something saves.' 'Salvation' as the message remained." Kurtz, *Not-God*, 50.

96. "Bill W. was always adamant about the fact that each person was free to develop a God of his or her own understanding. Alcoholics are told that their God can be a radiator, or the power of the group—G.O.D. can be an acronym for Good Orderly Direction, or even for Group of Drunks, they are told—or anything they like." Cheever, *My Name Is Bill*, 134.

97. "People suggested that I find a Higher Power. I was not fooled. I knew when they said Higher Power they meant God." *Alcoholics Anonymous Big Book*, 227.

98. Igor S., "What We Were Like: Emmet Fox and Alcoholics Anonymous."

> This was such a new thought that I got all sorts of books on Higher Powers, and I put a Bible by my bedside, and I put a Bible in my car. It is still there. And I put a Bible in my locker at the hospital. And I put a Bible in my desk. And I put a Big Book by my night stand, and I put a Twelve Steps and Twelve Traditions in my locker at the hospital, and I got books by Emmet Fox, and I got books by God-knows-who, and I got to reading all these things.[99]

An integral part of "The New Truth Movement" in the early twentieth century, Fox received notability for his Divine Science church located in New York City which rose to prominence during the Great Depression.[100]

Fox wrote numerous books that intertwined the Bible and New Age philosophies: *Stake Your Claim: Exploring the Gold Mine Within* and *Life is Consciousness*.[101] In his book *The Sermon on the Mount: The Keys to Success*, he wrote,

> The first thing that we have to realize is a fact of fundamental importance, because it means breaking away from all the ordinary prepossessions of orthodoxy. The plain fact is that Jesus taught no theology whatever. His teaching is entirely spiritual or metaphysical. Historical Christianity, unfortunately, has largely concerned itself with theological and doctrinal questions which, strange to say, have no part whatever in Gospel teaching. . . . There is absolutely no system of theology of doctrine to be found in the Bible; it is simply not there.[102]

He advocated for readers to have daily affirmations pairing Scripture with pre-written prayers/mantras.[103]

Fox articulated his inspiration for the concept of a power greater than oneself, or Higher Power, in his book *Power Through Constructive Thinking*:

---

99. *Alcoholics Anonymous Big Book*, 160.

100. *Alcoholics Anonymous Big Book*, 160.

101. Fox, *Stake Your Claim*; Emmet Fox, *Life is Consciousness*.

102. Fox, *The Sermon on the Mount*, 3. Fox's influence on the early members of AA appears in letters and essays in *AA Grapevine* rather than in *The Big Book*. For example: "I've just finished Emmet Fox's 'Sermon on the Mount,' and through that, attending church again and listening here and there about prayer, I have come much closer to God as I understand Him." R. A. B., "Me, a Crusader?"

103. "Peace: God I feel your peace as it moves gently through my soul. I feel a sense of serenity now as I let go of all cares and challenges. All tension is released. I am filled with inner peae [sic] that overflows into everything I do. Throughout this day I will be unfolding in your loving care. 1 Samuel 25:6 Peace be to you, and peace be to your house, and peace be to all that you have." Fox, *The Sermon on the Mount*, 3.

> The conscious discovery by you that you have this Power within you, and your determination to make use of it, is the birth of a child.... So your ability to contact the mystic Power within yourself, frail and feeble at first, will gradually develop until you find yourself permitting that Power to take your life into its care.[104]

When Bill W. explained his embrace of a higher power, he said:

> It was only a matter of being willing to believe in a Power greater than myself. Nothing more was required of me to make my beginning. I saw that growth could start from that point. Upon a foundation of complete willingness I might build what I saw in my friend. Would I have it? Of course I would! Thus was I convinced that God is concerned with us humans when we want Him enough.[105]

Although relatively unknown today, Fox and his unbiblical New Thought Movement heavily impacted AA and the idea of a higher power.

Using the same classifications that applied to instances where God was found in *The Big Book*, the term "Higher Power" underwent the same analysis:

TABLE FOUR: DISTRIBUTION OF CATEGORIES WITH HIGHER POWER BY NUMBER AND FREQUENCY

Rank	Category	Number	Frequency
1	Ambiguous Concept of God	47	85.5%
2	New Age Concept of God	8	14.5%
3	Incorrect View of God	0	0%
4	Common Sayings	0	0%
5	Taking God's Name in Vain	0	0%
6	Questioning God	0	0%
7	Possible Evangelical Concept	0	0%
8	From the Bible	0	0%

Splitting the use of "Higher Power" between the teaching section and testimonial section presents a fascinating picture. The term "Higher Power"

---

104. Fox, *Power Through Constructive Thinking*, 3.
105. *Alcoholics Anonymous Big Book*, 7.

was used only twice in the teaching section of *The Big Book*.¹⁰⁶ In the second portion of *The Big Book*, "Higher Power" was used forty out of fifty-two times (76.9 percent) without the accompanying mention of "God." Kurtz wrote:

> Yet AA's total omission of "Jesus," its toning down to even "God" to a "Higher Power," which could be the group itself, and its ever-changing of the verbal first message into hopeless helplessness rather than salvation: these ideas and practices adopted to avoid any "religious" association, [sic] were profound.¹⁰⁷

Kurtz's claim thirty years ago rings true. AA deliberately presented an ambiguous or New Age concept of God. The group did not want to offend or discourage anyone from joining its fellowship. Combining the examples of "Higher Power" with the instances of the use of "God" in the second half of *The Big Book* presents a very telling picture of how AA viewed God.

TABLE FIVE: DISTRIBUTION OF GOD AND HIGHER POWER BY NUMBER AND FREQUENCY

Rank	Category	Number	Frequency
1	Ambiguous Concept of God	141	57.3%
2	New Age Concept of God	36	14.6%
3	Incorrect Concept of God	29	11.7%
4	Possible Evangelical Concept	18	7.3%
5	Common Sayings	13	5.2%
6	Taking God's Name in Vain	5	2%
7	Questioning God	3	1.2%
8	From the Bible	1	.4%

---

106. "Once more: The alcoholic at certain times has no effective mental defense against the first drink. Except in a few rare cases, neither he nor any other human being can provide such a defense. His defense must come from a Higher Power." *Alcoholics Anonymous Big Book*, 24; In "Chapter VII. Working With Others," one passage reads, "When we look back, we realize that the things which came to us when we put ourselves in God's hands were better than anything we could have planned. Follow the dictates of a Higher Power and you will presently live in a new and wonderful world, no matter what your present circumstances!" *Alcoholics Anonymous Big Book*, 126.

107. Kurtz, *Not-God*, 50.

Of the 246 times the terms "God" or "Higher Power" appeared in the testimonial section of *The Big Book*, only 7.3 percent of the terms appeared to align with the evangelical concept of God and only .4 percent referred to God in the Bible.

For those seeking to get sober, they must know the truths about God and understand what a relationship with Him looks like. An acquaintance with God brings about a total life change and allows one to comprehend God and His Word with a correct view.[108] Knowing God informs the individual about His attributes and His character. God does not reveal Himself as a tolerant God permissive toward sin, as promoted by AA, but One who requires obedience to all things found in the Bible.[109]

William D. Silkworth and Sin Versus Disease

Within the entire *Big Book*, the mention of "sin" appears only four times and never in reference to addiction. One example from the testimonial section reads: "I learned that alcoholism isn't a sin, it's a disease."[110] Kurtz stated in his dissertation, "Alcoholics Anonymous not only suggests that alcoholism itself is not sinful but indicated the modern society that would implicitly call it such by the manipulation of psychological terms of the real "sin"—denying the meaning of the human."[111] AA's lack of a biblical doctrine of sin justified placing the onus of addiction on a disease. *The Big Book* brings up the disease model in thirty-three instances.[112] The man most responsible for this mentality in AA is Silkworth. His belief in the disease model for addiction also led to the mindset that AA provides the solution for addiction.[113]

---

108. Lambert, *A Theology of Biblical Counseling*, 104.

109. AA advocated for the concept of a tolerant God. "So we clean house with the family, asking each morning in meditation that our Creator show us the way of patience, tolerance, kindliness and love." *Alcoholics Anonymous Big Book*, 43.

110. *Alcoholics Anonymous Big Book*, 182.

111. Kurtz, *Not-God*, 218.

112. The only times that disease was not used in relation to addiction were the two times the individual discussed having cirrhosis of the liver. *Alcoholics Anonymous Big Book*, 250.

113. In a speech that Silkworth gave in 1950, he stated: "The fact remains—to the best of my knowledge—that no cure has yet been discovered. Not a single one. However, the disease has been arrested in nearly 100,000 alcoholics by a group that expounds no theory except absolute abstinence—Alcoholics Anonymous. It is not so difficult to

From Sin to Disease

In the preface of *The Big Book*, Silkworth contributed a section called the "Doctor's Opinion," having served as the chief physician of a prominent national hospital which specialized in drug and alcohol addiction.[114] Throughout his journal entry, Silkworth identified those with addiction problems as patients—patients who struggled with alcoholism.[115] Elsewhere, Silkworth stated, "Alcoholism is not just a vice or a habit. This is a compulsion; this is pathological craving; this is disease. An obsession of the mind that condemns one to drink and an allergy of the body that condemns one to die."[116] This classification is found within the text of AA and by default any ministry that has its foundation built upon AA.[117]

In a speech in 1950, Silkworth explained in greater detail his belief concerning those who suffer from addiction:

> My conception of alcoholism is contained in the findings I published thirteen years ago. I have confirmed them after observing some 17,000 cases under treatment. Alcoholism is a disease, essentially physical in origin, a manifestation of an allergy. This accounts for the phenomenon of the ten percent of the population who, if they drank, lose control over alcohol. The psychological involvement is caused by the refusal of the alcoholic to ascribe his difficulties to alcohol and his psychic dependence on it when he has reached the compulsive state of his addiction.[118]

Silkworth's description of those with substance abuse issues mimicked the prevailing theories at the time. The first diagnosis for addictions in the

---

understand or recognize the early symptoms of this disease. But let me first clarify a situation that has led to a great deal of confusion. Many of the psychological descriptions of the alcoholic are characteristic marks of the constitutional psychopath." Silkworth, "The Prevention of Alcoholism: A Challenge to the Catholic Clergy."

114. Mitchel, *Silkworth*, 1.

115. Anonymous, *The Book That Started It All*, 226.

116. Silkworth, *Alcoholism as a Manifestation of Allergy*, 145.

117. "The explanation that alcoholism was a disease of a two-fold nature, an allergy of the body and an obsession of the mind, cleared up a number of puzzling questions for me. The allergy we could do nothing about. Somehow our bodies had reached the point where we could no longer absorb alcohol in our systems. The why is not important; the fact is that one drink will set up a reaction in our system that requires more, that one drink is too much and a hundred drinks are not enough." *Alcoholics Anonymous Big Book*, 187.

118. Silkworth, "The Prevention of Alcoholism."

DSM, published two years later, categorized those with addiction as having a Sociopathic Personality Disturbance.[119]

Silkworth believed that no cure for addiction existed, and addicts would suffer from an incurable problem for the rest of their lives. He explained:

> In common with certain other diseases, clinically we have no cure for chronic alcoholism. Since the amalgamation of alcoholics into groups, we are able to meet many alcoholics who are completely sober for periods of from two to twenty years. But, following one drink of alcoholic beverage, the phenomenon of craving promptly returns. They cannot drink in moderation. The disease was merely arrested. Let us arouse ourselves. Let us recognize the urgent need of an educational campaign. Alcoholism is incurable but it can be prevented.[120]

Silkworth's view that addiction is incurable permeates the mindset of AA today. According to their belief: once an alcoholic, always an alcoholic. Those who attend AA have no hope of ever being free from their disease. As the *Big Book* stated, "Eventually the alcoholic loses all of his capacities as his disease gets progressively worse, and this is a tragedy that is painful to watch: the disintegration of a sound mind and body."[121] In one story about a housewife who drank at home alone, she lamented, "Because it was only through feeling defeat and feeling failure, the inability to cope with my life and with alcohol, that I was able to surrender and accept the fact that I had this disease and that I had to learn to live again without alcohol."[122] The defeatism shared by those who tell their story is the antithesis of the freedom that can be found in Christ.[123]

Despite Silkworth's incorrect view of addictions being a disease with no hope of freedom, he undeniably loved and had compassion for those who suffered. In the book titled *The Little Doctor Who Loved Drunks*, the author demonstrated Silkworth's exemplary passion for working with those

119. Robinson and Adinoff, "The Classification of Substance Use Disorders," 18.
120. Silkworth, "The Prevention of Alcoholism."
121. *Alcoholics Anonymous Big Book*, 144.
122. *Alcoholics Anonymous Big Book*, 155.
123. "It cannot be overstated just how entrenched your member's thought processes have become in such precepts as, 'Without my meetings I will relapse and lose hope,' and 'AA is the only way.' So, getting him to put off his newfound hope in something other than Christ, and putting on what the Scriptures say, will require perseverance, patience, tolerance, and love." Bowen, "Helping People Recover from Recovery," 73.

From Sin to Disease

addicted to alcohol: "We know that he was a prodigious and relentless worker, but still it was a shock to discover that in his lifetime of work with those who suffer our disease, he had talked with 51,000 alcoholics—45,000 at Towns Hospital and 6,000 at Knickerbocker!"[124] Although he sacrificed a lot of his time and energy to serve a discarded and uncared for people group during that time, Silkworth's legacy will be epitomized by the lasting idea that addiction is a disease, as exemplified by Ralph B.'s following testimony:

> We usually hear, "I stopped going to meetings," but not always. Dr. Silkworth reminded us that we have a disease like tuberculosis, cardiac disease or diabetes, where the patient must follow directions in order to arrest it and recover. We get a complete set of directions in the Twelve Steps. It's up to me whether I want to follow.[125]

The preceding quote came from *The International Journal of Alcoholics Anonymous* in October of 2019. Silkworth passed away more than 70 years ago, but his influence persists today.

Disease is not a sin, and sin is not a disease. Focusing on Christ brings freedom from sin, while thinking of alcoholism as a disease brings no lasting hope. The Bible offers genuine and real hope but AA can only offer what they call a temporary reprieve from alcoholism. Distinguishing sin from disease provides the proper understanding to find freedom from sin as a new creation in Christ. The Bible counters what AA proposes—"Once an alcoholic, always an alcoholic."[126] Those who attend Twelve-Step meetings have no hope to remain sober outside of continuing to participate in AA meetings and following its program.[127]

Since addiction problems stemmed from a disease rather than a sin issue, AA texts found solutions in a medical approach. Silkworth argued for both a physiological and psychological aspect to addictions and believed following AA's plan helped with the psychological compulsions to drink. Addressing the psychological component was due to Silkworth's belief that

---

124. Mitchel, *Silkworth*.
125. Ralph B., "Dear Grapevine."
126. *Alcoholics Anonymous Big Book*, 30.
127. While not found in AA literature, sponsors or others in AA meetings commonly say: "Those who attend meetings, stay sober," or "If you are struggling with your sobriety, get to a meeting."

AA provided group and moral psychology.[128] Those who struggle with addiction were told to place their hope and trust in the Twelve Steps and the community of AA Chapter 5 of *The Big Book*, titled "How It Works," asserted:

> RARELY HAVE we seen a person fail who has thoroughly followed our path. Those who do not recover are people who cannot or will not completely give themselves to this simple program, usually men and women who are constitutionally incapable of being honest with themselves. There are such unfortunates. They are not at fault; they seem to have been born that way. They are naturally incapable of grasping and developing a manner of living which demands rigorous honesty. Their chances are less than average. There are those, too, who suffer from grave emotional and mental disorders, but many of them do recover if they have the capacity to be honest.[129]

Every Twelve-Step meeting begins by reading this short section. Common readings are ingrained in the members of AA that the solution to their problem is directly tied to the ability of the fellowship to follow the simple steps of the program.

Carl Jung and Solutions

Bill W. earlier credited The Oxford Group, Silkworth, and James for their influence on the development of the Twelve Steps. In addition, he named Sam Shoemaker and Carl Jung as significant influencers in the creation of AA and the solutions presented in *The Big Book*.[130] Jung reinforced Bill W.'s belief that the AA program needed spirituality. In a letter to Jung in 1961, Bill W. explained that Jung's interaction with Roland H. played a substantial role in AA's development.[131] Bill W. went on to express how he co-opted the idea of a spiritual/religious experience from a discussion between Jung and

---

128. Miller and Gold, "The Disease and Adaptive Models of Addiction," 31.

129. *Alcoholics Anonymous Big Book*, 31.

130. In correspondence with Jung, Bill W. wrote, "As you will now dearly see, this astonishing chain of events actually started long ago in your consulting room, and it was directly founded upon your own humility and deep perception." See Silkworth.net, "Bill W.'s Letter to Dr. Carl Gustav Jung,"

131. Silkworth.net, "Bill W.'s Letter to Dr. Carl Gustav Jung."

From Sin to Disease

Roland.[132] AA presented the concept of spirituality as a solution—what Bill W. called a program of action:

> Then they outlined the spiritual answer and program of action which a hundred of them had followed successfully. Though I had been only a nominal churchman, their proposals were not, intellectually, hard to swallow. But the program of action, though entirely sensible, was pretty drastic. It meant I would have to throw several lifelong conceptions out of the window. That was not easy. But the moment I made up my mind to go through with the process, I had the curious feeling that my alcoholic condition was relieved, as in fact it proved to be.[133]

As previously stated, the problem with AA's presentation about God, or a spiritual answer, reveals the uncertainty about the type of spirituality presented. While Jung had a positive slant toward religion, he did not believe in any specific religion.[134] Additionally, in a 1955 letter to Pastor Walter Bernet, he classified Christianity as a faith with foundations rooted in myths.[135]

Jung had much to say about spirituality and AA.[136] However, he did not advocate for a spirituality/religion founded in biblical doctrine.[137] His core beliefs resembled a mixture of world religions:

---

132. "When he then asked you if there was any other hope, you told him that there might be, provided he could become the subject of a spiritual or religious experience—in short, a genuine conversion. You pointed out how such an experience, if brought about, might re-motivate him when nothing else could. But you did caution, though, that while such experiences had sometimes brought recovery to alcoholics, they were, nevertheless, comparatively rare. You recommended that he place himself in a religious atmosphere and hope for the best. This I believe was the substance of your advice. . . . You will also be interested to learn that, in addition to the 'spiritual experience,' many AAs report a great variety of psychic phenomena, the cumulative weight of which is very considerable. Other members have—following their recovery in AA—been much helped by your practitioners. A few have been intrigued by the I Ching and your remarkable introduction to that work." See Silkworth.net, "Dr. Carl Jung's Letter to Bill W."

133. *Alcoholics Anonymous Big Book*, 23.

134. Schaer, *Religion and the Cure of Souls in Jung's Psychology*, 73; Szasz, *The Myth of Psychotherapy*, 173.

135. Szasz, *The Myth of Psychotherapy*, 173.

136. "You see, 'alcohol' in Latin is spiritus, and you use the same word for the highest religious experience as well as for the most depraving poison. The helpful formula therefore is: spiritus contra spiritum." See Silkworth.net, "Dr. Carl Jung's Letter to Bill W."

137. Fuller, *Spiritual, but Not Religious*, 113–114.

> One major misinterpretation is that Jung was a Christian apologist, i.e., a defender of Christian truths within a contemporary setting using modern concepts and language. Jung does not place himself within the Christian theological circle.... Unlike the theologians Jung does not look to the Bible or to Christian tradition for authority or inspiration.[138]

Jung and Bill W. agreed that a spiritual approach instead of a religious approach was the best direction for AA to take.[139]

The most outlandish solution Bill W. investigated, participated in, and encouraged considered the use of LSD as a possible cure for alcohol addiction.[140] Evidence of the possible reality of a spiritual realm captivated Bill W. His interest in exploring a conscious afterlife drew him into a friendship with mystic Gerald Heard, who introduced him to Aldous Huxley.[141] Huxley eventually became one of the closest confidants of Bill W. and remained so for the rest of his life.[142] Through Bill W.'s connection with Huxley, Timothy Leary entered the scene, and Bill W. began dabbling with LSD and other hallucinogenic drugs.

Hartigan explained in further detail: "Bill seems to have become well-practiced in making way for spiritual experiences. Twenty years after the experience of the Divine that struck him sober, he wrote that in the intervening years, he had been 'subject to an immense amount of psychic phenomena of all sorts.'"[143] Bill W.'s belief in LSD as a possible solution led him to urge physicians within the AA community to verify the legitimacy of LSD as a therapy for AA members.[144]

---

138. Stein, *Jung on Christianity*, 4.

139. Fred W., a former patient of Dr. Jung, went on record stating, "Jung portrays the drinker who is seeking a spiritual release through alcohol, he was deeply convinced that this is a part of the motivation that most heavy drinkers have. Therefore alcohol is not always taken for escape or obliteration—rather it is an attempt, very often at least, to reach higher valuer—Aldous Huxley held to this identical view." Rokeach, *The Open and Closed Mind*, 116–17.

140. "Bill's interest in helping alcoholics find relief from the need to drink was also what motivated him to explore the possibilities presented by LSD." Hartigan, *Bill W.*, 241.

141. Kurtz, *Not-God*, 136.

142. "It was Wilson's scientific interest in spiritual things that made him an intellectual cohort of Aldous Huxley, but his quest for an understanding of the mystical realm was shared by other early AA members as well." Kurtz, *Not-God*, 240.

143. Hartigan, *Bill W.*, 117.

144. Kurtz, *Not-God*, 137.

Bill W. reasoned that LSD might allow those who struggled with addiction to mimic the spiritual awakening he experienced during the night he found the god of his own understanding. He purposed to use LSD to remove any blockage stopping people from feeling spiritually alive. He believed and agreed with Huxley that LSD allowed "doors of perception" to open.[145] Eventually, Bill W. stopped pushing the use of LSD when the suggestion stirred controversy within AA.[146]

AA helped millions of addicts over the last eighty years. Undoubtedly, the organization operated as a powerful force that positively impacted those struggling with substance abuse. However, a problem arises when individuals claim AA as a Christian organization created with biblical principles in mind.[147] The information presented reveals that AA is incompatible with scripture.

The Influence of AA in the SBC through Celebrate Recovery

For close to fifty years, AA remained the primary option for both believers and non-believers to participate in a program helping individuals with substance abuse issues.[148] From AA's humble beginnings, they boast just under two million members today.[149] Despite the success of AA helping people achieve sobriety, Christians still wanted a place where they could talk about sobriety and Jesus. John Baker, the co-founder of Celebrate Recovery (CR), compared his small-group Bible study with what happened in AA meetings in an interview: "In my men's small group I couldn't talk about my struggle, and at AA, I couldn't talk about my Savior."[150] Coming out of his desire to

---

145. Hartigan, *Bill W.*, 243.

146. Kurtz, *Not-God*, 137.

147. Kurtz argued that the biblical principles came from the influence of The Oxford Group. Kurtz, *Not-God*, 39.

148. Kaskutas and Galanter, *Recent Developments in Alcoholism*.

149. AA has a General Service office that conducts membership surveys every three years. Since AA does not keep a formal membership list, the membership surveys provide an estimate rather than a definitive number. The most current estimated membership is based on the 2021 survey. Alcoholics Anonymous "Estimated Worldwide AA Individual and Group Membership."

150. Shellnutt and Baker, "How Celebrate Recovery Helped Evangelicals Open Up About Addiction."

talk about both his struggle and Jesus, Baker teamed up with Rick Warren to develop CR, an approach to helping those with addictions in the SBC.[151]

Celebrate Recovery

Headquartered at Saddleback Church in California, CR stands as one of the most well-known ministries to help those who struggle with addictions. In the forward to CR literature, Warren wrote:

> What we need is a biblical and balanced program to help people overcome their hurts, habits, and hang-ups. Celebrate Recovery® is that program. Based on the actual words of Jesus rather than psychological theory, the recovery program contained in this kit is unique, and it is more effective in helping people change than anything else I've seen or heard of. . . . Most people are familiar with the classic Twelve-Step program of AA and other groups. While undoubtedly many lives have been helped through the Twelve Steps, I've always been uncomfortable with that program's vagueness about the nature of God, the saving power of Jesus Christ, and the ministry of the Holy Spirit. So I began an intense study of the Scriptures to discover what God had to say about "recovery." To my amazement, I found the principles of recovery—in their logical order—given by Christ in His most famous message, the Sermon on the Mount. . . . Celebrate Recovery is based on God's Word, the Bible.[152]

In this part of the forward, Warren's concern about AA motivated him to start CR in order to establish a program with a biblical foundation.

CR maintains a large reach in the SBC for those who suffer from addiction—a notable achievement.[153] The program devoted countless man hours and financial resources to assist over five million members who completed their program. The organization reached a large segment of addicts seeking to address their life-dominating sin with Christ as their "higher

---

151. CR has been the predominate Christian approach to substance abuse with thousands of churches worldwide implementing its program since its founding in 1991.

152. Baker, *Celebrate Recovery Leader's Guide,* 12. The leader's guide contains the entire curriculum found in the eight volumes of the participant's guide.

153. According to CR literature as of 2015, over 22,000 churches in all 50 states use CR curriculum. More than 1 million people have completed their program.

power."[154] CR provides an opportunity for Christians to talk about both their addictions and their relationship with Jesus Christ.

Warren and Baker determined to provide a program for those who desired the freedom to share about their relationship with Jesus Christ, an option unavailable to those in AA. However, aspects of CR show similarities to AA, despite Warren's desire for CR to avoid any distinct influence from AA.[155] An important question requires an answer: Did CR adopt AA ideas despite Warren's discomfort with their ambiguity on the nature of God? CR claims to be a biblically-based recovery program, but their texts do not support their assertion that they are not influenced by psychological theory.

Celebrate Recovery's Adoption of Alcoholics Anonymous

Warren based the groundwork for CR on what he called the Eight Principles of the Beatitudes.[156] On the surface, the Eight Principles appear solely based on the Bible and devoid of any influence by AA. However, each principle presents a similar foundation found in the Twelve Steps.[157] Warren simply wanted to emphasize the Eight Principles he wrote, but Baker went beyond Warren's intent and connected each of the Eight Principles with the Twelve Steps. Baker wrote the following in the introduction of *Celebrate Recovery Leader's Guide*:

> **Principle 1:** Realize I'm not God. I admit that I am powerless to control my tendency to do the wrong thing and that my life is unmanageable. *"Happy are those who know they are spiritually poor"* (Matthew 5:3).
> Step 1. We admitted we were powerless over alcohol—that our lives had become unmanageable.[158]

---

154. Celebrate Recovery, "History of Celebrate Recovery."

155. Baker, *Celebrate Recovery Leader's Guide*, 12.

156. "When Jesus taught the Sermon on the Mount, He began by stating eight ways to be happy. Today we call them the Beatitudes. From a conventional viewpoint, most of these statements don't make sense. They sound like contradictions. But when you fully understand what Jesus is saying, you'll realize that these eight principles are God's road to recovery, wholeness, growth, and spiritual maturity." Baker, *Your First Step to Celebrate Recovery*, 15.

157. Baker, *Celebrate Recovery Leader's Guide*, 19–23.

158. Baker, *Celebrate Recovery Leader's Guide*, 19; emphasis original.

Principle 2: Earnestly believe that God exists, that I matter to Him, and that He has the power to help me recover.
"Happy are those who mourn, for they shall be comforted" (Matthew 5:4)
Step 2. Came to believe that a Power greater than ourselves could restore us to sanity and Made a decision to turn our will and our lives over to the care of God as we understood Him.[159]

Principle 3: Consciously choose to commit all my life and will to Christ's care and control.
"Happy are the meek" (Matthew 5:5).
Step 3. Made a decision to turn our will and our lives over to the care of God as we understood Him.[160]

Principle 4: Openly examine and confess my faults to myself, to God, and to someone I trust.
"Happy are the pure in heart" (Matthew 5:8).
Step 4. Made a searching and fearless moral inventory of ourselves.
Step 5. Admitted to God, to ourselves, and to another human being the exact nature of our wrongs.[161]

Principle 5: Voluntarily submit to every change God wants to make in my life and humbly ask Him to remove my character defects.
Happy are those whose greatest desire is to do what God requires. (Matthew 5:6)
Step 6. We were entirely ready to have God remove all these defects of character.
"Humble yourselves before the Lord, and he will lift you up. (James 4:10)
Step 7. We humbly asked Him to remove all our shortcomings.
"If we confess our sins, he is faithful and just and will forgive us our sins and purify us from all unrighteousness." (1 John 1:9)[162]

Principle 6: Evaluate all my relationships. Offer forgiveness to those who have hurt me and make amends for harm I've done to others, except when to do so would harm them or others.
"Happy are the merciful." (Matthew 5:7) "Happy are the peacemakers." (Matthew 5:9)
Step 8. We made a list of all persons we had harmed, and became willing to make amends to them all.

---

159. Baker, *Celebrate Recovery Leader's Guide*, 20; emphasis original.
160. Baker, *Celebrate Recovery Leader's Guide*, 20; emphasis original.
161. Baker, *Celebrate Recovery Leader's Guide*, 20; emphasis original.
162. Baker, *Celebrate Recovery Leader's Guide*, 21; emphasis original.

From Sin to Disease

"Do to others as you would have them do to you." (Luke 6:31)
Step 9. We made direct amends to such people wherever possible, except when to do so would injure them or others.
"Therefore, if you are offering your gift at the altar and there remember that your brother has something against you, leave your gift in front of the altar. First go and be reconciled to your brother; then come and offer your gift." (Matthew 5:23–24)[163]

Principle 7. Reserve a daily time with God for self-examination, Bible reading, and prayer in order to know God and His will for my life and to gain the power to follow His will.[164]

Principle 8. Yield myself to God to be used to bring this Good News to others, by both my example and my words.
"Happy are those who are persecuted because they do what God requires." (Matthew 5:10)
Step 10. We continued to take personal inventory and when we were wrong, promptly admitted it.
"So, if you think you are standing firm, be careful that you don't fall!" (1 Corinthians 10:12)
 Step 11. We sought through prayer and meditation to improve our conscious contact with God, praying only for knowledge of His will for us and power to carry that out.
"Let the word of Christ dwell in you richly." (Colossians 3:16)
Step Twelve. Having had a spiritual experience as the result of these steps, we try to carry this message to others and to practice these principles in all our affairs.
"Brothers, if someone is caught in a sin, you who are spiritual should restore him gently. But watch yourself, or you also may be tempted." (Galatians 6:1)[165]

Despite Warren's concerns about the foundations of AA, his desire to create a bridge with those in Twelve-Step groups created an overlap between AA's Twelve Steps and CR's Eight Principles.[166] In the process, Baker explained

---

163. Baker, *Celebrate Recovery Leader's Guide*, 23; emphasis original.
164. Baker, *Celebrate Recovery Leader's Guide*, 23; emphasis original.
165. Baker, *Celebrate Recovery Leader's Guide*, 23; emphasis original.
166. "Throughout this material, you will notice several references to the Christ-centered 12 Steps. Our prayer is that Celebrate Recovery will create a bridge to the millions of people who are familiar with the secular 12 Steps (I acknowledge the use of some material from the 12 Suggested Steps of Alcoholics Anonymous) and in so doing, introduce them to the one and only true Higher Power, Jesus Christ. Once they begin that relationship, asking Christ into their hearts as Lord and Savior, true healing and recovery can begin!" Baker, *Celebrate Recovery: The Journey Begins Participant's Guide*, 215.

the Twelve Steps of AA in a way to make them compatible with the Eight Principles of CR and Scripture:

> The second step tells us that we have come to believe that a power greater than ourselves could restore us to sanity. . . . Step Two isn't saying that you're crazy. Let me try to explain what the word "sanity" means in this step. As a result of admitting our powerlessness in Principle 1, we can move from chaos to hope in Principle 2.[167]

The similarities of Principle Four of CR and Step Four of AA provide another example of Baker helping CR members navigate the Twelve Steps of AA: "To do a 'searching and fearless' inventory, you must step out of your denial, because we cannot put our faults behind us until we face them."[168] These few examples represent many other examples of AA's Twelve Steps overlapping with similar CR Principles.

Baker gave his rationale for determining what to include in CR curriculum by saying AA's *The Big Book* had twelve great promises.[169] Accepting these promises posed a problem since one of the "great promises" of the Twelve Steps of AA ensures members that they can find a God of one's own understanding.[170] Additionally, Baker went on to assert that material for any recovery-based ministry should assist one to teach and encourage movement through AA's Twelve Steps.[171] While Warren expressed apprehensions about AA, Baker, the co-author of CR, did not have an issue with AA other than their exception to talk about Jesus. [172] A disconnect appears between Warren's statements in the forward and the content Baker implemented in CR curriculum. In reality, the foundations of CR Christianized AA, something Warren wanted to avoid.[173]

---

167. Baker, *Celebrate Recovery Leader's Guide*, 77–78.
168. Baker, *Celebrate Recovery Leader's Guide*, 110.
169. Baker, *Celebrate Recovery Leader's Guide*, 29.
170. *Alcoholics Anonymous Big Book*, 31.
171. "Some books do a great job of teaching about the 12 Steps and specific areas of recovery; however, they do not encourage movement through the steps. I have seen many individuals get to the fourth step and get bogged down, dwelling in the mud of their past." Baker, *Celebrate Recovery Leader's Guide*, 30.
172. In *Your First Steps to Celebrate Recovery*, Baker detailed the positive aspects of AA's 12 Steps but did not address any of the possible conflicts with Christianity found in AA
173. Baker, *Celebrate Recovery Leader's Guide*, 14.

Doctrine of God

One may accurately assume the founders of CR, Warren and Baker, properly understand God. In his book *The Purpose Driven Life*, Warren wrote: "The ultimate goal of the universe is to show the glory of God. ... What is the Glory of God? It is who God is, it is the essence of his nature, the right of his importance, the radiance of his splendor, the demonstration of his power, and the atmosphere of his presence."[174] Warren's writings infer that God's glory is not merely part of who He is, but the totality of God's eternal and inherent qualities. Warren went on to say that "we are commanded to recognize his glory, honor his glory, declare his glory, praise his glory, reflect his glory, and live for his glory." [175] In an interview, John Piper asked Warren how America can avoid a superficial view of the nature of God. He answered, "I believe 'take up your cross and deny yourself and follow me,' and I believe 'come unto me all who are weary and heavy-laden and I will give you rest.'"[176] Unlike the voices responsible for AA's incorrect and purposefully theologically-uninformed view of God, Warren and CR should have a correct doctrine of God.

Another notion reinforces CR's correct doctrine of God due to the fact that the CR text prohibits members from believing in a God of their own understanding. CR materials explicitly affirm that the only Higher Power in CR is Jesus Christ, a position AA rejects. CR's primary text refers to a "Higher Power" forty-four out of fifty-six times in a similar way as the proceeding quote: "I now knew I was forgiven by the work of Jesus Christ—the one and only true Higher Power."[177] But while the quote clearly intends for Jesus Christ to fill the role of a Higher Power, some concerns still remain. As evidenced in AA's influence, CR borrowed AA terminology in five of the fifty-six instances of using the term "Higher Power," such as in the following statement:

> As we work Step 2, we begin to trust in our relationships with others and our Higher Power. "It is dangerous to be concerned with what others think of you, but if you trust the LORD, you are safe" (Proverbs 29:25, GNB). As we *"let go and let God"* and admit

---

174. Warren, *The Purpose Driven Life*, 53.
175. Warren, *The Purpose Driven Life*, 54.
176. Piper and Warren, "John Piper Interviews Rick Warren on Doctrine."
177. Baker, *Celebrate Recovery Leader's Guide*, 16.

that our lives are unmanageable and we are powerless do anything about it, we learn to trust ourselves and others.[178]

The phrase "let go and let god" appears in the *Big Book* and is often heard in AA meetings.[179]

The two CR founders faced a conundrum: Warren wanted to distance CR from AA and the organization's ambiguity towards God, while Baker attempted to build bridges between the two programs. The tension between two viewpoints manifests in the use of the term "Higher Power" in CR literature. CR also used "Higher Power" in acrostics:

Higher Power
Openness to Change
Power to Change
Expect to Change.
Strength
Acceptance
New Life
Integrity
Trust
Your Higher Power[180]

CR's use of AA terminology, with the dubious history behind the term "Higher Power," is questionable, especially since the idea of a Higher Power came from the unbiblical influences of James and Fox.[181] CR articulated a correct doctrine of God, but aspects of their use of "Higher Power" remain problematic.

Doctrine of Sin

As mentioned in the foreword of the book, Warren intended CR not just for those who struggle with drugs and alcohol but also for those who fall under what he called a "large umbrella," equipping CR to address "all types

---

178. Baker, *Celebrate Recovery Leader's Guide*, 78; emphasis original.

179. *Alcoholics Anonymous Big Book*, 182. The phrase "let go and let god" was not exclusive to AA The phrase was also widely used by followers of Keswick Theology, part of the Higher Life Theology movement of the late 1800s. See Barabas, *So Great Salvation*, 75.

180. Baker, *Celebrate Recovery Leader's Guide*, 74.

181. James, *The Varieties of Religious Experience*, 118; Fox, *Power Through Constructive Thinking*, 3.

From Sin to Disease

of habits, hurts, and hang-ups."[182] At the close of his forward, he wrote that through CR "you are going to see hopeless marriages and people set free from all kinds of sinful habits, hang-ups, and hurts as they allow Jesus to be Lord in every area of their lives."[183] Warren mentioned sin 158 times and the phrase "hurts, hang-ups, and habits" fifty-eight times. Only one instance in the entire book, used during a CR member's testimony, brought up the idea of the disease model.[184] AA did not impact CR's doctrine of sin when it relates to addiction.

Solutions

Warren assured those who participate in CR that "Celebrate Recovery is based on God's Word, the Bible."[185] The Bible plays an instrumental role in CR. CR leader literature mentioned God 500 times—not in an ambiguous or New Age understanding such as in AA, but as the God of the Bible. Additionally, CR encouraged members to pray 102 times—not to a god of one's own understanding, but to the God found in the Bible.[186] CR presented the Bible as the authoritative Word of God in sixty-four instances, but not a as moral manual as presented by AA: "There is a wide variety of resources from which to choose, but I believe the foundation for an effective recovery ministry curriculum should always be the same: the Bible. God's Word needs to be at the center of your recovery program."[187] Bill W. called Jesus a great man with excellent moral teachings, not Lord and Savior.[188] In contrast, CR's leader guide material used the title "Christ" 239 times and called members to submit and surrender their lives to Him: "Celebrate Recovery emphasizes spiritual commitment to Jesus Christ. The third principle calls

---

182. Warren commonly used this phrase in videos, advertisements, and other communication.

183. Baker, *Celebrate Recovery Leader's Guide*, 13.

184. Baker, *Celebrate Recovery Leader's Guide*, 96.

185. Baker, *Celebrate Recovery Leader's Guide*, 13.

186. "Reserve a daily time with God for self-examination, Bible reading, and prayer to know God and His will for my life and to gain the power to follow His will." Baker, *Celebrate Recovery Leader's Guide*, 9.

187. Baker, *Celebrate Recovery Leader's Guide*, 29.

188. *Alcoholics Anonymous Big Book*, 6.

for people to make a total surrender of their lives to Christ."[189] CR fulfilled part of the pledge to base their teachings on God's Word, the Bible.

Baker mentioned his background in AA during his testimony, betrayed further by the phrases and ideas he used throughout the CR text. For example, Baker used phrases such as "Drink like a gentleman" and "We are as sick as our secrets," which come directly from AA literature.[190] The importance of a sponsor demonstrates further similarities between the two organizations. CR advocates that a sponsor is the "best guard against relapse."[191] CR's understanding of the sponsor's role compares with AA's understanding, which states that attending meetings and working with a sponsor were integral parts to sobriety.[192] While accountability plays an important factor in sobriety, CR's use of the word "best" minimizes the power of prayer and the sufficiency of scripture.

Warren and Baker's hard work became the precursor to other addiction-focused ministries forming in local churches around the nation.[193] The CR founders set out to provide a biblically-informed program to fill a void which existed for addicts looking for a Christian alternative to AA.[194] Despite concerns about the influence of AA, their approach to addictions, as an issue of sin, coincides with scripture. However, CR curriculum does not uphold the sufficiency of scripture, as evidenced by the many similarities and overlaps with AA. When CR took practical elements from AA that supposedly helped in the process of sobriety, CR missed an opportunity to provide an unadulterated biblical approach to addictions.[195] In summary, while many use Warren and Baker's material, and while it offers some corrective to AA, the CR program is not based on the sufficiency of scripture.

---

189. Baker, *Celebrate Recovery Leader's Guide*, 13.

190. Baker, *Celebrate Recovery Leader's Guide*, 14, 59; *Alcoholics Anonymous Big Book*, 11, 17, 111.

191. Baker emphasized this statement in bold letters. Baker, *Taking an Honest and Spiritual Inventory*, 16.

192. *Alcoholics Anonymous Big Book*, 215.

193. The Steps by The Village Church, RU Recovery Ministries, and Mission at the Cross are a few of the ministries dedicated to help those with substance abuse issues.

194. Baker, *Celebrate Recovery Leader's Guide*, 21.

195. No peer reviewed studies present statistical comparisons between the success rate of AA versus CR.

Conclusion

AA undeniably influenced the SBC and its churches. Many churches who help addicts still incorporate elements of AA into their ministries to alcoholics. A purely biblical approach to substance abuse is difficult to find and attempts from within the evangelical community fall short of having a foundation solely based on the Bible. As demonstrated, the church needs to address addiction, but should they combine scripture with the Twelve Steps? From a pragmatic point of view, based on the supposed success of AA, some may argue in favor of this direction. The marketing is complete and widely accepted. For some, the Twelve Steps help the agnostic come to know Jesus.[196] However, knowing the underlying truths behind AA, the best interest of the church is to not adopt any ideological foundations from AA. Regardless of what an individual church decides, incorporating the Twelve Steps presents another example of unbiblical ideology influencing the church's approach to substance abuse.

The way churches approach AA falls within two main camps: those who support or advocate for AA and those who view the organization unfavorably. Even when churches view AA negatively, like Warren, they still incorporate the Twelve Steps to some degree within their ministries. AA left an unmistakable ideological and organizational impact on the church.

Churches who use CR need to answer a few questions: Is the use of the Twelve Steps as the foundation for a biblical recovery program wise? Would the church support New Age underpinnings in any other ministry? If churches answer no to the latter question, why do they use AA as their guide to helping those who struggle with addiction? The SBC and its churches have fulfilled Reverend Shoemaker vision from almost fifty years ago:

> I think AA has been wise to confine its organized activity to alcoholics, but I hope and I believe that we may yet see a wide effect of AA on medicine, on psychiatry, on correction, on education, on the ever present problem of human nature and what we shall do about it, and not least of all on the church itself. Perhaps the time

---

196. Frank B, "The bizarre thing is that more people come to Jesus through the path of the 12 Steps rather than having to choose Jesus from the start of their journey. It is something that we need to consider and recognize. For some who have the concept of God as the ocean or the universe, they are more likely to come to church six months later and accept Christ, rather than if they had been forced to choose God in the beginning."

has come for the church to be reawakened and revitalized by the insights and practices found in AA[197]

Over the last two decades, CR satisfied the church's attempts to come alongside or provide a Christian form of AA. While the SBC needed to enter the addiction field, the church could do more by presenting a model completely built on the scripture and entirely absent of any unbiblical influences.

---

197. Bill W., *Alcoholics Anonymous Comes of Age*, 269–70.

Chapter 4

The *DSM*'s Influence on the Medicalization of Addiction in America

Introduction

MENTAL HEALTH PROFESSIONALS TOOK possession of soul care, including the care of addicts.[1] In regard to psychology and psychiatry and its effects on helping those with addiction, the church does not possess the leading voice on how to address the life-dominating sin of substance abuse.[2] John MacArthur proposed that Christian psychology hinders the effort to restore soul care to the church.[3] Instead, the churches' support for secular theorists permits church members to use unbiblical theories.[4] Richard Ganz, in his book *Psychobabble*, pointed out that psychologists disagree with each

---

1. Greggo, "The Biblical Counseling Movement: History and Context," 130–32; Midgley, "The Biblical Counseling Movement: History and Context," 561–62; Williams, "The Biblical Counseling Movement: History and Context," 78–79.

2. Rowe, "Getting Christ off the Couch," 74.

3. "Over the past decade a host of evangelical psychological clinics have sprung up. Though almost all of them claim to offer biblical counsel, most merely dispense secular psychology disguised in spiritual terminology." MacArthur and Mack, *Introduction to Biblical*, 7.

4. "Some of the most influential, early psychologies in theological graduate schools included the psychoanalysis of Sigmund Freud, the analytical psychology of Carl Jung, the nondirective psychotherapeutic counseling of Carl Rogers, the physiological psychology of the liberal theologian-turned-psychologist G. T. Ladd, and the existential psychology of Søren Kierkegaard. Pastors, trained under these psychologies, influenced an entire generation of parishioners to think and act according to the therapeutic instead of according to the Gospel." MacArthur, *Think Biblically!* 32.

other regarding their anthropology. One of the few matters Christian counselors and biblical counselors agree upon in matters related to counseling is that people are separate from God.[5]

With addiction classified as a disease by the *DSM*, Christians who follow this classification run in the wrong direction. Instead of relying on the Word of God to guide their steps, they run toward psychiatry and follow the example of the culture:

> Science is our sacred cow, and psychotherapists, with their apparent roots in scientific knowledge and method, can lay their claims to preach whatever codes they do, not merely on the grounds of great truth, or on the assurances across guilds that they will not compete for the same pulpits, but also on the apparent facts that the clergy have tended to abdicate their claim to moral competence in favor of psychology and that the congregations have, by and large, resigned from their clergy.[6]

The psychiatrists serve as brain mechanics who find the psychological disconnects and short circuits in the brain.[7] Additionally, pastors now have church members greatly influenced by secular treatment options.[8] The secular perspective teaches addicts to put themselves first as the sole determinant in their sobriety. In this view, addicts need to admit they will remain addicts for the rest of their lives and will require attending Twelve-Step meetings in order to stay sober.[9] Those who struggle with substance abuse are told to take counsel for their souls from their sponsors, who may or may not follow Christ.[10] One approach rests on biblical truth, while the other rests on the knowledge of man.

---

5. MacArthur, *Think Biblically!* 5.

6. London, *The Modes and Morals of Psychotherapy*, 172.

7. Ganz, *Psychobabble*, 45.

8. Anonymous, *Members of the Clergy Ask,* 18; Tim P, "As I transitioned from working in the clinical field of addictions to becoming a pastor, it is amazing how much of the congregation's attitudes are more aligned with psychology than what the Bible teaches."

9. Treatment centers that advocate for AA typically have a similar FAQ: "Are You Destined to Relapse if You Stop Going to Recovery Meetings? Relapse is not necessarily inevitable if you stop attending your meetings, but the chances do increase greatly. If you feel like you are outgrowing your meetings, then the best thing to do would be to adjust your recovery plan, instead of avoiding recovery meetings altogether." Thecabinchiangmai.com, "Do I Need Recovery Meetings to Stay Sober?"

10. Bowen, "Helping People Recover from Recovery," 71.

With children as young as three years old prescribed psychotropic medications (antipsychotics, antidepressants, and stimulants), an entire generation will have the early stages of their lives filtered through the lens of mental illness, with prescription pills as the answer to those illnesses.[11] Diagnostic manuals and psychiatrists will determine what "normal" means and will become the primary source to determine which psychiatric medications to prescribe for various mental illnesses.[12] The classification system used to diagnose psychiatric illness is known as the *Diagnostic and Statistical Manual of Mental Disorders (DSM-V)*, published by the American Psychiatric Association (APA).[13] Mental health specialists, psychiatrists, and even some biblical counselors use the *DSM* as a guide to understand and diagnose mental illnesses, specifically addictions and related mental illnesses.[14]

The *DSM* is recognized as the authoritative manual for statistical analysis and research. The *DSM* provides the standard criteria and terminology, among other things, used by those in the mental health field that

---

11. "The total annual percentage of prescriptions filled by youth for any of the three medication classes was by age 3–5 years (0.8 percent), 6–12 years (5.4 percent), 13–18 years (7.7 percent), and 19–24 years (6.0 percent). Stimulant use was highest for older children (age 11 = 5.7 percent). Antidepressant use tended to increase with age and was highest for young adults (age 24 = 4.8 percent). Annual antipsychotic prescription percentages were lower than antidepressant or stimulant percentages for all age groups, with a peak in adolescence (age 16 = 1.3 percent). Annual stimulant and antipsychotic percentages for males were higher than corresponding percentages for females, but converged for young adults. Psychiatrists and child psychiatrists accounted for most of the prescriptions of antidepressants (22.2 percent–53.2 percent) and antipsychotics (51.7 percent–70 percent), but fewer of the stimulant prescriptions (30.4 percent–36.2 percent)." Sultan, "National Patterns of Commonly Prescribed Psychotropic Medications," 158.

12. As editor of the *DSM-IV*, Allen Frances's comments provide essential understanding: "Even though we had been boringly modest in our goals, obsessively meticulous in our methods, and rigidly conservative in our product, we failed to predict or prevent three new false epidemics of mental disorder in children—autism, attention deficit, and childhood bipolar disorder. And we did nothing to contain the rampant diagnostic inflation that was already expanding the boundary of psychiatry far beyond its competence." Frances, *Saving Normal*, 7.

13. *Diagnostic and Statistical Manual of Mental Disorders: DSM-V-TR* (Washington, DC: American Psychiatric Association, 2013).

14. "The contemporary language of mental illness is one example of this reductionism. The compendium for mental illnesses that our culture recognizes as authoritative is The Diagnostic and Statistical Manual for Mental Disorders (DSM). This manual makes many accurate observations about the numerous problems that afflict people. For biblical counselors, the DSM paints an incomplete and misleading picture." Lambert, *A Theology of Biblical Counseling*, 323.

assist in the diagnosis and assessment of mental illness.[15] While seen as the authoritative voice for the APA, a growing segment within the mental health field take issue with the *DSM* and its utility.[16] By tracing the massive increase of medical diagnoses for issues formerly identified as sin or moral issues, this chapter will reveal why the disease model of addiction found within the *DSM*, widely accepted even within the SBC and its churches, should not be used as the foundation for substance abuse treatment in the church.[17]

History of Changes to Addiction Classifications in the DSM

Since its inception in 1952, the *DSM* continues to play a monumental role in how society views addiction, how clinicians treat addiction, and how the church regards addictions. Sean Robinson and Bryon Adinoff wrote a journal article categorizing how the *DSM* classified addictions over the years.[18]

> DSM-I 1952
> **Terminology:** Alcoholism; Drug Addiction
> **Categorization:** Sociopathic Personality Disturbance
> **Role of Personality Disorders (PD) in relation to Substance Use Disorders (SUD):** Primary. Alcoholism and drug addiction considered a "reaction" (secondary diagnosis)
> **Main Sub-categories:** Not specified
> **Course Specifiers:** Not specified
> **Severity Specifiers:** Not specified
> **Duration:** Not specified[19]

---

15. Dziegielewski, *DSM-5 in Action*.

16. Khoury, Langer, and Pagnini, "The DSM: Mindful Science or Mindless Power?" 8; Carlat argued that "the DSM shows both scientific and clinical limits, its wide use and the blind approval of its categories and criteria must be carefully reconsidered." This view continues to gain wider acceptance within the field of psychiatry. The *DSM* no longer represents the only authoritative manual, and one should reference it carefully and ask questions. See Carlat, *Unhinged*, 53; Greenberg, *The Book of Woe*; Davies, *Cracked*, 15.

17. Jellinek, *The Disease Concept of Alcoholism*, 160; Playfair and Bryson, *The Useful Lie*, 28; Anonymous, *Al-Anon Family Groups*, 8; Baker, *Celebrate Recovery Leader's Guide*, 96.

18. Robinson and Adinoff, "The Classification of Substance Use Disorders," 18.

19. Robinson and Adinoff, "The Classification of Substance Use Disorders," 18.

DSM-II 1968
Terminology: Alcoholism; Drug Dependence
Categorization: Personality Disorder and Certain other Non-psychotic Mental Disorders
Role of Personality Disorders (PD) in relation to SUD: Primary. Although Alcoholism is secondary, additional/separate diagnosis encouraged
Main Sub-categories: Excessive drinking (Episodic, Habitual), Alcohol addiction
Course Specifiers: Not specified
Severity Specifiers: Not specified
Duration: Not specified[20]

DSM-III 1980
Terminology: Substance Use Disorders; Substance Abuse, Substance Dependence **Categorization:** Classified Independently
Role of Personality Disorders (PD) in relation to SUD: Personality disturbance is listed as "Associated features" which are often present, and may be intensified by the SUD
Main Sub-categories: Substance Abuse, Dependence
Course Specifiers: Continuous, Episodic, In remission, Unspecified
Severity Specifiers: Not specified
Duration: At least one month[21]

DSM-III-R 1987
Terminology: Psychoactive Substance Use Disorders; Substance Dependence, Substance Abuse
Categorization: Classified Independently
Role of Personality Disorders (PD) in relation to SUD: Personality disturbance is listed as "Associated features" which are often present, and may be intensified by the SUD
Main Sub-categories: Psychoactive Substance Abuse, Dependence
Course Specifiers: Partial and Full Remission
Severity Specifiers: Mild, Moderate, Severe
Duration: At least one month[22]

DSM-IV 1994
Terminology: Substance-Related Disorders; Substance Use Disorders, Substance Dependence and Substance Abuse
Categorization: Classified Independently

20. Robinson and Adinoff, "The Classification of Substance Use Disorders," 18.
21. Robinson and Adinoff, "The Classification of Substance Use Disorders," 18.
22. Robinson and Adinoff, "The Classification of Substance Use Disorders," 18.

Role of Personality Disorders (PD) in relation to SUD: Antisocial and Borderline PD are listed as "associated mental disorders" which are often co-morbid with and can complicate SUD
Main Sub-categories: Substance Abuse, Dependence
Course Specifiers: Early Full Remission, Early Partial Remission, Sustained Full Remission, Sustained Partial Remission, On Agonist Therapy, In a Controlled Environment
Severity Specifiers: With, Without Physiological Dependence
Duration: 12-month period[23]

DSM-V 2013
Terminology: Substance-Related and Addictive Disorders
Categorization: Classified Independently
Role of Personality Disorders (PD) in relation to SUD: SUDs are commonly seen in individuals with antisocial PDs which are associated with poorer prognosis
Main Sub-categories: Substance Use Disorders with Severity/Specifiers
Course Specifiers: Early remission, Sustained remission, On maintenance therapy, In a controlled environment
Severity Specifiers: Mild, Moderate, Severe
Duration: Within a 12-month period[24]

Looking specifically at the terminology, it progressed from alcoholism and drug addiction in the *DSM-I* to dependence in the *DSM-II* and to a disorder by the *DSM-III*, which remained a disorder in the *DSM-IV* and *DSM-V*. The terminology gradually evolved as the medicalization of substance abuse treatment took place. When the classifications first came out, the *DSM-I* listed alcoholism as a Sociopathic Personality Disturbance and Personality Disorder, and the *DSM-II* listed it as Certain other Non-psychotic Mental Disorders, meaning the person struggled with mind-altering substances.[25]

Those who disagreed with the medicalization of substance abuse noticed the changes to the classifications of addictions within the *DSM*. Marc Lewis, a professor of developmental psychology and a neuroscientist, adamantly opposed the *DSM*'s incorrect assumption that addiction is best addressed as a disease.

---

23. Robinson and Adinoff, "The Classification of Substance Use Disorders," 18.

24. Robinson and Adinoff, "The Classification of Substance Use Disorders," 18.

25. *Diagnostic and Statistical Manual of Mental Disorders: DSM-I*, 73; *Diagnostic and Statistical Manual of Mental Disorders: DSM-II*, 45.

Perhaps surprisingly, the most recent rewrite of the *DSM* avoids the term addiction with respect to drug and alcohol dependencies. Rather, it calls them substance-use disorders (SUDs). But let's not mince words: substance-use disorders are precisely what most of us mean by "addiction." Instead, the current *DSM* refers to gambling as an addiction. Does that mean that gambling is more addictive than heroin? And "Internet gaming disorder" has been added to the list, as a "condition for further study." Which means they're not quite sure what to call it, but it seems to be in the same ballpark as crystal meth. The psychiatrists who continue refining the map of mental disorders may be almost as confused as their patients. Or, to put it more kindly, psychiatrists are becoming aware that addictive issues are defined by behavioral patterns, not particular substances. [26]

Lewis's book, *The Biology of Desire: Why Addiction Is Not a Disease*, exemplified a paradigm shift in the fields of psychiatry and psychology, where voices in the psychology field rejected what the *DSM* asserts about substance abuse.[27]

With classifications in the DSM transforming addiction into a medical problem, the health care industry abdicated that addiction should be dealt with in the medical field without peer reviewed scientific proof,.[28] The realm of genetics and psychopathology first attempted to offer a solution to the disease model of addiction.[29] When those failed to irrefutably prove a biological explanation for addiction, neuroscientists tried the next

---

26. Lewis, *The Biology of Desire*, 165–66.

27. Snoek and Matthews, "Testing and Refining Marc Lewis's Critique," 2; Heather, "Challenging the Brain Disease Model of Addiction," 249; Tekin, "Brain Mechanisms and the Disease Model of Addiction," 401; Lewis, "Brain Change in Addiction as Learning, Not Disease," 1552.

28. Anderson, Swan, and Lane, "Fads and the Medicalization of Drug Addiction," 476.

29. Schaler stated, "Pathology, as revolutionized by Rudolf Virchow (1821–1902), requires an identifiable alteration in bodily tissue, a change in the cells of the body, for disease classification. No such identifiable pathology has been found in the bodies of heavy drinkers and drug users. This alone justifies the view that addiction is not a physical disease." Schaler, *Addiction Is a Choice*, 16. Lewis wrote, "The environmental factors that predispose people to addiction have been well understood for decades. Yet the role of genetics continues to be emphasized by the medical community, while the role of experience (including life events and quality of life) continues to be played down." Lewis, *The Biology of Desire*, 168.

approach. Yet, all additional attempts failed to prove conclusively that addiction is a disease.[30]

> In mainstream medicine, a name will only be given to a disease after its pathological roots have been identified in the body, such as in in organ, tissue, cells, etc. With few exceptions, that is how general medicine operates: once you have discovered the physical origins of a problem, only then do you give it a name. Psychiatry first names a so-called mental disorder before it has identified any pathological basis in the body. So even when there is no biological evidence that mental disorder exists, that disorder can still enter the DSM and become part of our medical culture. [31]

Despite the failure of the medical field to prove substance abuse is definitively a medical condition, addictions were medicalized and treated as a disease.[32]

Evaluation of the DSM

Evaluating the foundation, doctrine of sin, and solutions which undergird the *DSM* uncovers the dangers of uniting psychological diagnoses and classifications with recovery ministries. [33] A closer look at the methodological flaws behind the compiling of the various editions of the *DSM*, as uncovered by some within the mental health field itself, introduces concerns regarding the reliability of their diagnostic manual.[34]

---

30. Heather, "Q: Is Addiction a Brain Disease or a Moral Failing? A: Neither," 115–117; Pickard, Ahmed, and Foddy, "Alternative Models of Addiction,"; Satel and Lilienfeld, "Addiction and the Brain-Disease Fallacy."

31. Davies, *Cracked*, 29.

32. Snoek and Matthews, "Introduction," 2; Heather, "Challenging the Brain Disease Model of Addiction," 249; Tekin, "Brain Mechanisms and the Disease Model of Addiction," 402; Lewis, "Brain Change in Addiction as Learning, Not Disease," 1552.

33. A content analysis done on the *DSM-V* revealed zero mentions of the following words: Bible, Jesus, God, sin, or salvation.

34. Reznek, *Peddling Mental Disorder*, 95; Davies, "How Voting and Consensus Created the Diagnostic and Statistical Manual of Mental Disorders (DSM-III)," 32; Cooper, "Understanding the DSM-V: Stasis and Change," 64; Timimi, "No More Psychiatric Labels: Why Formal Psychiatric Diagnostic Systems Should Be Abolished," 215; Surís, Holliday, and North, "The Evolution of the Classification of Psychiatric Disorders," 5; Kupfer, First, and Regier, *A Research Agenda for DSM-V*, 31–84; Hyman, "The Diagnosis of Mental Disorders: The Problem of Reification,"155–79. Greenberg, *The Book of Woe*, 86; Davies, *Cracked*, 15; Frances, *Saving Normal*, 20.

Foundation

The foundation of the *DSM* relied upon the belief that no one needs God and diagnosing problems occurs best without the Word of God. [35] Eric Johnson, a professor at Houston Baptist University, identified the *DSM*'s void in regard to spirituality or ethics: "Let us reflect on one of its most puzzling, yet clearly defining features: the virtual lack of any ethical or spiritual evaluative language in a manual for identifying what is psychologically abnormal for human beings."[36] The authors of the *DSM* believed they adequately provided a foundation to address mental health issues without the Bible.[37]

The Bible views those who struggle with addiction as people who have a life-dominating sin of drunkenness.[38] While the current medical concept of addiction did not exist when the Bible was written, the *DSM* presents addiction as a means to reward unfilled neurological pathways, not sin.[39]

> All drugs that are taken in excess have in common direct activation of the brain reward system, which is involved in the reinforcement of behaviors and the production of memories. They produce such an intense activation of the reward system that normal activities may be neglected. Instead of achieving reward system activation through adaptive behaviors, drugs of abuse directly activate the reward pathways. [40]

---

35. A content analysis of *DSM-V* showed one instance where "God" was mentioned: "Ideas that appear to be delusional in one culture (e.g., witchcraft) may be commonly held in another. In some cultures, visual or auditory hallucinations with a religious content (e.g., hearing God's voice) are a normal part of religious experience." See *DSM-V-TR*, 146. The word "religion" appeared 18 times in the *DSM-V*.

36. Johnson, *Foundations for Soul Care*, 241.

37. All of the main psychological theorists and their theories are presented as truth. "The *DSM* has been used by clinicians and researchers from different orientations (biological, psychodynamic, cognitive, behavioral, interpersonal, family/systems), all of whom strive for a common language to communicate the essential characteristics of mental disorders presented by their patients." *DSM-V-TR*, xli.

38. Shaw, *The Heart of Addiction*, 57, Kindle; Welch, *Addictions: A Banquet in the Grave*, 17; Bowen, "Helping People Recover from Recovery," 71.

39. The Bible presents drunkenness as a moral issue, not a medical disease. See Galatians 5:21.

40. *DSM-V-TR*, 481.

The *DSM*'s Influence on Medicalization of Addiction

Mark Shaw and Ed Welch argued against the fallacy that addictions should only be attributed to psychological and physiological reasons, countering the view of supporters of the *DSM*.[41]

Some suggest the APA intended to project the authoritative voice on all issues of the soul. Greenberg summarized the statements of Darrel Regier, vice-chair of the *DSM-V*:

> By making the *DSM-V* a living document, we will ensure that the *DSM* will remain a common language in the field—and then to the rest of us: Reiger [sic] said "It will hasten our response to breakthroughs in research." What exactly we were supposed to do before those breakthroughs could occur, he didn't exactly say. The framers of the *DSM-V* may have been replacing the Bible with a living document, but they were still asking us to take them on faith.[42]

Even the leading theorists using the *DSM* do not hide their disdain for Christians.[43]

---

41. Shaw, *The Heart of Addiction*, 3, Kindle; Welch, *Addictions*, 45–46.

42. Greenberg, *The Book of Woe*, 86.

43. "Religious creeds encourage some of the craziest kinds of thoughts, emotions, and behaviors and favor severe manifestations of neurosis, borderline personality states and sometimes even psychosis. . . . In the final analysis, then, religion is neurosis. This is why I remarked, at a symposium on sin and psychotherapy held by the American Psychological Association a few years ago, that from a mental health standpoint Voltaire's famous dictum should be reversed: for if there were a god, it would be necessary to uninvent him." Ellis, *The Case against Religion*, 15. Freud wrote, "Religion is an attempt to get control over the sensory world, in which we are placed, by means of the wish-world, which we have developed inside us as a result of biological and psychological necessities. . . . If one attempts to assign to religion its place in man's evolution, it seems not so much to be a lasting acquisition, as a parallel to the neurosis which the civilized individual must pass through on his way from childhood to maturity." Freud, *Freud: Dictionary of Psychoanalysis*, 155. Skinner wrote, "Science, not religion, has taught me my most useful values, among them intellectual honesty. It is better to go without answers than to accept those that merely resolve puzzlement. I like Bertrand Russell's reply to Pascal's wager. Pascal argued that the consequences of believing in God were so immense that only a fool would not believe; but, said Russell, suppose God values intellectual honesty above all else and that he has given us shoddy evidence of His existence and is planning to damn to hell all those who believe in Him only for the sake of the glittering prizes." Skinner, "What Religion Means to Me," 13.

From Sin to Disease

Doctrine of Sin

Looking at disorders within the *DSM* reveals the exclusion of sin as the reason for an individual's troubles. Alcoholism represents a prime example of a life-dominating sin designated as a disorder. Prior to the *DSM*'s designation of alcoholism as a disorder, alcoholism exhibited a spiritual ailment in an individual where the church and clergy acted as the primary agents to address the problem.[44]

In the late 1940s, doctors were asked the question, "Do you think alcoholism should be regarded as an illness and treated by a physician?" Forty percent replied that they believe addiction is a medical problem, twenty-five percent called addiction a psychiatric issue, and nine percent believed it was a combination of the two.[45] While the thought seems ludicrous to see addiction as anything but a disease by the medical field, the debate to label addiction as a disease occurred less than fifty years ago. Alcoholics Anonymous (AA) acted as one of the major driving forces to change the designation of alcoholism.[46] The combination of the *DSM* changing the mindset of the medical field and AA influencing the culture led to a shift in how society, and specifically the church, viewed alcoholism.

Exploring how the *DSM* views addiction shows that a doctrine of disease replaced the doctrine of sin.[47] Society now sees addiction as an incurable disease instead of as a life-dominating sin.[48] In this new view, addicts have no hope of ever living a life free from the bondage of drugs and alcohol.

---

44. Carroll, "Presuppositions One and Two," 68. DiClemente, *Addiction and Change*, 3; Shaw, *The Heart of Addiction*, 515–20, Kindle; Vogel, "Finding the Whole Person," 181–82; Fingarette, *Heavy Drinking: The Myth of Alcoholism as a Disease*; Rohan, "Comment on 'The N.C.A. Criteria for the Diagnosis of Alcoholism,'" 213; Vaillant, *The Natural History of Alcoholism*, 20; Berg, *Changed into His Image*, 29.

45. Jellinek, *The Disease Concept of Alcoholism*, 162.

46. Jellinek, *The Disease Concept of Alcoholism*, 160.

47. A word search in the *DSM-V* found the term "alcohol use disorder" used 142 times with zero mention of sin as a possible cause.

48. Some of the common phrases at AA or Narcotics Anonymous (NA) meetings express, "I will be an addict for the rest of my life," and "My disease is always working to take me back out." Those who struggle with substance abuse truly believe they will have their disease forever. Their sobriety is tied to attending meetings, working with their sponsor and working through their program. *Alcoholics Anonymous Big Book*, 30; Baker, *Celebrate Recovery: The Journey Begins Participant's Guide*, 16.

The *DSM*'s Influence on Medicalization of Addiction

What is this new addiction industry meant to accomplish? More and more addictions are being discovered, and new addicts are being identified, until all of us will be locked into our own little addictive worlds with other addicts like ourselves, defined by the special interests of our neuroses. What a repugnant world to imagine, as well as a hopeless one. Meanwhile, all of the addictions we define are increasing. In the first place, we tell people they can never get better from their "diseases."[49]

The *DSM* and AA have influenced the minds of millions, convincing them that without the Twelve Steps, treatment facilities, or psychotherapy those who struggle with alcoholism will suffer permanently from their disease.[50]

Solutions

In most cases, the default solution for taking care of addicts involves treating them as if they have a disease that will plague them for the rest of their lives.[51] Additionally, the medicalization of addiction resulted in the use of pharmaceutical drugs as a solution.[52] The use of pharmaceutical drugs as

---

49. Peele, *Diseasing of America*, 4, Kindle.

50. Tim P. shared his experience working in the drug and alcohol facilities as the clinical director for over a decade: "I've heard that excuse way too many times. In the first place, I don't subscribe to the disease model; I'm not convinced. Is it a learned behavior or disease? I'm not convinced it is a disease. The disease model used to support treatment and treatment professions to run with the disease. When a guy says his disease took him out, that's a cop out. Even if the disease model was real, it's like saying my diabetes made me eat sugar." Vonasch, "Ordinary People Associate Addiction," 56–66; *Alcoholics Anonymous Big Book*, 30; Baker, *Taking an Honest and Spiritual Inventory*, 16; DiClemente, *Addiction and Change*, 3; Playfair and Bryson, *The Useful Lie*, 33; Jellinek, *The Disease Concept of Alcoholism*, 4; Fingarette, *Heavy Drinking*, 2; Shaw, *The Heart of Addiction*, 421–24, Kindle; Hammer, "Addiction: Current Criticism of the Brain Disease Paradigm," 27.

51. DiClemente, *Addiction and Change*, 3; Playfair and Bryson, *The Useful Lie*, 33; Jellinek, *The Disease Concept of Alcoholism*, 4; Fingarette, *Heavy Drinking*, 2; *Alcoholics Anonymous Big Book*, 30; Baker, *Taking an Honest and Spiritual Inventory*, 16; Shaw, *The Heart of Addiction*, 421–24, Kindle; Hammer, "Addiction," 27.

52. The use of Buprenorphine (Suboxone) is one of the primary treatment options for those who struggle with opiate addiction. See Jones, "Practical Consideration for the Clinical Use of Buprenorphine," 4. Naltrexone, also known as Antabuse, is a prescription medication used to help alcoholics. See Cummings, *Progress in Neurotherapeutics and Neuropsychopharmacology*, 260. Moore and Mattison wrote, "Most psychiatric drug use reported by adults was long term, with 84.3 percent (95 percent CI, 82.9 percent–85.7 percent) having filled 3 or more prescriptions in 2013 or indicating that they had started

a solution contradicts what biblical counselors see as a heart issue needing to be addressed by the Holy Spirit through the Word of God.[53] In the cases where actual counseling takes place, the main focus emphasizes how to make the counselee feel better and to be happy.[54] In contrast, biblical counselors encourage the counselee to obey the Word of God. The solutions presented in the *DSM* find no basis in obedience to the Word of God; instead, they lead followers of Christ away from the truth.

One of the mental illnesses classified as a co-occurring disorder in addiction also found in the Bible is anxiety.[55] Allen Frances wrote about the dangers of the reclassifications of anxiety in the *DSM-V*. "There is the new Generalized Anxiety Disorder which threatens to turn the aches and pains and disappointments of everyday life into mental illness." [56] According to the *DSM*, anxiety disorders "include disorders that share features of excessive fear and anxiety and related behavioral disturbances. Fear is the emotional response to a real or perceived imminent threat, whereas anxiety is the anticipation of future threat."[57] This definition sounds very similar to the biblical definition of anxiety, as articulated in the Holman Bible Dictionary: "State of mind wherein one is concerned about something or someone. This state of mind may range from genuine concern to obsessions

---

taking the drug during 2011 or earlier." Moore and Mattison, "Adult Utilization of Psychiatric Drugs," 274.

53. "He teaches, guides, and illumines us. This truth makes it possible for the counselor to discern how to minister to the counselee, including what the real heart issue is, what Scripture best applies to that issue, and how to guide the counselee toward the truth of God's Word concerning the issue. The Spirit's illumination makes it possible for the Word to come to life and to be recognized as truth by the counselee so he will desire to change. A number of Scriptures teach this truth (John 14:25–26; Romans 8:14; 1 Corinthians 2:12–14; Hebrews 10:15)." Babler and Ellen, *Counseling by the Book*, 1923–1927, Kindle.

54. *Feeling Good: The New Mood Therapy* by David Burns has sold over 4 million copies since its publication in 1980.

55. Anxiety is one of the main co-occurring issues for addicts who enter treatment. "As noted in the American Psychiatric Press Textbook on Psychiatry, long-term treatment can be erroneously maintained or reinstated when drug-induced rebound anxiety occurs. Addiction is the ultimate outcome." Breggin, *Toxic Psychiatry*, 332; DuPont, "Anxiety and Addiction," 53; Forsyth, Parker, and Finlay, "Anxiety, Sensitivity, Controllability, and Experiential Avoidance," 853; Book, "Severity of Anxiety in Mental Health," 1159.

56. Davies, *Cracked*, 58.

57. *DSM-V-TR*, 189.

that originate from a distorted perspective of life."[58] Despite the similar definitions, the solutions for overcoming anxiety differ dramatically. Biblical counselors argue that the use of medications to combat anxiety are not prudent as a long-term solution.[59] However, David Powlison did not oppose to the use of medication as a short-term solution to help those with psychiatric problems.[60] With anxiety disorders making up 40 percent of all new referrals in general outpatient practice, medication and psychotherapy provide the two main forms of treatment.[61]

Questionable Methodology and Classifications

Robert L. Spitzer

One of the primary architects of the current classification of mental disorders is Robert L. Spitzer, who chaired the APA's task force for the *DSM-III*.[62] Spitzer's reputation elevated while he worked as the co-developer of the computer program Diagno II, which, based on a logical decision tree, determined a diagnosis from scores from the Psychiatric Status Schedule he co-published in 1970.[63] He also received credit for co-developing the Mood Disorder Questionnaire (MDQ), a screening technique to diagnose bipolar disorder.[64] Spitzer co-developed another screening diagnosis, the Patient Health Questionnaire (PRIME-MD), for individuals to self-administer and determine if they have a mental illness.[65] Some sections of the PRIME-MD which focus on depression have now been accepted as

---

58. Brand, Draper, and England, "Anxiety," 78.

59. Fitzpatrick and Hendrickson, *Will Medicine Stop the Pain*, 45–46; Smith, *The Christian Counselor's Medical Desk Reference*, 82–85; Lambert, *A Theology of Biblical Counseling*, 110.

60. "Does that mean that medication is always wrong? No. If you are in complete panic and medication helps to calm you down, that can be a good thing. But don't kid yourself by thinking that, because of [sic] medication takes off the edge of your anxiety, you don't have to do the hard work of learning to trust God and depend on him." Powlison, *Overcoming Anxiety*, 208. Kindle.

61. *Anxiety Disorders: DSM-5 Selections*, 5; Mayo Clinic "Generalized Anxiety Disorder."

62. Decker, *The Making of DSM-III*, 81.

63. Spitzer and Endicott, "DIAGNO II: Further Developments," 12–21; Spitzer, "The Psychiatric Status Schedule," 41.

64. Spitzer, "Development and Validation,"1873.

65. Spitzer, Kroenke, and Williams, "The PHQ-9," 613.

the go-to screening and diagnosis for clinical depression and monitoring response to treatment.[66]

Spitzer, the lead contributor to the *DSM-III*, noted, "There are only a handful of mental disorders in the *DSM* known to have a clear biological cause. These are known as organic disorders (like epilepsy, Alzheimer's, and Huntington's disease). These are few and far between."[67] Despite billions of dollars earmarked for psychiatric research, studies failed to produce any evidence that any mental disorders qualify as a discrete disease with a unitary cause.[68] Spitzer was asked, "So, let me get this clear, there are no discovered biological causes for many of the remaining mental disorders in the *DSM*." Spitzer replied, "Not for many, for any! No biological markers have been identified." [69] He admitted that the *DSM* incorrectly classified large parts of typical human experiences like depression, sadness, anxiety, and grief as criteria of mental health disorders, which resulted in the over-medicalization of normal human experiences.[70]

If biology and science did not help the *DSM-III* task force come up with new disorders, what did? Spitzer revealed: "I guess our general principle was that if a large enough number of clinicians felt that a diagnostic concept was important in their work, then we were likely to add it as a new category. That was essentially it. It became a question of how much consensus there was to recognize and include a particular disorder."[71] Sometime after the first two editions of the *DSM*, which appeared more scientifically driven, a shift occurred involving less science.[72] Spitzer felt no remorse when acknowledging the deficiencies in how the *DSM-III* was created.

66. Spitzer, "Utility of a New Procedure," 1749.

67. Davies, *Cracked*, 15.

68. Frances, *Saving Normal*, 20; Kupfer, First, and Regier, *A Research Agenda for DSM-V*, 31–84; Hyman, "The Diagnosis of Mental Disorders," 155–79.

69. Davies, *Cracked*, 27.

70. "What happened is that we made estimates of the prevalence of mental disorders totally descriptively without considering that many of these conditions might be normal reactions which are not disorders. That is the problem, because we are not looking at the context in which those conditions developed. You have effectively medicalized much of ordinary human sadness, fear, ordinary experiences; you've medicalized them. I think we have, to some extent, a serious problem. It is not known . . . I don't know if it's twenty percent, thirty percent? I don't know but that a considerable amount." Spitzer, "The Trap: What Happened to Our Dream of Freedom."

71. Davies, *Cracked*, 17.

72. Surís, Holliday, and North, "The Evolution of the Classification of Psychiatric Disorders," 5.

The *DSM*'s Influence on Medicalization of Addiction

> Our team was certainly not the typical of psychiatry community, and that was one of the major arguments against the *DSM-III*: it allowed a small group with a particular viewpoint to take over psychiatry and change it in a fundamental way. What did I think of the charge? Well it was absolutely true! It was a revolution, that's what it was. We took over because we had power.[73]

Instead of relying on studies and research, the *DSM* devolved into a process to determined diagnoses based on what gained the most votes in committees.[74]

Allen Frances

Allen Frances spent his early career at the Cornell University Medical College, where he headed the outpatient department and developed specialty research clinics for depression, anxiety disorder, schizophrenia, and AIDS.[75] He eventually became the chairman for the Department of Psychiatry at Duke University's School of Medicine. Frances became most well known as the lead editor for the *DSM-IV*, and he holds an exemplary stature within the world of psychiatry. In his paper titled "The New Crisis of Confidence in Psychiatric Diagnosis," Frances went on record stating, "Psychiatric diagnosis still relies exclusively on fallible subjective judgments rather than objective biological tests."[76] Frances echoed Spitzer, a somewhat surprising response, considering their standing within the psychiatric community.

The medicalization of "normal" behavior took place in the *DSM-III* and *DSM-IV*. Frances was asked, "Are you saying that the way that the *DSM* is being used has led to the medicalization of a number of people who really don't warrant their diagnosis?" Frances replied, "Exactly. There is no right answer to who should be diagnosed. There is no gold standard for psychiatric diagnosis. So it's impossible to know for sure, but when the diagnosis rates triple over the course of fifteen years, my assumption is that medicalization is going on."[77] Both Spitzer and Frances admitted to the weakness

---

73. Davies, *Cracked*, 39.

74. Reznek, *Peddling Mental Disorder*, 95; Davies, "How Voting and Consensus," 32; Cooper, "Understanding the DSM-V," 64; Timimi, "No More Psychiatric Labels," 215; Greenberg, *The Book of Woe*, 82.

75. Frances, *Saving Normal*, 176.

76. Frances, "The New Crisis of Confidence in Psychiatric Diagnosis."

77. Davies, *Cracked*, 54.

of the editions of the *DSM*, and when pressed why the APA would allow the printing of the *DSM* knowing its deficiencies, the answer came down to money and funding.[78]

Frances continued his criticism of the *DSM* in his book *Saving Normal: An Insider's Revolt against Out-of-Control Psychiatric Diagnosis, DSM-V, Big Pharma, and the Medicalization of Ordinary Life*.[79] The title itself conveys a great deal about what the man behind the *DSM-IV* thought about the direction taken by the *DSM-V*. "Innocent kids might become obese and die early receiving unnecessary medication for a fake diagnosis. *DSM-V* was going to create public-health problems, and the public needed to have a say."[80] His rationale for his exposé on the inner workings of the *DSM* speaks volumes on the medicalization of what he called an "ordinary life" and the dangers posed to society.

While the *DSM-III* was seen as a manual based on consensus, the *DSM-IV* received criticism for its influences from pharmaceutical drug companies.[81] Frances, the lead contributor to the *DSM-IV*, stated, "A number of powerful outside forces flexed their muscles, grabbed hold of [the] *DSM-IV*, and used clever methods to encourage its misuse. They succeeded in changing diagnostic habits in ways we never imagined possible and lacked the tools to control."[82] The extensive growth in diagnostic classification coincided with a rise of psychotropic drugs.[83] This rise also produced massive profits which enabled and motivated the pharmaceutical industry to inflate the diagnostic bubble to an even greater scale.[84]

---

78. Spitzer stated, "Well they already should had [sic] to postpone publication several times, because of all the problems. So I think the DSM committee should ask the APA for an extension until all the work has been done properly. But this is not happening, and I think it is because the APA wants it published next year—it needs the huge amount of money sales will bring." Frances agreed with Spitzer when he said, "Will it protect profits first and prematurely rush a second or third rate product into print?" After spending $25 million on the *DSM-V*, the APA released it a few months after Frances was interviewed. Davies, *Cracked*, 54.

79. Frances, *Saving Normal*.
80. Frances, *Saving Normal*, 8.
81. Peterson, *Our Daily Meds*, 162.
82. Frances, *Saving Normal*, 49.
83. Statista.com "Prescription Drug Expenditure U.S., 1960–2017."
84. Frances, *Saving Normal*, 49.

The *DSM*'s Influence on Medicalization of Addiction
External Influences

Politics and money, not science, have become the primary influencers for determining what to include in the *DSM*.[85] This is a startling assertion, but one that *DSM* detractors point to that started with changes in the classification of homosexuality in the *DSM-III*. In the *DSM-I* and *DSM-II*, the psychiatric community agreed that homosexuality was a mental disorder.[86] The reason for its removal came, in part, from pressure outside the psychiatric community.[87] In a vote taken at the 1973 APA convention, 5,854 psychiatrists voted against classifying homosexuality as a mental disease while 3,810 voted in dissent. Ronald Bayer, who wrote the book *Homosexuality and American Psychiatry: The Politics of Diagnosis* stated, "If groups of people march and raise hell, they can change anything in time. Will schizophrenia be next?"[88] This change represents just one example of how the *DSM*, which supposedly reflects a scientific, unbiased manual without political influence, is challenged from within the psychiatric community as a non-scientific manual.[89]

Another example of the *DSM*'s misrepresentation as a true diagnostic manual based on science appears in the classification of depression. In a 2010 interview, Davies asked Spitzer what the criteria for the minimum threshold for depression should be. He answered, "It was just a consensus. We would ask clinicians and researchers, 'How many symptoms do you think patients ought to have before you would give them the diagnosis of

---

85. Davies, "How Voting and Consensus," 32; Greenberg, *The Book of Woe*, 66; Davies, *Cracked*, 15.

86. The *DSM-I* classified homosexuality under paraphilia (a condition characterized by abnormal sexual desires, typically involving extreme or dangerous activities). In the *DSM-II*, it was classified as a "sexual orientation disturbance." Drescher, "Out of DSM," 569.

87. Drescher, "Out of DSM," 570–71; Mayes and Horwitz, "Correction to the DSM-III," 258–59.

88. Bayer, *Homosexuality and American Psychiatry*, 141.

89. Dome, "Are DSM and Logic Not on Good Terms?" 91–92; Drescher, "Out of DSM," 565–75; Davies, "How Voting and Consensus," 32.

What makes this important is that this type of pushback against the APA used to be relegated to a few voices who were usually seen as rebels and troublemakers. With Spitzer and Frances speaking out against the *DSM*, well-respected voices are now shedding light on the inaccuracies of the *DSM*. There was even an article written for the Huffington Post by Bruce Levine, a clinical psychologist, titled "*DSM-V*: Science or Dogma? Even Some Establishment Psychiatrists Embarrassed by Newest Diagnostic Bible." Society itself is now questioning the *DSM*. Bruce Levine, "*DSM-V*: Science or Dogma?"

depression?' and we came up with the arbitrary number of five."[90] When questioned if the *DSM-III* contributors had done any studies to come up with that threshold, Spitzer said:

> We did reviews on the literature, and in some cases, we received funding from the NIMH (National Institute of Mental Health) to do field trials. . . . It would be nice if we had a biological gold standard, but that doesn't exist, because we don't understand the neurobiology of the depression.[91]

The words from the individual responsible for the *DSM-III*, the man who came up with screening processes to determine depression, revealed that the authoritative voice in psychiatry—the *DSM*, held up in such high esteem as a scientific manual—cares less about science and more about consensus.[92]

The scientific method remains consistent: observe natural phenomena, formulate a hypothesis, test hypothesis with rigorous experimentation, and then establish theory based on repeated validation of results.[93] This method allows for repeatedly conducting experiments to verify if previous experimental results are true or false. However, the scientific method cannot apply to many of the diagnoses in the *DSM-III* and *DSM-IV*, undermining its claim as the authoritative scientific source on mental health.[94]

While mainstream mental health professionals hope that misclassification of issues and false diagnoses rarely occur, these misclassifications and false diagnoses happen frequently. Three essential members of various editions of the *DSM* recorded what the *DSM* contained. Theodore Milion, a member of the *DSM-III* task force, reflected: "There was very little systemic research, and much of the research that existed was really a hodgepodge—scattered, inconsistent, and ambiguous. I think the majority of us recognized that the amount of good, solid science upon which we were making our decisions was pretty modest."[95] *DSM-IV* editor Frances went

---

90. Carlat, *Unhinged*, 53.

91. Carlat, *Unhinged*, 53.

92. Paris and Phillips, *Making the DSM-5*, 161; Hersen and Gross, *Handbook of Clinical Psychology*, 350; Eriksen and Kress, *Beyond the DSM Story*, 38; Davies, "How Voting and Consensus, 32.

93. Carey, *A Beginner's Guide to Scientific Method*, 3–5.

94. Davies, "How Voting and Consensus," 32; Greenberg, *The Book of Woe*, 66; Davies, *Cracked*, 15; Petersen, *Our Daily Meds*, 162; Spitzer, "The Trap."

95. Lane, *Shyness*, 43–44.

on to say: "Loose diagnosis is causing a national drug overdose of medication. Six percent of our people are addicted to prescription drugs, and there are more emergency room visits and deaths due to legal prescription drugs than to illegal street drugs."[96] Charles O'Brien, lead editor of the *DSM-V* substance abuse team, stated: "Let's take depression or anger or any of the other things we diagnose. They're all subjective. You have to get hints from what the patient says and how they say it, but you have no test for it."[97] The manual considered in some circles as the primary tool for diagnosing mental illness was written with less than stellar research and, in some cases, built upon behind-the-scenes dealings in backroom meetings.[98]

Pharmaceutical Companies' Influence on the DSM

The amount of money spent on mental health in America shows a massive increase in spending with each edition of the *DSM*.[99] Despite more money than ever spent on mental health, the results, according to those in the mental health field, have been less than stellar.[100] Frances warned against those in the mental health field blindly following everything in the *DSM*.[101] Those within the field go as far as calling for the abolition of di-

---

96. Frances, *Saving Normal*, 6.

97. Greenberg, *The Book of Woe*, 178.

98. Steingard, *Critical Psychiatry* Controversies, 42; Faust, *Ziskin's Coping*, 227; Krueger, Millon, and Simonsen, *Contemporary Directions in Psychopathology*, 61.

99. Cosgrove and Krimsky, "A Comparison of DSM-IV and DSM-5 Panel Members."

100. According to the National Institute of Mental Health, "An estimated 26 percent of homeless adults staying in shelters live with serious mental illness, and an estimated 46 percent live with severe mental illness and/or substance use disorders. Approximately 20 percent of state prisoners and 21 percent of local jail prisoners have 'a recent history' of a mental health condition. 70 percent of youth in juvenile justice systems have at least one mental health condition, and at least 20 percent live with a serious mental illness. Only 41 percent of adults in the U.S. with a mental health condition received mental health services in the past year. Among adults with a serious mental illness, 62.9 percent received mental health services in the past year. Just over half (50.6 percent) of children aged 8–15 received mental health services in the previous year." Nami.org, "NAMI."

101. "The *DSM-V* will considerably increase medicalization and may turn our current diagnostic inflation into hyperinflation. Overdiagnosis transforms normal grief into major depressive disorder, normal temper tantrums into disruptive mood dysregulation disorder, normal forgetfulness of old age into minor neurocognitive disorder, poor eating habits into binge eating disorder, and expectable worry about physical symptoms into somatic symptom disorder." Frances, "*DSM*, Psychotherapy, Counseling and the Medicalization of Mental Illness," 282–84.

agnostic manuals like the *DSM*.[102] The medicalization of America increased with every release of the *DSM*, which resulted in more money spent on medical services. Greenberg stated, "Lowered thresholds for old diagnoses and its brand-new, untested diagnoses, the *DSM-V* would be like honey to the drug company flies and like gold to lawyers."[103] But the general public grows increasingly aware of the huge profits pharmaceutical companies make with each *DSM* release.[104]

Due to the attention given to the potential conflicts of interest between the *DSM* task force members and pharmaceutical companies, professors from the University of Massachusetts and Tufts decided to research financial ties between *DSM* task force members and the pharmaceutical industry.[105] The researchers looked at 170 members who participated in providing the diagnostic criteria found in the *DSM-IV*.[106] Ninety-five of the 170 *DSM* members (55 percent) had at least one financial association with pharmaceutical companies. Of the task force members on the panels for "Schizophrenia and Other Psychotic Disorders" and "Mood Disorders," 100 percent had ties to pharmaceutical companies. When broken down by payment categories, 42 percent received payment for research funding, 22 percent for consultancies, and 16 percent for speaking engagements.[107]

The authors of the study concluded that strong financial ties existed between pharmaceutical companies and those responsible for modifying and developing the criteria used to diagnose mental illness.[108] Further-

102. Timimi, "No More Psychiatric Labels," 208–15; Eriksen and Kress, *Beyond the DSM Story*, 87; Paul Genova, "Dump the DSM!" *Psychiatric Times* 20, no. 4 (April 2003): 72.

103. Greenberg, *The Book of Woe*, 80.

104. Wieczner, "Drug Companies Look to Profit from DSM-V."

105. Fava, "Conflicts of Interest," 55–72, Angell, *The Truth about the Drug Companies*, 16; Krimsky, *Science in the Private Interest: Has the Lure of Profits Corrupted Biomedical Research?*

106. Cosgrove, "Financial Ties between DSM-IV Panel Members," 155.

107. Cosgrove, "Financial Ties between DSM-IV Panel Members," 156.

108. "Our inquiry into the relationships between DSM panel members and the pharmaceutical industry demonstrates that there are strong financial ties between the industry and those who are responsible for developing and modifying the diagnostic criteria for mental illness. The connections are especially strong in those diagnostic areas where drugs are the first line of treatment for mental disorders. Full disclosure by DSM panel members of their financial relationships with for-profit entities that manufacture drugs used in the treatment of mental illness is recommended." Cosgrove, "Financial Ties between DSM-IV Panel Members," 159.

The DSM's Influence on Medicalization of Addiction

more, the drug companies and task force members had the strongest connections in cases where medication is the first line of treatment for certain mental illnesses. Investigators suggested that full financial disclosures and connections be made before future publishing any material that deals with diagnoses or classifications of mental disorders.[109]

Despite putting the APA on notice that researchers were investigating financial ties between previous *DSM* contributors and pharmaceutical companies, the *DSM-V* reflected no difference in ties between contributors and pharmaceutical companies.[110] Greenberg provided an example of the APA's deception:

> Charles O'Brien is a University of Pennsylvania psychiatrist and head of the *DSM-V* workgroup for substance-related disorders. "People should understand that when they read things in the newspaper about Pharma influence, I don't believe it," he said, as he made the conflict-of-interest disclosure required of every speaker. "We stopped that a long time ago, even though in the past we might have had some consultancies." O'Brien didn't say exactly what they had stopped, but it clearly wasn't the consultancies. Indeed, he was still working for three drug companies.[111]

Despite the APA's disclosure policy concerning possible financial conflicts of interest with the *DSM-V*, the policy did not lower the conflicts of interest of the members on the *DSM-V* panel. Cosgrove and Krimsky argued, "Transparency alone cannot mitigate the potential for bias and is an insufficient solution for protecting the integrity of the revision process."[112] At this point, the *DSM* severely damaged its reputation, and mental health experts questioned its validity.

The intertwining of pharmaceutical companies, the *DSM*, and doctors prescribing medication for addicts is undeniable. For every new classification, another drug suddenly becomes available to treat the supposed new disorder. In rehab centers and sober living homes, one of the most abused multi-use medications is Seroquel, or Quetiapine.[113] Initially approved for those with bipolar disorder or schizophrenia, doctors found a use for the

---

109. Cosgrove, "Financial Ties between DSM-IV Panel Members," 154.
110. Cosgrove, "Conflicts of Interest and Disclosure," 229.
111. Greenberg, *The Book of Woe*, 177.
112. Cosgrove and Krimsky, "A Comparison of DSM-IV and DSM-5 Panel Members."
113. Soeiro-De-Souza, "Role of Quetiapine beyond Its Clinical Efficacy," 643–52.

From Sin to Disease

drug to treat anxiety or chronic insomnia.[114] As another multiuse drug example, Naltrexone initially received approval as a drug to treat opioid and alcohol dependence, but other off-label uses include compulsive gambling, kleptomania, fibromyalgia, cancer, multiple sclerosis, and HIV.[115] Most people remain unaware of the off-label uses of the same medication for various unrelated issues.[116] Pharmaceutical companies deliberately deceive the consumer by using different names of the same drug for different medical conditions.[117]

Those who enter treatment for substance abuse complain that they went in for an addiction to an illicit or certain prescription drugs; but by the time they left treatment, they were on even more drugs than when they first went in.[118] An unquestionable link exists between Big Pharma, the *DSM*, and those who use it as their main guidebook to come up with diagnoses. The symbiosis of Big Pharma, the APA, and the *DSM* effects society financially and negatively impacts those seeking help from psychiatrists.

---

114. Lee, "Off-Label Use of Quetiapine," 1390.

115. Slomski, "Opioid Agonist and Antagonist," 333; Grant and Kim, "Medication Management of Pathological Gambling," 44–48; Grant, "Outcome Study of Kleptomania Patients," 11–14; Younger, "Low-Dose Naltrexone for the Treatment of Fibromyalgia," 529–38; Zagon and Mclaughlin, "Naltrexone Modulates Tumor Response," 671–73; Gekker, Lokensgard, and Peterson, "Naltrexone Potentiates Anti-HIV-1," 257–63.

116. Cavalla, *Off-Label* Prescribing, 42.

117. Goldacre, *Bad Pharma*, 181. Trazadone was initially marketed to help those that suffered from depression. One of its other treatment uses includes serving as a sleep aid. See Sadock, *Kaplan & Sadock Concise Textbook of Clinical Psychiatry*, 554. Wellbutrin was first prescribed as an anti-depressant but now used to help individuals quit smoking or who struggle with anxiety. See Wyatt, *Wyatt's Practical Psychiatric Practice*, 145. Klonopin is used to control and prevent seizures. However, it is also used to treat anxiety and panic disorders. See Berman, *100 Questions & Answers about Panic*, 85.

118. In the book *Inside Rehab*, the author interviewed parents of those who were given prescription medication while in treatment. "She and her husband had paid for an expensive alternative regime including prescription medications and nutrition supplements. Initially some of the expenses were covered by health insurance: about $30,000, but another $200,000 came from their own funds." Fletcher, *Inside Rehab*, 61. One of the most widely prescribed medications to help with alcoholism are a class of drugs which include Seroquel. Seroquel is also one of the medications being abused by those in treatment. See Carl, Gallo, and Johnson, *Practical Pharmacology in Rehabilitation*, 287.

The *DSM*'s Influence on Medicalization of Addiction

Suboxone

While therapy and Twelve-Step treatments have been the dominant force in addressing addictions, the use of medication became a newer approach. The medicalization of addiction finalized with the introduction of drugs as an answer to help those struggling with substance abuse. One of the most used prescription medications for the opiate crisis has been Buprenorphine (Suboxone).[119] Due to the high relapse rate, an increase of overdoses, and more deaths, addicts have been more willing to use medication to combat what the medical realm defined as a disease. Suboxone has actually been around since the 1970s. Doctors prescribed the drug as a substitute for heroin and morphine for pain management. The drug provided a safer alternative by requiring fewer regulations due to the built-in "abuse deterrence properties" as an opioid agonist-antagonist.[120]

The company that manufactured Suboxone, Reckitt Benckiser, worked alongside addiction treatment centers and sought an exception to enable individual suppliers, instead of designated federal clinics, to write prescriptions for Buprenorphine.[121] With the passing of the Drug Addiction Treatment Act of 2000, doctors were allowed to prescribe certain opiates to treat what the *DSM* classified as the Opioid Use Disorder.[122] Thus, the medical field embraced the use of Suboxone as a solution to opiate addiction. However, those in Twelve-Step communities look down upon the drug.[123] A large division took place between the two distinct realms (Twelve Steps and the medical field) of how addiction should be treated.

Suboxone surfaced in the news recently due to a $1.4 billion judgment against the manufacturers of the drug. The attorney general of Connecticut, George Jepsen, stated, "The circumstances alleged in this case are particularly egregious in that, in the midst of an epidemic of opioid abuse

---

119. J Velander, "Suboxone: Rationale, Science, Misconceptions," 23. Velander believes in the disease model: "As with other chronic medical illnesses, opioid addiction, once developed, has no cure and requires ongoing monitoring and treatment."

120. Jasinski, "Human Pharmacology and Abuse Potential of the Analgesic Buprenorphine," 501.

121. Velander, "Suboxone," 25.

122. Authority for Physicians who dispense or prescribe certain narcotic drugs for maintenance treatment or detoxification treatment. Suboxone is still the only opiate authorized under this waiver. Nida.nih.gov "Effective Treatments for Opioid Addiction."

123. Within certain 12-Step circles, those who take Suboxone for their addiction are not considered sober. The underlying reasoning for discouraging Suboxone use comes from a hard line against any mind-altering substances.

and addiction ... consumers and taxpayers have had to pay more for a drug that may help to mitigate some of the problem."[124] Cutting corners in the regulatory process for pharmaceutical companies is not something new, as drug manufacturers commonly tweak a formula slightly to maintain a grasp on their patents. This example left an egregious toll on the nation at a cost of $600 billion a year to combat the opiate epidemic.

Two of the most influential contributors to the *DSM-III* and *IV* went on record stating how the *DSM* contains errors and responded to influences by forces outside the psychological field.[125] Several authors argued that the *DSM* was created during behind-closed-doors bargaining sessions, influenced by multibillion-dollar drug corporations.[126] These same authors view the *DSM* as more of an advertisement for Big Pharma products than as an actual diagnostic manual to help treat those who have a mental illness.[127]

The DSM's Impact on How the SBC Approaches Addiction and Its Co-Occurring Disorders

Those in the mental health field see the *DSM* and its diagnoses as the main authority on how to deal with mental illness.[128] Even within some SBC churches, the Word of God becomes secondary to *DSM* classifications and treatments.[129] What was once traditionally accepted as a spiritual issue transformed into what the recovery field deemed a medical issue.[130] The

---

124. Moraff, "Suboxone Creator's Shocking Scheme to Profit off of Heroin Addicts,"

125. Robert Spitzer and Allen Frances, as noted earlier in this chapter, have both spoken against how the *DSM* decides what a disorder is.

126. Fava, "Conflicts of Interest," 56; Angell, *The Truth About the Drug Companies*, 16; Krimsky, *Science in the Private Interest*, 2; Cosgrove, "Financial Ties between DSM-IV Panel Members," 159.

127. "While the successive framers of the *DSM* have attempted to base it on scientific evidence, political and economic factors have also shaped the conceptualization of mental illness. These economic and institutional forces have reinforced the *DSM*'s use of a medical model in understanding psychopathology." Pilecki, Clegg, and McKay, "The Influence of Corporate and Political Interests,"194.

128. "The American Psychiatric Association's Diagnostic and Statistical Manual of Mental Disorders (*DSM*) is a classification of mental disorders with associated criteria designed to facilitate more reliable diagnoses of these disorders. With successive editions over the past 60 years, it has become a standard reference for clinical practice in the mental health field." *DSM-V-TR*, 5.

129. Johnson, *Foundations for Soul Care*, 240.

130. Playfair and Bryson, *The Useful Lie*, 28. Jellinek wrote, "The contacts of the

acceptance of the disease model within the church is so prevalent that even AA literature discusses this reality.[131] A shift occurred with the release of the *DSM-V*.[132] The criteria used to determine if an individual falls under this category replicates almost a carbon copy of the AA checklist. Since the shift of redefining the underlying cause of addiction, churches have been more likely not to address the problem. They have relented to those in the medical realm.[133]

While the psychiatric industry tears itself apart from the inside, pastors and church congregations embraced the "science" of psychology and psychiatry and ignored the heeding of biblical counselors as well as some powerful voices within the field of psychiatry.[134] Russell Moore, the former head of the Ethics and Religious Liberty Commission of the Southern Baptist Convention, classified depression as a chemical issue while interviewing Rick Warren after the death of his son via suicide:

> So how would you know there are some people who, for instance, may be suffering from depression because of a reason . . . it's they've lost a spouse, or maybe even somebody who does have a spiritual problem—he feels guilty for something that's happening. And you have someone whose [sic] experiencing a chemical issue or a medical issue.[135]

---

clergymen with Alcoholics Anonymous groups, and their acquaintances with the spiritual outlook and the striking success of that fellowship, have contributed to the changes in denominational attitudes." Jellinek, *The Disease Concept of Alcoholism*, 171.

131. Anonymous, *Al-Anon Family Groups*.

132. Alcoholism is now classified as one of the Substance-Related and Addictive Disorders. *DSM-V-TR*, 515. The classification changed due to the expansion from just psychoactive substances. It now includes behaviors such as gambling, kleptomania, and internet gaming.

133. As stated in a previous chapter, the last time the SBC addressed alcoholism was in a 2006 resolution. The SBC has remained silent ever since.

134. "Some Christians have embraced modern psychology's findings and theories with uncritical enthusiasm, naively trusting that its texts are a perfect reflection of human reality. Others have argued that any appropriation of modern psychology is 'psychoheresy,' since it necessarily poisons the Christians who imbibe it. This book will examine neither extreme but will consider the vast territory between them, specifically the five well-thought-through views from evangelicals who offer a fairly comprehensive representation of the ways that most Christians understand psychology and counseling in our day." Johnson, *Psychology & Christianity*, 10.

135. Moore, Warren, and Rose, "Dealing with Mental Health Issues as a Christian," to Breggin, "Many people who take the drugs become desperately depressed and suicidal, violently aggressive, or wildly out of control without realizing their medication is causing

Rick and Kay Warren emphasized that their son's suicide could have been prevented with a diagnosis of Borderline Personality Disorder and continued medication.[136] Understandably, parents look for causality for such a tragic loss. The reassurance found in science appeals to those in grief.[137] Unfortunately, the interviews with the Warrens and Moore showcased how intertwined the *DSM* had become in the Christian approach to mental health.[138]

Without looking at the theological errors in the *DSM* and solely focusing on the methodological errors, one would expect Christians in the field of counseling to reject the use of the *DSM*, but that is not the case. Eric Johnson included a section in his book *Foundations For Soul Care* titled "The Virtues and Vices of the Diagnostic and Statistical Manual."[139] A primary voice for a wing of Christian counseling within the SBC that advocates for psychology, Johnson proclaimed that the *DSM* is both scientific and an important addition to the field of psychology.[140] He went so far as to say that the *DSM* "has to be considered a monumental scientific achievement."[141] Despite members of the *DSM-III* and *DSM-IV* task forces stating flaws in methodology and science, Johnson and some of his colleagues continue to support the *DSM*.

An outcome of embracing the *DSM* involved the acceptance of psychotropic medications, which played a significant role in treating addictions by individual voices in the field of biblical counseling. Brad Hambrick's definition of mental health mirrors the *DSM*.[142] In a study guide,

---

them to think, to feel, and to act in unusual and otherwise abhorrent ways." Breggin, *Medication Madness*, 1. Due to the risk of suicide, one of the causes of death for those who struggle with addictions, those encouraged to take psychotropic medication should know all of the essential facts.

136. Warren, "Psychiatry and Faith."

137. Farias, "Scientific Faith," 1210–13; Rutjens, Van Harreveld, and Van Der Pligt, "Step by Step," 250–55.

138. Lambert, "Mental Illness, Psychiatric Drugs, and Counseling Education."

139. Johnson, *Foundations for Soul Care*, 240.

140. Johnson, *Psychology & Christianity*. Johnson also stated, "It is to be seen as a tremendous scientific achievement that 'For our present purposes, we will simply assume its overall empirical basis and scientific legitimacy.'" Johnson, *Foundations for Soul Care*, 241.

141. Johnson, *Foundations for Soul Care*, 241.

142. "Mental illness may have its cause in the physical body (i.e., brain chemistry, habituated neural pathways, genetics, glandular system, viral or bacterial infection, etc.), environmental causes (i.e., trauma, poor socialization, abusive-neglectful home life, etc.),

which accompanied a seminar he taught, he wrote an entry titled "Six Steps to Wise Decision Making About Psychotropic Medications." Hambrick acknowledged that no known biological tests determine mental illness.[143] However, this did not stop Hambrick from providing a step-by-step plan of action for those he counsels to determine if they should start taking psychotropic medication.[144] Hambrick's view on medication does not address information or literature on its dangers. Oddly, for an article titled "Six Steps to Wise Decision Making About Psychotropic Medications," he mentions nothing about the dangers of taking them, despite ample evidence that these medications are not always safe.[145]

The field of Christian counseling is filled with practitioners who are no different from secular psychologists and psychiatrists.[146] Christian counselors readily embrace the *DSM* and the use of pharmaceutical drugs as the answer to some of the issues that coincide with addictions. A cause for concern results when individuals such as Johnson and Hambrick influence pastors and church members without pointing out concerns that even their secular counterparts bring to light. Hambrick answered the question "What is a mental illness?" by stating, "As close as we can get to an accepted definition would be the one given in the Diagnostic and Statistical Manual: Fifth Edition (*DSM-V*) by the American Psychiatric Association (APA)." [147]

---

personal choices (i.e., the consequences of sinful or foolish decisions on a spectrum from isolated bad choices with significant emotional-relational implication to addiction), or a combination of these causes." Hambrick, "Towards a Christian Perspective on Mental Illness."

143. Hambrick, "6 Steps to Wise Decision Making about Psychotropic Medications," Hambrick said, "Most struggles known as mental illness do not have a body-fluid test (i.e., blood, saliva, or urine) to verify their presence."

144. Hambrick stated, "Step One – Assess Life and Struggle. Step Two – Make Needed Non-Medical Changes. Step Three – Determine the Non-Medicated Base-Line for Your Mood and Life Functioning. Step Four – Begin a Medication Trial. Step Five – Assess Level of Progress Against the Medication Side Effects. Step Six – Determine Whether to Remain on Medication." Hambrick, "6 Steps to Wise Decision Making about Psychotropic Medications."

145. Breggin, *Medication Madness*, 1. In fairness, steps 1–3 can be affirmed as a wise approach to the problem.

146. Johnson even stated, "[The *DSM*] is a scientific text, and as such is far superior to the biblical text for the scientific task of the diagnosis of most mental disorders." Johnson, *Foundations for Soul Care*, 243. See also Myers, *Psychology in Modules with Updates on DSM-V*; Jones, "A Constructive Relationship for Religion," 184–99; Roberts, "The Idea of a Christian Psychology," 37–40.

147. Hambrick, "Towards a Christian Perspective on Mental Illness." According to

Instead of providing a biblical view on mental illness, Hambrick defaulted to the *DSM* for the primary definition.

Conclusion

The *DSM*'s classifications for addiction and anxiety exemplify the medicalization of struggles found in the Bible. Despite controversies, arguments concerning the validity of the *DSM*, and questionable financial maneuvering with those writing the *DSM*, Americans continue to embrace it as the definitive manual to diagnose mental illnesses. Since the release of the *DSM-I* in 1952, more categories emerged for disorders and an increase of new medicines, yet a question needs to be asked: Is America better off than before the *DSM*'s release? Life-dominating sins have been classified as diseases. The SBC and its churches have been removed as the primary caretaker of souls. America has become dependent on faulty science and medicine and less dependent on God.

The church's reliance on the *DSM* to determine what classifies as a disease impacted how the church takes care of those with addiction issues. The introduction of the disease model immobilized the SBC's churches and rendered them mainly absent in combating the life-dominating sin of substance abuse. Churches have an easier time referring church members to Twelve-Step programs, both secular and faith-based, rather than having the courage to engage addicts and alcoholics. As demonstrated in the previous chapter, even the curriculum of faith-based programs mimics AA. The combination of AA and the *DSM* paralyzed the SBC, damaging churches and, in some cases, removing soul care from the church.

---

the *DSM-V*: "A mental disorder is a syndrome characterized by clinically significant disturbance in an individual's cognition, emotion regulation, or behavior that reflects a dysfunction in the psychological, biological, or developmental processes underlying mental functioning. Mental disorders are usually associated with significant distress in social, occupational, or other important activities. An expectable or culturally approved response to a common stressor or loss, such as the death of a loved one, is not a mental disorder. Socially deviant behavior (e.g., political, religious, or sexual) and conflicts that are primarily between the individual and society are not mental disorders unless the deviance or conflict results from a dysfunction in the individual, as described above." *DSM-V-TR*, 16.

Chapter 5

Conclusion

Summary

BEFORE THE LATE NINETEENTH century, society viewed addiction as a moral issue—an issue best cared for by the church. Addiction to drugs and alcohol was once considered a spiritual battle where pastors served as the primary physicians to address the problem.[1] Over the last two and half centuries, addiction transformed into what the medical field calls a disease.[2] Alcoholics Anonymous (AA) and other self-help groups contributed to Christians embracing addiction as a disease, while the infiltration of the church by secular techniques can be traced to the *Diagnostic and Statistical Manual of Mental Disorders (DSM)*.[3] The removal of sin as the primary cause for addiction neglects biblical truth and enables the secular therapist to take over the soul care of addicts. Three main models show how

---

1. DiClemente, *Addiction and Change*, 3. Shaw, *The Heart of* Addiction, 515–20, Kindle; Vogel, "Finding the Whole Person," 181–82; Fingarette, *Heavy Drinking*, 3; Rohan, "Comment on 'The N.C.A. Criteria,'" 212; Mendelson and Mello, *The Diagnosis and Treatment of Alcoholism*, 14; Vaillant, *The Natural History of Alcoholism*, 20; Berg, *Changed into His Image*, 29.

2. DiClemente, *Addiction and Change*, 3; Playfair and Bryson, *The Useful Lie*, 33; Vaillant, *The Natural History of Alcoholism*, 20; Towns and Lambert, *Habits that Handicap*, 177; McCarthy, "Early Alcoholism Treatment, 60; Dubiel, *The Road to Fellowship*; Stern, "STERILIZED in the Name of Public Health," 1128–138.

3. Jellinek, *The Disease Concept of Alcoholism*, 160; Playfair and Bryson, *The Useful Lie*, 28; *Diagnostic and Statistical Manual of Mental Disorders: DSM-V-TR*.

the church today views addiction and influence how the church addresses addiction.

Three Views of Addiction

Addiction as Sin

Christians embraced the notion that addiction is a disease even though the Bible contradicts this view.[4] One of the goals of biblical counseling takes back the behavioral issues designated as medical issues.[5] Christians believing that addiction is a disease can be traced back to medical doctors who contributed up to one-fifth of the contributions in the *Journal of Pastoral Practice*.[6] Some of the topics included addiction and alcoholism, which began removing the soul care of addicts from the clergy. Personal sin remains the root cause of most of the day-by-day counseling problems that arise.[7]

Jay Adams proposed that sin covers a multitude of problems and bad behaviors.[8] These problems and bad behaviors did not matter whether they were conscious or unconscious deeds. The foundational issue reveals the selfish desires of man to please himself, which affirms the absolute depravity of man. In essence, no new diseases or mental illnesses manifest in the world.[9] Ultimately, humanity faces the same problems today that the biblical characters also faced.[10] Sin is the root cause, and the proper way to address life-dominating sins is through obedience to God and His Word.[11]

In his book *The Heart of Addiction*, Mark Shaw proposed that if someone is not sure that addiction should be classified as a sin, they should present scientific studies that prove it is a disease.[12] The disease model for

---

4. Playfair and Bryson, *The Useful Lie*, 33.
5. Powlison, *The Biblical Counseling Movement*, 10.
6. Powlison, *The Biblical Counseling Movement*, 10.
7. Adams, *The Christian Counselor's Manual*, 136.
8. Powlison, *The Biblical Counseling Movement*, 100.
9. Priolo, "Presupposition Five: Sickness and Sin," 63.
10. Luther stated: "The main object sought at present was to bring about better discipline among the members of the various congregations and to put down the sins of drunkenness, unchastity, frivolous swearing, and witchcraft." Kolstlin, *Life of Luther*, 343.
11. Adams, "Sin and Counseling," 57; Powlison, *The Biblical Counseling Movement*, 101; Priolo, "Sin and Misery," 98.
12. Shaw, *The Heart of Addiction*, 19, Kindle.

addiction amounts to an unproven man-made theory. When looking at addiction, the issue that needs addressing is determining whether or not addiction results from a "sin nature" or a "disease concept." The problem of drunkenness and idolatry cannot be ignored. Addiction is a heart issue where the world's approach and scripture cannot be merged together.[13] The "disease concept" gained credibility because society embraced it as a medical issue backed by real science. In reality, the disease concept prevails as a lie based on a hopeless view of addiction, which offers the addict no expectations of ever overcoming the disease.[14]

Addiction as Choice

Christians who deny that addiction is a disease suffer ridicule for their "backward thinking" or "anti-science" perspective. In a review of the book *Cracked*, the reviewer wrote a scathing exposé on the truths of psychiatry: "I'd read several similar books, and did not want to waste my time on one contrasting biopsychiatry with some 'positive' Christian vision."[15] A growing section of the secular world agrees that addiction is not a disease and offer valuable contributions to the discussion, even from those who discredit Christian counselors. Some of the proponents of this way of thinking include Stanton Peele, James Davies, and Herbert Fingarette. Fingarette wrote:

> All attempts to identify and define "alcoholism" have failed because the concept itself is fundamentally flawed. "Alcoholism" exist [sic] in our language and in our minds, but not in the objective world around us.
>
> ... So many words have been written and spoken about "alcoholism" that language alone "confirms it as a reality."[16]

Previously seen as a topic only Christians would argue against, the disease model is becoming a current topic amongst those in the addiction field.

---

13. Shaw, *The Heart of Addiction*, 3, Kindle.

14. Shaw, *The Heart of Addiction*, 3, Kindle.

15. Salty Current "Review of *Cracked* by James Davies," While reviews are not always found in academic resources such as journals or books, the critical review in this blog exemplifies a common theme when looking over blogs and websites that deal with addictions.

16. Fingarette, *Heavy Drinking*, 49.

This conversation presents a strong opportunity for the church to clarify its stance on addiction and reassert its claim on the care of souls for addicts.

Since a subsection of the psychiatry and psychology fields advocate against labeling issues like addiction and depression as a disease, the church has an opportunity to reassert itself as a primary answer for addictions. Biblical counselors may reembrace what Martin Luther proposed almost six hundred years ago: prayer and faith offer the best way to address a sin issue, not pills or medical doctors.[17] George E. Vaillant, a respected psychiatrist in the addiction field, said: "I willingly concede, however, that alcohol dependence lies on a continuum and that in scientific terms, behavior disorder will often be a happier semantic choice than disease."[18] One of the primary voices speaking against the disease model, as stated in Chapter 1 comes from Stanton Peele, who has written extensively that addiction is not a disease.[19] Peele's view contrasts what is often publicly said by the so-called leaders in the field of addiction.[20] Unfortunately, with so many paraprofessionals in the realm of addictions, they neglect to look at some of the data that science reveals on the topic.[21] Instead, addiction as a disease is based on personal knowledge from working with an addict rather than looking at the scientific data—which they deem irrelevant, obscure, or contradictory to their personal belief.[22]

Addiction as a Disease

The National Institute of Drug Abuse considers addiction a complex illness.[23] The characteristics of addiction manifest as an intense and sometimes uncontrollable desire which persists even though potentially

---

17. Tappert, *Luther: Letters of Spiritual Counsel*, 46.
18. Vaillant, *The Natural History of Alcoholism*, 20.
19. Peele, *Diseasing of America*, 774, Kindle.
20. Thirty years have passed since Fingarette and Peele questioned the validity of the disease model, but more clinicians and doctors are pushing back that addiction is a disease. Fingarette, *Heavy Drinking*, 26; Rohan, "Comment on 'The N.C.A. Criteria for the Diagnosis of Alcoholism," 211–18; Mendelson and Mello, *The Diagnosis and Treatment of Alcoholism*; Peele, *Diseasing of America*, 774, Kindle.
21. Burnette, "Mindsets of Addiction," 367; Holden, "Addiction Is Not a Disease," 679; Levy, "Addiction Is Not a Brain Disease (and It Matters)," Lewis, "Brain Change in Addiction as Learning, Not Disease," 1551; Lewis, *The Biology of Desire*, 164.
22. Pattison, Sobell, and Sobell, *Emerging Concepts of Alcohol Dependence*.
23. National Institute on Drug Abuse, *Principles of Drug Addiction Treatment*.

Conclusion

devastating consequences result.[24] Accordingly, the experts describe addiction as a brain disease that starts with the repeated use of drugs or alcohol. Over time the drug use consumes the individual and becomes a compulsive behavior.[25] The prolonged consumption of the drugs compromises the brain function and causes the brain to short circuit. This rewiring of the brain will affect learning, memory, motivation, and inhibitory control over the individual's behavior.[26] Scientists propose that genetics, age, and environmental factors determine whether one does or does not become an addict.[27] However, the specific conditions which predispose certain people to succumb to an addiction more than others with similar genetics remains unclear.

According to medical professionals, addiction is a learned behavior, and the recovery process will take time.[28] The reason that the process will take time is due to memories of the past or physical dependency, requiring therapy and professional treatment to overcome addiction. As mentioned in Chapter 1, Rusk said mental problem like depression and anxiety need the same type of treatment like pneumonia or appendicitis. Both mental health and physical ailments are medical issues that need medical care.[29] The link between addiction and other mental illnesses are commonplace within addiction treatment. Treatment centers that focus on both mental illness and addiction classify as dual diagnosis centers who have a medical doctor in addition to a Certified Alcohol/Drug Abuse Counselor (CADC).[30]

From Sin to Disease

The idea that addiction is a disease was initially proposed in the 1800s when Benjamin Rush thought individuals who consumed too much alcohol were in fact diseased.[31] He promoted prohibition as one of his main platforms since the term alcoholic previously did not exist. Drunkards previously

---

24. DiClemente, *Addiction and Change*, 3.
25. DiClemente, *Addiction and Change*, 3.
26. Miller, "How Addiction Hijacks the Brain," 1–3.
27. Miller, "How Addiction Hijacks the Brain."
28. Miller, "How Addiction Hijacks the Brain."
29. Whitaker, *Anatomy of an Epidemic*, 46.
30. For further information on Dual Diagnosis Treatment centers, see Rehabs.com, "Choosing the Best Dual Diagnosis Rehab Program,"
31. Baldwin Research Institute, "Alcoholism Is Not a Disease."

received the designation as inebriates, not alcoholics.[32] Drunkenness signaled that the person engaged in poor behavior, not as the underlying cause for deviant behavior.[33] The traditional view considered drug users and people who consumed too much alcohol to be immoral individuals. The sinful nature underlying one's immorality was the impetus that brought about chemical dependency. Those in the addiction field today widely reject the traditional perspective, despite its unquestioned acceptance until the late 1800s.[34]

Another foundational shift which occurred in the 1900s resulted from the evolving definition of a disease.[35] The first generation of those in the field of psychology viewed addiction as a disease. Parts of the body malfunctioned, accompanied by symptoms seen physically such as chickenpox, cancer, and pneumonia. These diseases prompted the discovery of medical treatments to address the problem. According to Stanton Peele, the second generation was classified as emotional disorders that focused on thoughts and feelings. These disorders included schizophrenia, depression, and phobias treated with pills or surgery. Addiction fell within the third generation of diseases.[36] Symptoms were not classified by physical manifestations but were based on abnormal or distorted behavior.[37] By the early 1920s, the church lost its jurisdiction for the care of souls due to its perceived impotence with regard to addressing the problems addicts faced.[38]

The expansion from the first generation of diseases to the third generation influenced the perception of a disease. Once defined as having a physical malfunction with symptoms, diseases became an illness absent physicals signs—replacing physiological symptoms with behavior. Identifiers for those who suffer from third generation diseases included: losing control of one's involvement in the activity, requirements to attend

32. Jellinek, *The Disease Concept of Alcoholism*, 8.
33. Playfair and Bryson, *The Useful Lie*, 8.
34. Peele, *Diseasing of America*, 685–689, Kindle.
35. Fingarette, *Heavy Drinking*, 1–2; Peele, *Diseasing of America*, 353–59, Kindle.
36. "The third generation of diseases—addictions—strays still farther from the model of physical disorder to which the name disease was first applied by modern medicine. That is, unlike a mental illness such as schizophrenia, which is indicated by disordered thinking and feelings, addictive disorders are known by the behaviors they describe." Peele, *Diseasing of America*, 364–67, Kindle.
37. Playfair and Bryson, *The Useful Lie*, 35; Peele, *Diseasing of America*, 484–93, Kindle.
38. Abbott, *The System of Professions*, 308.

CONCLUSION

Twelve-Step meetings for the rest of one's life to manage one's illness, being born with addictive behavior, easily addicted to mind altering substance, and denial that one suffers from a disease until confronted by fellow addicts or by an addiction expert.[39]

The psychological jargon that infiltrated the Church directly opposes the Word of God. Society changed addiction from a sin to a genetic predisposition, disorder, or disease. This changed removed the addict's responsibility and allowed the addict to become a victim.[40] While seemingly ludicrous to see addiction as anything but a disease by the medical field today, this was still debated in 1955.[41] As presented in Chapter 3, AA represented the driving force that infiltrated the Church as a proponent of the disease model.[42] What was once traditionally accepted as a spiritual issue transformed into what the recovery field deemed a medical issue.[43] Since the shift of redefining the underlying cause of addiction, churches have been less likely to address the problem and relented to those in the medical realm.

Implications

Those who ingest any mind-altering substances can become dependent to the substance ingested into their body. The introduction of mind-altering substances causes physical, mental, and emotional changes to occur. Eye movements, tremors, hallucinations, hearing of voices, and mood swings represent a few examples which show something impacting with the body. According to the medical profession, these physical, mental, and emotional changes could be symptoms of an individual suffering from a disease. In order to have a true medical diagnosis, it entails "any deviation from or interruption of the normal structure or function of any body part, organ, or

39. Playfair and Bryson, *The Useful Lie*, 35–36, 45; Jellinek, *The Disease Concept of Alcoholism*, 37-38; Fingarette, *Heavy Drinking*, 41; Spickard and Thompson, *Dying for a Drink*, 41.

40. Priolo, "Presupposition Four: The Bible and Psychology," 63.

41. "A more fundamental reason why research on alcoholism has not achieved the degree of biological perspective available for research on tuberculosis, cancer, poliomyelitis, is the slow development of the concept that alcoholism is a disease." Jellinek, *The Disease Concept of Alcoholism*, 158. See also Lape, "The American Foundation on Medical Research in Biological Perspective," 9–12.

42. Jellinek, *The Disease Concept of Alcoholism*, 160.

43. Playfair and Bryson, *The Useful Lie*, 28.

system."[44] Individuals who propose that addiction is a disease miss the fact that the person chooses to drink or do drugs. Their choice brings upon the physical, emotional, and mental maladies which can eventually kill them, a consequence of the mind-altering substance they consume.

The SBC and its churches have deviated from what the Bible presents as a life-dominating sin. The author proposed that instead of embracing that the root problem of addiction is sin, integrationists and some biblical counselors present a superficial version of the Bible in order to receive acceptance from the clinical world. Both integrationists and some biblical counselors have conceded that addiction is not a disease but neglect to focus on the sin component and how the Word of God speaks as the absolute authority on the topic. Church programs that address addiction are more likely to present a Twelve-Step model fashioned after AA or attempt to use techniques formulated in the secular world.[45] While CR has been the primary resource used by churches, newer Christian programs such as The Villages "Steps" and Watermark's Regen are propped up as the new way of battling addiction. Churches still commonly use what AA has been deceiving the church with for years. Their solution has its basis on the acceptance of the Twelve Steps as an inherent part of any addiction ministry.

For centuries, the church and the church alone possessed the responsibility to care for souls. Over the last two hundred and fifty years, the church relented and allowed secular theories and techniques to seize control and speak as the primary voice on soul care. In the realm of addictions, this infiltration led to the influencing of the minds of Christ followers. AA, medical professionals, and some in the church continue to lie to those struggling with addictions, telling addicts that their problem, as an incurable disease, will remain with them for the rest of their lives. Both the secular world and even some in the church tell adducts and their families that their only solution is to attend Twelve-Step meetings or to embrace the secular therapies.

The departure from viewing scripture as sufficient for all things indicates how far the church strayed from the truth. Over five hundred years ago, Luther eloquently noted: "But they do not understand that Satan is sometimes the cause and disease at once, and he can turn fever into chills and health into illness. To deal with Satan there must be a higher medicine,

---

44. *Merriam-Webster's Medical Dictionary*, 181.
45. Street, "Market-Driven Madness," 19.

Conclusion

namely, faith and prayer."[46] The departure from scripture unnecessarily caused too many addicts to put all their hope in the Twelve Steps or psychology instead of God.

Is engaging the culture important enough to include unbiblical thoughts and phrases into a Bible-based program? CR and other similar programs embrace the same psychological terms, various parts of what is taught in AA, and the utilization of the Twelve Steps. Scripture is sovereign over all life-dominating sins and the solutions presented by man.[47] Adams said, "No matter how bad the crisis may appear to be, it is never beyond His ability to resolve it."[48] Even in the midst of an addiction, God has a purpose for the addict amidst his struggle. Obedience to God's Word will equip the addict to overcome and defeat the temptations of drugs and alcohol. As Adams stated: "The counselor's task is to relate God fully to the crisis. It is crucial for Him to restructure the entire picture as one in which God is at work achieving His purposes. To do this so profoundly changes the crisis that it takes on an entirely new dimension. It becomes a crisis in which God is involved."[49] The foundational issue behind every life-dominating sin is that the addict is a sinner in need of a Savior. In order to properly address addiction, the church does not need to have a firm grasp on the Twelve Steps or secular psychology but rather a very thorough understanding of what the Word of God says about sin.[50]

The true impact the SBC can have on those who struggle with addiction cannot manifest with the current approach taken. Those who attend recovery ministries attend meetings with a foundation characteristic of AA. A common phrase mentioned during times of struggle expresses: "I need to get to a meeting." The addict tends to idolize AA meetings or calling their sponsor for encouragement to work through the Twelve Steps. By doing so, addicts neglect placing their recovery solely in the hands of God.

After spending six years running sober living homes and serving as a pastor of a recovery church, the author witnessed first-hand the

---

46. Tappert, *Luther*, 46.

47. John MacArthur stated, "A truly Christian worldview begins with the conviction that God Himself has spoken in Scripture. As Christians, we are committed to the Bible as the inerrant and authoritative Word of God. We believe it is reliable and true from cover to cover, in every jot and tittle (cf. Matt 5:18). Scripture, therefore, is the standard by which we must test all other truth-claims." MacArthur, *Think Biblically!* Kindle, 244.

48. Adams, *Coping with Counseling Crises*, 21.

49. Adams, *Coping with Counseling Crises*, 21.

50. Adams, "Sin and Counseling," 58.

ramifications of attempting to replace Christ with the Twelve Steps. A "god of one's own understanding" acts as a Higher Power to fit the needs of those struggling. AA and those who attend their meetings often see the God of the Bible as unloving, judgmental and out to ruin fun, so they substitute the God of the Bible with a laissez faire god of their own choosing with minimal or no regulations.

Christ alone is sufficient for all things. Churches do not need programs influenced by AA, nor do churches need to embrace the disease model been presented by the *DSM*. At its core, what the world calls addiction truly means placing the mind-altering substance as an idol above God. For the last eighty years the church embraced and utilized AA as the primary resource for recovery ministries, and the end result has been the glorification of an unbiblical approach to addictions and the failure of the church to speak as the primary voice to combat addictions. The percentage of individuals addicted to mind altering substances continues to rise, more people die of overdoses, and the memberships of churches dwindle while AA meetings grow.

Bibliography

Aa.org. "Estimated Worldwide A.A. Individual and Group Membership." https://www.aa.org/sites/default/files/literature/smf-132_Estimated_Membership_EN_1221.pdf.

Abadinsky, Howard. *Drug Use and Abuse: A Comprehensive Introduction*. Boston: Cengage Learning, 2018.

Abbott, Andrew Delano. *The System of Professions: An Essay on the Division of Expert Labor*. Chicago: University of Chicago Press, 1988.

Abraham, Karl. "The Psychological Relations between Alcoholism and Sexuality." *Journal of Nervous and Mental Disease* 74.2 (1931) 233.

Acker, Caroline Jean, and Sarah W. Tracy. *Altering American Consciousness: The History of Alcohol and Drug Use in the United States, 1800–2000*. Amherst, MA: University of Massachusetts Press, 2004.

Adams, Jay. *The Big Umbrella: And Other Essays on Christian Counseling*. Grand Rapids: Baker, 1972.

———. *The Christian Counselor's Manual*. Grand Rapids: Baker, 1973.

———. *Competent to Counsel*. Phillipsburg, NJ: Presbyterian and Reformed, 1970.

———. *Coping with Counseling Crises: First Aid for Christian Counselors*. Grand Rapids: Baker, 1976.

———. "Sin and Counseling." *Journal of Modern Ministry* 2.1 (2005): 58.

———. *A Theology of Christian Counseling: More than Redemption*. Grand Rapids: Ministry Resource Library, 1986.

Adams, Todd "A Christian's Response to Chronic Illness." *Journal of Modern Ministry* 4.3 (2007) 123.

Alcohol Safety Action Projects Evaluation Methodology and Overall Program Impact. Washington, DC: U.S. Department of Transportation, National Highway Traffic Safety Administration, 1979.

Alcoholics Anonymous Big Book. 4th ed. New York: Alcoholics Anonymous World Services, 2001.

Alcoholics Anonymous. *"Pass It On": The Story of Bill Wilson and How the A.A. Message Reached the World*. 9th ed. New York: Alcoholics Anonymous World Services, 1984.

American Public Health Association. "Substance Abuse as a Public Health Problem." American Public Health Association Policy, 7121. January 1, 1971.

Anderson, Tammy, Holly Swan, and David C. Lane. "Institutional Fads and the Medicalization of Drug Addiction." *Sociology Compass* 4.7 (February 2010): 476–494.

BIBLIOGRAPHY

Angell, Marcia. *The Truth about the Drug Companies: How They Deceive Us and What to Do about It.* New York: Random House Trade Paperbacks, 2005.

Annual of the 1886 Southern Baptist Convention: Thirty-First Session; Forty-First Year. Atlanta: Jas P. Harrison, 1886.

Annual of the 1890 Southern Baptist Convention: Thirty-Fifth Session; Forty-Fifth Year. Atlanta: Franklin, 1890.

Annual of the 1896 Southern Baptist Convention: Forty-First Session; Fifty-First Year. Atlanta: Franklin, 1896.

Annual of the 1905 Southern Baptist Convention: Fiftieth Session; Sixtieth Year. Nashville: Executive Committee, Southern Baptist Convention, 1905.

Annual of the 1921 Southern Baptist Convention: Sixty-Sixth Session; Seventy-Sixth Year. Nashville: Marshal & Bruce, 1921.

Annual of the 1935 Southern Baptist Convention: Eightieth Session; Ninetieth Year. Nashville: Executive Committee, Southern Baptist Convention, 1935.

Annual of the 1946 Southern Baptist Convention: Eighty-Ninth Session; One Hundred First Year. Nashville: Executive Committee, Southern Baptist Convention, 1946.

Annual of the 1955 Southern Baptist Convention: Ninety-Eighth Session; One Hundred Tenth Year. Nashville: Executive Committee, Southern Baptist Convention, 1955.

Annual of the 1968 Southern Baptist Convention: One Hundred Eleventh Session; One Hundred Twenty-Third Year. Nashville: Executive Committee, Southern Baptist Convention, 1968.

Annual of the 1972 Southern Baptist Convention: One Hundred Fifteenth Session; One Hundred Twenty-Seventh Year. Nashville: Executive Committee, Southern Baptist Convention, 1972.

Annual of the 1988 Southern Baptist Convention: One Hundred Thirty-First Session; One Hundred Forty-Third Year. Nashville: Executive Committee, Southern Baptist Convention, 1988.

Annual of the 1997 Southern Baptist Convention: One Hundred Fortieth Session; One Hundred Fifty-Second Year. Nashville: Executive Committee, Southern Baptist Convention, 1997.

Annual of the 2006 Southern Baptist Convention: One Hundred Forty-Ninth Session; One Hundred Sixty-First Year. Nashville: Executive Committee, Southern Baptist Convention, 2006.

Anonymous. *Al-Anon Family Groups: Formerly, Living with an Alcoholic.* New York: Al-Anon Family Group Headquarters, 1984.

Anonymous. *The Book That Started It All: The Original Working Manuscript of Alcoholics Anonymous.* Center City, MN: Hazelden, 2010.

Anonymous. "Dr. Silkworth's Rx for Sobriety." *AA Grapevine* (June 1945).

Anonymous. *Drug Addiction: Crime or Disease? Interim and Final Reports.* Bloomington, IN: Indiana University Press, 1961.

Anonymous. *Members of the Clergy Ask about Alcoholics Anonymous.* New York: Alcoholics Anonymous World Services, 1992.

Anonymous. *The Songbook of the Salvation Army.* New York: Salvation Army Supplies, 1954.

Anonymous. *Twelve Steps and Twelve Traditions.* New York: Alcoholics Anonymous World Services, 1981.

Anxiety Disorders: DSM-5 Selections. Arlington, VA: American Psychiatric Association, 2016.

Bibliography

Armor, David J., J. Michael Polich, and Harriet B. Braiker. *Alcoholism and Treatment: Prepared Under a Grant from the National Institute on Alcohol Abuse and Alcoholism, Department of Health, Education, and Welfare.* Santa Monica, CA: Rand, 1976.

Arms, Donn. "Idolatry and Counseling." *Journal of Modern Ministry* 2.3 (2005): 117–24.

Arterburn, Stephen, and Jim Burns. *Drug-Proof Your Kids: A Prevention Guide; An Intervention Plan.* Pomona, CA: Focus on the Family, 1989.

Arthur, T. S. *Strong Drink: The Curse and the Cure.* Philadelphia: Hubbard Brothers, 1877.

Asam.org. "The Definition of Addiction." https://www.asam.org/quality-care/definition-of-addiction.

Ashmead, Henry. *Proceedings, 1870–1875, American Association for the Cure of Inebriates.* New York: Arno, 1981.

B., Dick, and Ken B. *Pioneer Stories in Alcoholics Anonymous: God's Role in Recovery Confirmed!* Kihei, HI: Paradise Research, 2012.

B., R. A. "Me, a Crusader?" *AA Grapevine: The International Journal of Alcoholics Anonymous* (April 1957).

B., Ralph. "Dear Grapevine." *AA Grapevine: The International Journal of Alcoholics Anonymous* (October 2019).

Babler, John, and Nicolas Ellen. *Counseling by the Book.* Rev. ed. Fort Worth: CTW, 2014.

———, *Counseling by the Book.* Rev. ed. Fort Worth: CTW, 2014. Kindle.

Badgaiyan, Rajendra. "Correction: Do We Really Need to Continue Pharmacotherapy for Opioid Use Disorder (OUD) Indefinitely?" *Journal of Reward Deficiency Syndrome* 1.2 (2015).

Baekeland, Frederick. "Evaluation of Treatment Methods in Chronic Alcoholism." *Biology of Alcoholism* (1977): 385–440.

Baldwin Research Institute. "Alcoholism Is Not a Disease." http://www.baldwinresearch.com/alcoholism.cfm.

Baker, John. *Celebrate Recovery: The Journey Begins Participant's Guide Set.* Vol. 1–4. Grand Rapids: Zondervan, 2013.

———. *Celebrate Recovery: The Journey Begins Participant's Guide.* Vol. 2, *Taking an Honest and Spiritual Inventory.* Grand Rapids: Zondervan, 2013.

———. *Celebrate Recovery Leader's Guide: A Recovery Program Based on Eight Principles from the Beatitudes.* Grand Rapids: Zondervan, 2009.

———. *Your First Step to Celebrate Recovery: How God Can Heal Your Life.* Grand Rapids: Zondervan, 2013.

Barabas, Steven. *So Great Salvation: The History and Message of the Keswick Convention.* Eugene, OR: Wipf & Stock, 2005.

Barnard, William G. *Exploring Unseen Worlds: William James and the Philosophy of Mysticism.* Albany, NY: State University of New York Press, 1997.

Barry, Colleen L., and Haiden A. Huskamp. "Moving beyond Parity—Mental Health and Addiction Care under the ACA." *New England Journal of Medicine* 365.11 (2011): 973–75.

Barry, Colleen L., Haiden A. Huskamp, and Howard H. Goldman. "A Political History of Federal Mental Health and Addiction Insurance Parity." *Milbank Quarterly* 88.3 (2010): 404.

Barton, Walter E. *The History and Influence of the American Psychiatric Association.* Washington, DC: American Psychiatric Association, 1988.

Bibliography

Bauer, Walter. *A Greek-English Lexicon of the New Testament and Other Early Christian Literature* [BDAG]. 3rd ed. Revised and edited by Frederick William Danker. Chicago: University of Chicago Press, 2000.

Baumohl, Jim. "Inebriate Institutions in North America, 1840–1920." *Addiction* 85.9 (1990): 1187–1204.

Bayer, Ronald. *Homosexuality and American Psychiatry: The Politics of Diagnosis.* Princeton, NJ: Princeton University Press, 1987.

Baylor, Courtenay. *Remaking a Man: One Successful Method of Mental Refitting.* New York: Franklin, 1919.

Bear, Marjorie Warvelle. *A Mile Square of Chicago.* Oak Brook, IL: TIPRAC, 2007.

Beecher, Lyman. *Six Sermons on Intemperance, Delineating Its Nature, Occasions, Signs, Evils, and Remedy.* Edinburgh, UK: J. Dickson, 1849.

Bemis, Judith, and Amr Barrada. *Embracing the Fear: Learning to Manage Anxiety & Panic Attacks.* Minneapolis: Hazelden, 2011.

Benezet, Anthony. *The Mighty Destroyer Displayed: In Some Account of the Dreadful Havock Made by the Mistaken Use as Well as Abuse of Distilled Spirituous Liquors.* Philadelphia: Joseph Crukshank, 1774.

Benson, C. Irving. *The Eight Points of the Oxford Group: An Exposition for Christians and Pagans.* London: Oxford University Press, 1938.

Berg, Jim. *Changed into His Image: God's Plan for Transforming Your Life.* Greenville, SC: Bob Jones University Press, 2000.

Berman, Carol W. *100 Questions & Answers about Panic Disorders.* Burlington, MA: Jones and Bartlett, 2005.

Binger, Carl. *Revolutionary Doctor: Benjamin Rush (1746–1813).* New York: W. Norton, 1966.

Blamires, Harry. *The Christian Mind: How Should a Christian Think?* Vancouver: Regent College, 2005.

Blanchard, Kenneth H., and Phil Hodges. *Lead like Jesus: Lessons from the Greatest Leadership Role Model of All Times.* Nashville: Thomas Nelson, 2005.

Blocker, Jack S. *American Temperance Movements: Cycles of Reform.* Boston: Twayne, 1989.

Blocker, Jack S., David M. Fahey, and Ian R. Tyrrell. *Alcohol and Temperance in Modern History: An International Encyclopedia.* Santa Barbara, CA: ABC-CLIO, 2003.

Blumberg, Leonard. "The American Association for the Study and Cure of Inebriety." *Alcoholism: Clinical and Experimental Research* 2.3 (1978): 235–40.

———. *The Ideology of a Therapeutic Social Movement: Alcoholics Anonymous.* New Brunswick, NJ: Rutgers University Center of Alcohol Studies, 1977.

Bonhoeffer, Dietrich, and R. Gregor Smith. *Sanctorum Communio: A Dogmatic Inquiry into the Sociology of the Church.* London: Collins, 1963.

Bonner, Arthur. *Jerry McAuley and His Mission Front Cover.* Neptune, NJ: Loizeaux Bros., 1990.

Bonnie, Richard J., Morgan A. Ford, and Jonathan K. Phillips. *Pain Management and the Opioid Epidemic: Balancing Societal and Individual Benefits and Risks of Prescription Opioid Use.* Washington, DC: National Academies, 2017.

Book, Sarah W., Suzanne E. Thomas, Joshua P. Smith, and Peter M. Miller. "Severity of Anxiety in Mental Health versus Addiction Treatment Settings when Social Anxiety and Substance Abuse Are Comorbid." *Addictive Behaviors* 37.10 (2012): 1158–61.

Booth, William. *Today in Darkest England.* London: Salvationist, 1990.

Bibliography

Borchert, William. *The Lois Wilson Story: When Love Is Not Enough: The Authorized Biography of the Cofounder of Al-Anon*. Center City, MN: Hazelden, 2005.
Borgman, Brian. *Feelings and Faith: Cultivating Godly Emotions in the Christian Life*. Wheaton, IL: Crossway, 2009.
Bowen, Don. "Helping People Recover from Recovery." *Journal of Modern Ministry* 2.1 (2005): 71–78.
Boyer, Paul. *Urban Masses and Moral Order in America, 1820–1920*. Cambridge, MA: Harvard University Press, 1997.
Boyle, Kathleen, Margaret L. Polinsky, and Yih-Ing Hser. "Resistance to Drug Abuse Treatment: A Comparison of Drug Users Who Accept or Decline Treatment Referral Assessment." *Journal of Drug Issues* 30.3 (2000): 555–74.
Boyle, Peter, Paolo Boffetta, Albert B. Lowenfels, Harry Burns, Otis Brawley, Witold Zatonski, and Jürgen Rehm. *Alcohol Science, Policy and Public Health*. Oxford: Oxford University Press, 2013.
Brand, Chad, Charles Draper, and Archie England. "Anxiety." In *Holman Illustrated Bible Dictionary*. Nashville: Holman Bible, 2003.
Brannan, Rick. *Lexham Research Lexicon of the Hebrew Bible*. Lexham Research Lexicons. Bellingham, WA: Lexham, 2020.
Bratter, Thomas Edward, and Gary G. Forrest. *Alcoholism and Substance Abuse: Strategies for Clinical Intervention*. New York: Free, 1985.
Breggin, Peter. *Medication Madness: The Role of Psychiatric Drugs in Cases of Violence, Suicide, and Crime*. New York: St. Martin's Griffin, 2009.
———. *Toxic Psychiatry: Why Therapy, Empathy, and Love Must Replace the Drugs, Electroshock, and Biochemical Theories of the New Psychiatry*. New York: St. Martin's Griffin, 1994.
Bridges, Jerry. *The Pursuit of Holiness*. Colorado Springs: Navpress, 1978.
Broadening the Base of Treatment for Alcohol Problems. Washington, DC: National Academy, 1990.
Bronowski, Jacob. *The Ascent of Man*. Boston: Little & Brown, 1974.
Brooks, Thomas. *Precious Remedies against Satan's Devices*. London: Banner of Truth Trust, 1968.
Brown, Tim. "He's Coming Home: Are You Ready?" *Journal of Modern Ministry* 4.3 (2007): 59–68.
Brüne, Martin. "Substance-Related and Addictive Disorders." In *Oxford Clinical Psychology*. Oxford: Oxford University Press. 2016.
Bucer, Martin. *Concerning the True Care of Souls*. Edited by Peter Beale and David F. Wright. Carlisle, PA: Banner of Truth, 2009.
Bunting, Charles A. *Hope for the Victims of Alcohol, Opium, Morphine, Cocaine, and Other Vices: A Narration of Successful Efforts*. London: Forgotten, 2017.
Burnette, Jeni L. Rachel B. Forsyth, Sarah L. Desmarais, and Crystal L. Hoyt. "Mindsets of Addiction: Implications for Treatment Intentions." *Journal of Social and Clinical Psychology* 38.5 (2019): 367.
Burns, David. *Feeling Good: The New Mood Therapy*. New York: William Morrow, 1999.
Buschendorf, Christa, Astrid Franke, and Johannes Voelz, eds. *Civilizing and Decivilizing Processes: Figurational Approaches to American Culture*. Newcastle upon Tyne, UK: Cambridge Scholars, 2011.
Butterfield, Lyman Henry, ed. *Letters of Benjamin Rush*. Vol. 1. Princeton, NJ: Princeton University Press, 1951.

Bibliography

Cahalan, Don. *Understanding America's Drinking Problem: How to Combat the Hazards of Alcohol.* San Francisco: Jossey-Bass, 1988.

Campbell, Nancy D. *Discovering Addiction: The Science and Politics of Substance Abuse Research.* Ann Arbor, MI: University of Michigan Press, 2007.

Campbell, Nancy D., J. P. Olsen, and Luke Walden. *The Narcotic Farm: The Rise and Fall of America's First Prison for Drug Addicts.* New York: Abrams, 2008.

Caplan, Paula J., and Maureen Gans. "Is There Empirical Justification for the Category of 'Self-Defeating Personality Disorder'?" *Feminism & Psychology* 1.2 (1991): 263–78.

Carey, Stephen S. *A Beginner's Guide to Scientific Method.* Boston: Wadsworth Cengage Learning, 2012.

Carl, Lynette L., Joseph A. Gallo, and Peter R. Johnson. *Practical Pharmacology in Rehabilitation: Effect of Medication on Therapy.* Champaign, IL: Human Kenetics, 2013.

Carlat, Daniel. *Unhinged: The Trouble with Psychiatry—A Doctor's Revelations about a Profession in Crisis.* Riverside, CA: Free, 2010.

Carroll, Robert. "Presuppositions One and Two: God's Sovereignty and Man's Responsibilities." *Journal of Modern Ministry* 1.1 (2004): 67–75.

Carter, John D., and Bruce Narramore. *The Integration of Psychology and Theology: An Introduction.* Grand Rapids: Zondervan, 1979.

Catanzaro, Frank, III. "Introduction to Biblical Counseling." Lecture presented at Southwestern Baptist Theological Seminary, Fort Worth, TX, February 2, 2014.

Cavalla, David. *Off-Label Prescribing: Justifying Unapproved Medicine.* Chichester, West Sussex: John Wiley & Sons, 2015.

CCEF Live. "The Biblical Counseling Movement: History & Context by David Powlison." https://youtu.be/lzeqUwyfH_s.

Celebraterecovery.com. "History of Celebrate Recovery." https://www.celebraterecovery.com/about/history-of-cr.

Chandler, Matt. "The Steps Gospel Centered Recovery." https://youtu.be/sYnO6LS_bHo.

Chandler, Matt, and Michael Snetzer. *Steps Mentor Guide: Gospel-Centered Recovery.* Nashville: Lifeway Christian Resources, 2015.

Cheever, Susan. *My Name Is Bill: Bill Wilson—His Life and the Creation of Alcoholics Anonymous.* New York: Washington Square, 2005.

Clum, Franklin D. *Inebriety: Its Causes, Its Results, Its Remedy.* Philadelphia: J. B. Lippincott, 1888.

Cms.gov. "The Mental Health Parity and Addiction Equity Act (MHPAEA)." https://www.cms.gov/CCIIO/Programs-and-Initiatives/Other-Insurance-Protections/mhpaea_factsheet.

Coe, John H. *Educating the Church for Wisdom's Sake, or, Why Biblical Counseling Is Unbiblical.* Portland, OR: Theological Research Exchange Network, 1991.

Compton, Wilson A. "Applying a Public Health Approach to Drug Abuse Research." *Journal of Drug Issues* 35.3 (2005): 461–67.

Connors, Gerard J., Dennis M. Donovan, and Carlo C. DiClemente. *Addiction Treatment and the Stages of Change: Selecting and Planning Interventions.* New York: Guilford, 2001.

Coombs, Robert H. *Addiction Counseling Review: Preparing for Comprehensive, Certification, and Licensing Examinations.* Mahwah, NJ: Lawrence Erlbaum, 2005.

Cooper, Edith Fairman. *The Emergence of Crack Cocaine Abuse.* New York: Novinka, 2002.

Bibliography

Cooper, Rachel. "Understanding the DSM-V: Stasis and Change." *History of Psychiatry* 29.1 (2017): 64.

Corner, George W. *The Autobiography of Benjamin Rush: His Travels through Life Together with His Commonplace Book for 1789–1813.* Westport, CT: Greenwood, 1970.

Corwin, E. L. "Institutional Facilities for the Treatment of Alcoholism." *Research Council on Problems of Alcohol* 7 (1944): 19.

Cosgrove, Lisa, and Sheldon Krimsky. "A Comparison of DSM-IV and DSM-5 Panel Members' Financial Associations with Industry: A Pernicious Problem Persists." *PLoS Medicine* 9.3 (2012): 1–4.

Cosgrove, Lisa, Harold J. Bursztajn, Sheldon Krimsky, Maria Anaya, and Justin Walker. "Conflicts of Interest and Disclosure in the American Psychiatric Association's Clinical Practice Guidelines." *Psychotherapy and Psychosomatics* 78.4 (2009): 228–32.

Cosgrove, Lisa, Sheldon Krimsky, Manisha Vijayaraghavan, and Lisa Schneider. "Financial Ties between DSM-IV Panel Members and the Pharmaceutical Industry." *Psychotherapy and Psychosomatics* 75.3 (2006): 155.

Craddock, Nick, and Laurence Mynors-Wallis. "Psychiatric Diagnosis: Impersonal, Imperfect and Important." *British Journal of Psychiatry* 204.2 (2014): 93–95.

Crothers, T. D. "Diseases of Inebriety from Alcohol, Opium, and other Narcotic Drugs: Its Etiology, Pathology, Treatment, and Medico-Legal Relations." *JAMA* 20.21 (1893): 590.

Crystal, David. *Words in Time and Place: Exploring Language through the Historical Thesaurus of the Oxford English Dictionary.* Oxford: Oxford University Press, 2014.

Cummings, Jeffery. *Progress in Neurotherapeutics and Neuropsychopharmacology.* Vol. 2. Cambridge, MA: Cambridge University Press, 2007.

Dasgupta, Amitava, and Loralie J. Langman. *Pharmacogenomics of Alcohol and Drugs of Abuse.* Hoboken, NJ: Taylor and Francis, 2012.

Davenport-Hines, Richard. *The Pursuit of Oblivion: A Global History of Narcotics.* New York: Norton, 2004.

Davies, D. L. "Normal Drinking in Recovered Alcohol Addicts." *Quarterly Journal of Studies of Alcohol* 23 (March 1962): 94–104.

Davies, James. *Cracked: The Unhappy Truth about Psychiatry.* New York: Pegasus, 2013.

———. "How Voting and Consensus Created the Diagnostic and Statistical Manual of Mental Disorders (DSM-III)." *Anthropology & Medicine* 24.1 (2016): 32.

———. *The Importance of Suffering: The Value and Meaning of Emotional Discontent.* London: Routledge, 2012.

De Leon, George. *Community as Method: Therapeutic Communities for Special Populations and Special Settings.* Westport, CT: Praeger, 1997.

Decker, Hannah S. *The Making of DSM-III: A Diagnostic Manual's Conquest of American Psychiatry.* Oxford: Oxford University Press, 2013.

DeGroat, Charles R. "The New Exodus: A Narrative Paradigm for Understanding Soul Care." *Journal of Psychology and Theology* 37.3 (2009): 186–93.

DeJong, Alexander C. *Help & Hope for the Alcoholic.* Wheaton, IL: Tyndale House, 1982.

Dentzer, Susan. "Substance Abuse and other Substantive Matters." *Health Affairs* 30.8 (2011): 1398.

Diagnostic and Statistical Manual of Mental Disorders: DSM-I. Washington, DC: American Psychiatric Association, 1952.

Diagnostic and Statistical Manual of Mental Disorders: DSM-II. Washington, DC: American Psychiatric Association, 1968.

Bibliography

Diagnostic and Statistical Manual of Mental Disorders: DSM-III. Washington, DC: American Psychiatric Association, 1980.
Diagnostic and Statistical Manual of Mental Disorders: DSM-III-R. Washington, DC: American Psychiatric Association, 1987.
Diagnostic and Statistical Manual of Mental Disorders: DSM-IV. Washington, DC: American Psychiatric Association, 1994.
Diagnostic and Statistical Manual of Mental Disorders: DSM-V-TR. Washington, DC: American Psychiatric Association, 2013.
DiClemente, Carlo C. *Addiction and Change: How Addictions Develop and Addicted People Recover.* New York: Guilford, 2003.
DiClemente, Carlo C., Gerrard Conners, Mary Velasquez, and Dennis Donovan. *Substance Abuse Treatment and the Stages of Change.* 2nd ed. New York: Guilford, 2013.
Diehl, Heath A. *Wasted: Performing Addiction in America.* Farnham, UK: Ashgate, 2016.
Dome, Peter, Zoltan Demeter, Xenia Gonda, and Zoltan Rihmer. "Are DSM and Logic Not on Good Terms?" *British Journal of Psychiatry* 207.2 (2015): 91–92.
Doweiko, Harold E., and Amelia L. Evans. *Concepts of Chemical Dependency.* 10th ed. Boston: Cengage Learning, 2019.
Drescher, Jack. "Out of DSM: Depathologizing Homosexuality." *Behavioral Sciences* 5.4 (April 2015): 565–75.
Driberg, Tom. *The Mystery of Moral Re-Armament: A Study of Frank Buchman and His Movement.* New York: Knopf, 1965.
Drug Abuse and Treatment Act, 1972: Report Together with Minority Views to Accompany S. 525. Washington, DC: U.S. Government Printing Office, 1979.
Dubiel, Richard Michael. *The Road to Fellowship: The Role of the Emmanuel Movement and the Jacoby Club in the Development of Alcoholics Anonymous.* New York: iUniverse, 2004.
Dunnington, Kent. *Addiction and Virtue: Beyond the Models of Disease and Choice.* Downers Grove, IL: IVP Academic, 2011. Kindle.
DuPont, Robert. "Anxiety and Addiction: A Clinical Perspective on Comorbidity." *BMC* 59.2 (1995): 53.
Dusenbury, Linda, and Mathea Falco. "Eleven Components of Effective Drug Abuse Prevention Curricula." *Journal of School Health* 65.10 (1995): 420–25.
Dusenbury, Linda, Antonia Lake, and Mathea Falco. "A Review of the Evaluation of 47 Drug Abuse Prevention Curricula Available Nationally." *Journal of School Health* 67.4 (1997): 127–32.
Dziegielewski, Sophia F. *DSM-5 in Action.* Hoboken, NJ: Wiley Blackwell, 2015.
Eason, Andrew M. "The Strategy of a Missionary Evangelist: How William Booth Shaped the Salvation Army's Earliest Work at Home and Abroad." *International Bulletin of Missionary Research* 38.4 (2014): 183–86.
Eason, Andrew M., and Roger J. Green, eds. *Boundless Salvation: The Shorter Writings of William Booth.* New York: Peter Lang, 2012.
Edwards, Griffith. "Thomas Trotter's 'Essay on Drunkeness' Appraised." *Addiction* 107.9 (August 2012): 1562–579.
El-Guebaly, Nady, and Claudio Violato. "The International Certification of Addiction Medicine: Validating Clinical Knowledge Across Borders." *Substance Abuse* 32.2 (2011): 77–83.
Ellis, Albert. *The Case against Religion: A Psychotherapist's View and the Case against Religiosity.* Austin, TX: American Atheist, 1985.

Bibliography

———. *Reason and Emotion in Psychotherapy.* Secaucus, NJ: Carol, 1994.
Erickson, Carlton K. *The Science of Addiction: From Neurobiology to Treatment.* New York: W. W. Norton, 2018.
Erickson, Millard J. *Christian Theology.* Grand Rapids: Baker, 1998.
Eriksen, Karen, and Victoria E. Kress. *Beyond the DSM Story: Ethical Quandaries, Challenges, and Best Practices.* Thousand Oaks, CA: SAGE, 2005.
Evans, C. Stephen. *Søren Kierkegaard's Christian Psychology: Insight for Counseling & Pastoral Care.* Grand Rapids: Ministry Resources Library, 1990.
Eyrich, Howard, Edward E. Hindson, and William L. Hines. *Curing the Heart: A Model for Biblical Counseling.* Rossshire, UK: Mentor, 2002.
Eysenck, H. J. *Handbook of Abnormal Psychology: An Experimental Approach.* New York: Basic Books, 1961.
Fabiani, Cesar E. *Addictions and Buprenorphine.* Bloomington, IN: Xlibris, 2012.
Farias, Miguel, Anna-Kaisa Newheiser, Guy Kahane, and Zoe de Toledo. "Scientific Faith: Belief in Science Increases in the Face of Stress and Existential Anxiety." *Journal of Experimental Social Psychology* 49.6 (2013): 1210–213.
Farr, Clifford B. "Benjamin Rush and American Psychiatry." *American Journal of Psychiatry* 100.6 (1944): 5.
Faust, David. *Ziskin's Coping with Psychiatric and Psychological Testimony.* New York: Oxford University Press, 2010.
Fava, Giovanni A. "Conflicts of Interest." In *Ethics in Psychiatry*, 55–72. International Library of Ethics, Law, and the New Medicine. Vol 45. Edited by H. Helmchen and N. Sartorius. N.p.: Springer, Dordrecht, 2010.
Feighner, John P. "Diagnostic Criteria for Use in Psychiatric Research." *Archives of General Psychiatry* 26.1 (1972): 57.
Fichter, Joseph Henry. *The Rehabilitation of Clergy Alcoholics: Ardent Spirits Subdued.* New York: Human Sciences, 1982.
Finan, Christopher M. *DRUNKS: An American History.* Boston: Beacon, 2018.
Fingarette, Herbert. *Heavy Drinking: The Myth of Alcoholism as a Disease.* Berkeley, CA: University of California Press, 1988.
Fisher, Gary L., and Nancy A. Roget. *Encyclopedia of Substance Abuse Prevention, Treatment, & Recovery.* Los Angeles: SAGE, 2009.
Fitzpatrick, Elyse, and Laura Hendrickson. *Will Medicine Stop the Pain: Finding God's Healing for Depression, Anxiety, and Other Troubling Emotions.* Chicago: Moody, 2006.
Fitzpatrick, Michael. *Dr. Bob and Bill W. Speak: AA's Cofounders Tell Their Stories.* Center City, MN: Hazelden, 2012.
Fletcher, Anne M. *Inside Rehab: The Surprising Truth about Addiction Treatment: And How to Get Help That Works.* New York: Viking, 2013.
Forsyth, John P., Jefferson D. Parker, and Carlos G. Finlay. "Anxiety, Sensitivity, Controllability, and Experiential Avoidance and Their Relation to Drug of Choice and Addiction Severity in a Residential Sample of Substance-Abusing Veterans." *Addictive Behaviors* 28.5 (2003): 851–70.
Fosdick, Harry Emerson. *A Great Time to Be Alive.* New York: Harper & Bros, 1944.
———. *On Being a Real Person.* New York: Harper & Bros, 1943.
———. "Shall the Fundamentalists Win?" Sermon preached at the First Presbyterian Church, New York City, May 21, 1922.

Bibliography

———. "Those Marvelous 12 Steps." *AA Grapevine: The International Journal of Alcoholics Anonymous* (June 1960).
Fox, Emmet. *Life is Consciousness*. Eastford, CT: Martino Fine Books, 2011.
———. *Power Through Constructive Thinking*. New York: HarperOne, 1989.
———. *Stake Your Claim: Exploring the Gold Mine Within*. New York: HarperOne, 1992.
———. *The Sermon on the Mount: The Key to Success in Life; and, the Lord's Prayer, an Interpretation*. New York: HarperOne, 2012.
Fox, Ruth. "A Multidisciplinary Approach to the Treatment of Alcoholism." *American Journal of Psychiatry* 123.7 (1967): 769–78.
Frances, Allen. "DSM, Psychotherapy, Counseling and the Medicalization of Mental Illness: A Commentary from Allen Frances." *Professional Counselor* 4.3 (2014): 282–84.
———. "The New Crisis of Confidence in Psychiatric Diagnosis." *Annals of Internal Medicine* (2013).
———. *Saving Normal: An Insider's Revolt against Out-of-Control Psychiatric Diagnosis, DSM-5, Big Pharma, and the Medicalization of Ordinary Life*. New York: William Morrow, 2014.
Franklin, Cynthia, and Rowena Fong. *The Church Leader's Counseling Resource Book: A Guide to Mental Health and Social Problems*. New York: Oxford University Press, 2011.
Freed, Christopher R. "Addiction Medicine and Addiction Psychiatry in America: Commonalities in the Medical Treatment of Addiction." *Contemporary Drug Problems* 37.1 (2010): 139–63.
Freud, Sigmund. *Freud: Dictionary of Psychoanalysis*. Irvine, CA: Dickens, 2004.
———. *A General Introduction to Psychoanalysis*. New York: Washington Square, 1960.
———. *The Origin and Development of Psychoanalysis*. Chicago: Regnerry, 1955.
———. *The Problem of Lay-Analyses*. New York: Brentano, 1927.
Freud, Sigmund, and Josef Breuer. *Studies on Hysteria*. New York: Basic Books, 1957.
Freud, Sigmund, and A. A. Brill. *The Basic Writings of Sigmund Freud*. New York: Modern Library, 1938.
Freud, Sigmund, and James Strachey. *Beyond the Pleasure Principle*. New York: Liveright, 1950.
Frey, Dennis D. *Biblical Directionism: A Biblical Approach to Counseling Methodology*. Newburgh, IN: GMA & Inspiration, 2003.
Friedman, Mitchell. "The 12 Steps of Addiction Recovery Programs as an Influence on Leadership Development: A Personal Narrative." *International Journal for Transformative Research* 3.2 (2016): 15–23.
Fromm, Erich. *Psychoanalysis and Religion*. New Haven, CT: Yale University Press, 1950.
Fuller, Robert C. *Spiritual, but Not Religious: Understanding Unchurched America*. Oxford: Oxford University Press, 2010.
Galanter, Marc. *Psychotherapy for the Treatment of Substance Abuse*. Arlington, VA: American Psychiatric, 2011.
———. *Recent Developments in Alcoholism: Methodology, Psychosocial Treatment, Selected Treatment Topics, Research Priorities*. New York: Springer Science Business Media, 1989.
Ganz, Richard L. *Free Indeed: Escaping Bondage and Brokenness for Freedom in Christ*. Wapwallopen, PA: Shepherd, 2002.

Bibliography

———. *Psychobabble: The Failure of Modern Psychology and the Biblical Alternative.* Wheaton, IL: Crossway, 1993.

Gekker, Genya, James R. Lokensgard, and Phillip K. Peterson. "Naltrexone Potentiates Anti-HIV-1 Activity of Antiretroviral Drugs in CD4 Lymphocyte Cultures." *Drug and Alcohol Dependence* 64.3 (2001): 257–63.

Gellman, Marc, and J. Rick Turner. *Encyclopedia of Behavioral Medicine.* New York: Springer, 2013.

Genova, Paul. "Dump the DSM!" *Psychiatric Times* 20.4 (April 2003): 72.

Gifford, Sanford. *The Emmanuel Movement (Boston, 1904–1929): The Origins of Group Treatment and the Assault on Lay Psychotherapy.* Boston: Francis Countway Library of Medicine, 1997.

Glantz, Meyer D., and Christine R. Hartel. *Facing Drug Abuse: Origins and Interventions.* Washington, DC: American Psychological Association, 1999.

Goldacre, Ben. *Bad Pharma: How Drug Companies Mislead Doctors and Harm Patients.* New York: Faber and Faber, 2014.

Golub, Andrew Lang, and Bruce D. Johnson. "Alcohol Is Not the Gateway to Hard Drug Abuse." *Journal of Drug Issues* 28.4 (1998): 971–84.

Gomberg, Edith Lisansky, Helene Raskin White, and John A. Carpenter. *Alcohol, Science, and Society Revisited.* Ann Arbor, MI: University of Michigan Press, 1982.

Goodwin, Donald W. "Alcohol Problems in Adoptees Raised apart from Alcoholic Biological Parents." *Archives of General Psychiatry* 28.2 (January 1973): 238.

Gordis, E. "Accessible and Affordable Health Care for Alcoholism and Related Problems: Strategy for Cost Containment." *Journal of Studies on Alcohol* 48.6 (1987): 579–85.

Gould, Dudley C. *Science and the Soul.* St. Paul, MN: Paragon House, 2006.

Grant, Jon E. "Outcome Study of Kleptomania Patients Treated with Naltrexone." *Clinical Neuropharmacology* 28.1 (2005): 11–14.

Grant, Jon E. and S. W. Kim. "Medication Management of Pathological Gambling." *Minnesota Medicine* 89.9 (2006): 44–48.

Green, Roger J. *War on Two Fronts: The Redemptive Theology of William Booth.* Atlanta: Salvation Army Supplies, 1989.

Greenberg, Gary. *The Book of Woe: The Making of the DSM and the Unmaking of Psychiatry.* New York: Blue Rider, 2013.

Greggo, Stephen P. "The Biblical Counseling Movement: History and Context." *Trinity Journal* 32.1 (Spring 2011): 130–32.

Guess, Pam. "The Emperor's New Drugs: Exploding the Antidepressant Myth." *Ethical Human Psychology and Psychiatry* 13.1 (2011): 83–87.

H., Paul, and Scott N. *Simple but Not Easy: A Practical Guide to Taking the 12 Steps of Alcoholics Anonymous.* Cumberland, WI: Spiritual Progress, 2013.

Hall, Kathleen T., and Paul S. Applebaum. "The Origins of Commitment for Substance Abuse in the United States." *J Am Acad Psychiatry Law* 3 (2002): 33–45.

Hambrick, Brad. "6 Steps to Wise Decision Making about Psychotropic Medications." http://bradhambrick.com/6-steps-to-wise-decision-making-about-psychotropic-medications/.

———. "Overcoming Addiction." http://bradhambrick.com/addiction/.

———. "Step 3: UNDERSTAND the Origin, Motive, and History of My Sin." http://bradhambrick.com/addiction/.

———. "Towards a Christian Perspective on Mental Illness." http://bradhambrick.com/mentalillness/.

BIBLIOGRAPHY

Hamm, Richard F. *Shaping the Eighteenth Amendment: Temperance Reform, Legal Culture, and the Polity, 1880–1920.* Studies in Legal History. Chapel Hill, NC: University of North Carolina Press, 1995.

Hammer, Rachel, Molly Dingle, Jenny Ostergren, Brad Patridge, Jennifer McCormick, and Barbara Koenig. "Addiction: Current Criticism of the Brain Disease Paradigm." *AJOB Neuroscience* 4.3 (2013): 27.

Harmless, William. *Mystics.* New York: Oxford University Press, 2008.

Harrison, Maureen, and Steve Gilbert. *The Americans with Disabilities Act Handbook.* Beverly Hills, CA: Excellent Books, 1992.

Hartigan, Francis. *Bill W.: A Biography of Alcoholics Anonymous Cofounder Bill Wilson.* New York: Thomas Dunne Books, 2000.

Harwood, Henrick J., and Dean R. Gerstein. *Treating Drug Problems: Commissioned Papers on Historical, Institutional, and Economic Contexts of Drug Treatment.* Washington, DC: National Academy, 1992.

Hasin, Deborah S., Charles P. O'Brien, Marc Auriacombe, Guilherme Borges, Kathleen Bucholz, Alan Budney, Wilson M. Compton, Thomas Crowley, Walter Ling, Nancy M. Petry, Marc Schuckit, and Bridget F. Grant. "DSM-5 Criteria for Substance Use Disorders: Recommendations and Rationale." *American Journal of Psychiatry* 170.8 (2013): 834–51.

Hasin, Deborah S., Miriam C. Fenton, Cheryl Beseler, Jung Yeon Park, and Melanie M. Wall. "Analyses Related to the Development of DSM-5 Criteria for Substance Use Related Disorders: 2. Proposed DSM-5 Criteria for Alcohol, Cannabis, Cocaine and Heroin Disorders in 663 Substance Abuse Patients." *Drug and Alcohol Dependence* 122.1–2 (2012): 28–37.

Hatch, A. S. *Jerry McCauley: His Life and Work.* Edited by R. M. Offord. New York: New York Observer, 1885.

Headrick, Richard W. *America's Churches through the Eyes of a Bum.* Laurel, MS: Hellfighter, 2012.

Healthcare.gov. "Affordable Care Act (ACA)." https://www.healthcare.gov/glossary/affordable-care-act/.

Healy, David. *The Creation of Psychopharmacology.* Cambridge, MA: Harvard University Press, 2002.

———. *Pharmageddon.* Berkeley, CA: University of California Press, 2012.

———. *Psychiatric Drugs Explained.* Edinburgh, UK: Churchill Livingstone, 2002.

Heather, Nick. "Q: Is Addiction a Brain Disease or a Moral Failing? A: Neither." *Neuroethics* 10.1 (2017): 115–24.

Heather, Nick, and Ian Robertson. *Controlled Drinking.* London: Methuen, 1981.

Heather, Nick, David Best, Anna Kawlek, Matt Field, Marc Lewis, and Fredrick Rotgres. "Challenging the Brain Disease Model of Addiction: European Launch of the Addiction Theory Network." *Addiction Research & Theory* 26.4 (October 2017): 249–55.

Hegstad, Harold. *The Real Church: An Ecclesiology of the Visible.* Cambridge: James Clarke, 2013.

Henningfield, Jack E., Patricia B. Santora, and Warren K. Bickel. *Addiction Treatment: Science and Policy for the Twenty-First Century.* Baltimore: Johns Hopkins University Press, 2007.

Bibliography

Herbeck, Diane M., Yih-Ing Hser, and Cheryl Teruya. "Empirically Supported Substance Abuse Treatment Approaches: A Survey of Treatment Providers' Perspectives and Practices." *Addictive Behaviors* 33.5 (2008): 699–712.

Hersen, Michel, and Alan M. Gross. *Handbook of Clinical Psychology*. Vol. 1. Hoboken, NJ: J. Wiley & Sons, 2008.

Heyman, Gene M. *Addiction: A Disorder of Choice*. Cambridge, MA: Harvard University Press, 2010.

Hickman, Timothy A. "Keeping Secrets: Leslie E. Keeley, the Gold Cure and the 19th-century Neuroscience of Addiction." *Addiction* 113 (2018): 1739–49.

———. "'Mania Americana': Narcotic Addiction and Modernity in the United States, 1870–1920." *Journal of American History* 90.4 (January 2004): 1269.

Hidalgo, Don. *What the Hell Is Behavioral Health?: The Shell Game: A Metaphor for What Is Happening to the Counseling Profession*. Pittsburgh: Dorrance, 2019.

Hindson, Edward E., and Howard Eyrich. *Totally Sufficient*. Eugene, OR: Harvest House, 1997.

Hirsh, Joseph. "The Research Council on Problems of Alcohol." *Scientific Monthly* 65.3 (1947): 231.

Hoffer, Abram. *Vitamin B-3 & Schizophrenia: Discovery, Recovery, Controversy*. Kingston, ON: Quarry Health, 1998.

Holden, Tim. "Addiction Is Not a Disease." *Canadian Medical Association Journal* 184.6 (February 2012): 679.

Holifield, E. Brooks. *A History of Pastoral Care in America: From Salvation to Self-Realization*. Eugene, OR: Wipf and Stock, 2005.

Hughes, Richard, and Robert Brewin. *The Tranquilizing of America: Pill Popping and the American Way of Life*. New York: Harcourt Brace Jovanovich, 1979.

Humphries, Drew. *Crack Mothers: Pregnancy, Drugs and the Media*. Columbus: Ohio State University Press, 2011.

Huss, Magnus, and Gerhard von dem Busch. *Chronische Alkoholskrankheit Oder Alcoholismus Chronicus Ein Beitrag Zur Kenntniss Der Vergiftungs-Krankheiten, Nach Eigener Und Anderer Erfahrung*. Stockholm, SE: C. E. Fritze, 1852.

Hyman, Steven E. "The Diagnosis of Mental Disorders: The Problem of Reification." *Annual Review of Clinical Psychology* 6.1 (2010): 155–79.

Israelstam, S., and S. Lambert. "Homosexuality as a Cause of Alcoholism: A Historical Review." *International Journal of the Addictions* 18.8 (1983): 1087.

Jackson, Maurice. *Let This Voice Be Heard: Anthony Benezet, Father of Atlantic Abolitionism*. Philadelphia: University of Pennsylvania Press, 2010.

Jaffe, A. "Reform in American Medical Science: The Inebriety Movement and the Origins of the Psychological Disease Theory of Addiction, 1870–1920." *British Journal of Addiction to Alcohol and Other Drugs* 73.2 (1978): 139–47.

James, William. *The Varieties of Religious Experience: A Study in Human Nature*. New York: Longmans, Green, 1917.

———. *The Varieties of Religious Experience: A Study in Human Nature: Being the Gifford Lectures on Natural Religion Delivered at Edinburgh in 1901–1902*. London: Longmans, 1937.

Jasinski, Donald R. "Human Pharmacology and Abuse Potential of the Analgesic Buprenorphine." *Archives of General Psychiatry* 35.4 (1978): 501.

Jellinek, E. M. *The Disease Concept of Alcoholism*. New Haven, CT: Hillhouse, 1960.

Bibliography

Johnson, Eric L. *Foundations for Soul Care: A Christian Psychology Proposal.* Downers Grove, IL: IVP Academic, 2014.

———, ed. *Psychology & Christianity: Five Views.* Downers Grove, IL: IVP Academic, 2010.

Johnson, T. Dale, Jr. "Church and Community." Lecture presented at Southwestern Baptist Theological Seminary, Fort Worth, TX, August 29, 2017.

———. "History of Soul Care." Lecture presented at Southwestern Baptist Theological Seminary, Fort Worth, TX, August 27, 2014.

Jones, Hendree E. "Practical Consideration for the Clinical Use of Buprenorphine." *Science & Practice Perspectives* 2.2 (2004): 4–20.

Jones, Jeffery E. *Americans with Addiction in Their Family Believe It Is a Disease.* Washington, DC: Gallup Polling, August 11, 2006.

Jones, Stanton L. "A Constructive Relationship for Religion with the Science and Profession of Psychology: Perhaps the Boldest Model Yet." *American Psychologist* 49.3 (1994): 184–99.

Jones, Stanton L., and Richard E. Butman. *Modern Psychotherapies.* Westmont, IL: InterVarsity, 1991.

Kaminer, Wendy. *I'm Dysfunctional, You're Dysfunctional: The Recovery Movement and Other Self-Help Fashions.* Reading, MA: Addison-Wesley, 1992.

Kaskutas, Lee Anne, and Marc Galanter. *Recent Developments in Alcoholism: Research on Alcoholics Anonymous and Spirituality in Addiction Recovery.* New York: Springer-Verlag, 2009.

Katcher, B. S. "Benjamin Rush's Educational Campaign against Hard Drinking." *American Journal of Public Health* 83.2 (1993): 273–81.

Keeley, Leslie E. *The Non-Heredity of Inebriety.* Chicago: Scott, Foresman, 1902.

"The Keeley 'Gold Cure' for Inebriety." *British Medical Journal* 2.1645 (1892): 85.

Kellemen, Robert W. *Equipping Counselors for Your Church: The 4E Ministry Training Strategy.* Phillipsburg, NJ: P&R, 2011.

Keller, Mark, and John Doria. "On Defining Alcoholism." *Alcohol Health and Research World* 15.4 (1991): 253.

Kelly, John F., and Cassandra M. Westerhoff. "Does It Matter How We Refer to Individuals with Substance-Related Conditions?: A Randomized Study of Two Commonly Used Terms." *International Journal of Drug Policy* 21.3 (2010): 202–07.

Kerr, Norman Shanks. *Inebriety or Narcomania: Its Etiology, Pathology, Treatment, and Jurisprudence.* London: H. K. Lewis, 1894.

———. *Society for the Study and Cure of Inebriety: Inaugural Address Delivered in the Medical Society of London's Rooms, April 25th, 1884.* London: H. K. Lewis, 1884.

Khoury, Bassam, Ellen J. Langer, and Francesco Pagnini. "The DSM: Mindful Science or Mindless Power?: A Critical Review." *Frontiers in Psychology* 5.602 (June 2014): 8.

King, Martha J. "Receive the Olive Branch: Benjamin Rush as Reconciler in the Early Republic." *Early American Studies: An Interdisciplinary Journal* 15.2 (2017): 352–81.

Kirsch, Irving. *The Emperor's New Drugs: Exploding the Antidepressant Myth.* New York: Basic Books, 2010.

Kisacky, Jeanne Susan. *Rise of the Modern Hospital: An Architectural History of Health and Healing, 1870–1940.* Pittsburgh: University of Pittsburgh Press, 2017.

Kissin, Benjamin, and Henri Begleiter. *The Biology of Alcoholism.* New York: Springer, 1979.

Bibliography

Kohler-Hausmann, Julilly. *Getting Tough: Welfare and Imprisonment in 1970s America.* Princeton, NJ: Princeton University Press, 2017.
Kolstlin, Julius. *Life of Luther.* New York: C. Scribner's Sons, 1883.
Kraepelin, Emil. *Lectures on Clinical Psychiatry.* New York: Hafner, 1968.
———. *Manic-Depressive Insanity and Paranoia.* New York: Arno, 1976.
———. *One Hundred Years of Psychiatry.* New York: Philosophical Library, 1962.
Kreeft, Peter, and Ronald K. Tacelli. *Handbook of Christian Apologetics: Hundreds of Answers to Crucial Questions.* Westmont, IL: IVP Academic, 1994.
Krimsky, Sheldon. *Science in the Private Interest: Has the Lure of Profits Corrupted Biomedical Research?* Lanham, MD: Rowman & Littlefield, 2003.
Krueger, Robert F., Theodore Millon, and Erik Simonsen. *Contemporary Directions in Psychopathology: Scientific Foundations of the DSM-V and ICD-11.* New York: Guilford, 2010.
Kupfer, David J., Michael B. First, and Darrel A. Regier. *A Research Agenda for DSM-V.* Washington, DC: American Psychiatric Association, 2002.
Kurtz, Ernest. "Alcoholics Anonymous and the Disease Concept of Alcoholism." *Alcoholism Treatment Quarterly* 20.3–4 (2002): 14.
———. *The Collected Ernie Kurtz.* New York: Authors Choice, 2008.
———. *Not-God: A History of Alcoholics Anonymous.* Center City, MN: Hazelden Educational Services, 1991.
Kurtz, N. R., and M. Regier. "Policy Lessons of the Uniform Act: A Response to Comments." *Journal of Studies on Alcohol* 37.3 (1976): 382–92.
———. "The Uniform Alcoholism and Intoxication Treatment Act: The Compromising Process of Social Policy Formulation." *Journal of Studies on Alcohol* 36.11 (1975): 1428.
Kusserow, Richard. *Crack Babies: A National Epidemic.* Upland, PA: Diane, 1990.
Lambert, Heath. *A Theology of Biblical Counseling: The Doctrinal Foundations of Counseling Ministry.* Grand Rapids: Zondervan, 2016.
———. "Mental Illness, Psychiatric Drugs, and Counseling Education." www.biblicalcounselingcoalition.org/2013/07/09/mental-illness-psychiatric-drugs-and-counseling-education/.
Landry, Mim J. *Overview of Addiction Treatment Effectiveness.* Upland, PA: Diane, 1996.
Lane, Christopher. *Shyness: How Normal Behavior Became a Sickness.* New Haven, CT: Yale University Press, 2009.
Lape, Esther Everett. "The American Foundation on Medical Research in Biological Perspective." *AIBS Bulletin* 6.2 (1956): 9–12.
LaPlante, Debi A., Howard Shaffer, and Sarah E. Nelson. *APA Addiction Syndrome Handbook.* Vol. 1, Foundations, Influences, and Expressions of Addiction. Washington, DC: American Psychological Association, 2012.
Lassiter, Pamela S., and John R. Culbreth. *Theory and Practice of Addiction Counseling.* Thousand Oaks, CA: SAGE, 2018.
The Layman with a Notebook. *What Is The Oxford Group?* London: Oxford University Press, 1933.
Lee, Todd C., Ploa Desforges, Jennifer Murray, Ramy R. Saleh, and Emily G. McDonald. "Off-Label Use of Quetiapine in Medical Inpatients and Postdischarge." *JAMA Internal Medicine* 176.9 (2016): 1390.
Lemere, Frederick. "Aversion Treatment of Alcoholism: Some Reminiscences." *Addiction* 82.3 (1987): 257–58.

Bibliography

Lender, Mark Edward. *Dictionary of American Temperance Biography: From Temperance Reform to Alcohol Research, the 1600s to the 1980s*. Westport, CT: Greenwood, 1984.

Lender, Mark Edward, and James Kirby Martin. *Drinking in America: A History*. New York: Free, 1982.

Lesch, O. M., J. Kefer, S. Lentner, R. Mader, B. Marx, M. Musalek, and A. Nimmerrichter. "Diagnosis of Chronic Alcoholism: Classificatory Problems." *Psychopathology* 23.2 (1990): 88–96.

Leshner, Alan I. "Addiction Is a Brain Disease, and It Matters." *Science* 278.5335 (1997): 45–47.

Levin, Jerome David. *Introduction to Alcoholism Counseling: A Bio-Psycho-Social Approach*. Basingstoke, UK: Taylor & Francis, 1995.

Levine, Bruce. "*DSM-V*: Science or Dogma? Even Some Establishment Psychiatrists Embarrassed by Newest Diagnostic Bible." https://www.huffpost.com/entry/dsm-5_b_2657667.

Levine, H. G. "The Discovery of Addiction: Changing Conceptions of Habitual Drunkenness in America." *Journal of Studies on Alcohol* 39.1 (1978): 143–74.

———. "The Vocabulary of Drunkenness." *Journal of Studies on Alcohol* 42.11 (1981): 1038–51.

Levy, Leonard W., Kenneth L. Karst, and Adam Winkler. *Encyclopedia of the American Constitution*. New York: Macmillan Reference USA, 2000.

Levy, Neil. "Addiction Is Not a Brain Disease (and It Matters)." *Frontiers in Psychiatry* 4 (2013).

Lewis, Marc D. *The Biology of Desire: Why Addiction Is Not a Disease*. New York: Public Affairs, 2016.

———. "Brain Change in Addiction as Learning, Not Disease." *New England Journal of Medicine* 379.16 (2018): 1551–560.

Libby, Ronald T. "Treating Doctors as Drug Dealers: The Drug Enforcement Administration's War on Prescription Painkillers." *Independent Review* 10.4 (2006): 511–45.

Lobdell, Jared. *This Strange Illness: Alcoholism and Bill W*. New York: Aldine de Gruyter, 2004.

Logan, Enid. "The Wrong Race, Committing Crime, Doing Drugs, and Maladjusted for Motherhood: The Nation's Fury over 'Crack Babies.'" *Social Justice* 26.1 (1999): 115.

Lombardo, Paul A. *A Century of Eugenics in America: From the Indiana Experiment to the Human Genome Era*. Bloomington, IN: Indiana University Press, 2011.

London, Perry. *The Modes and Morals of Psychotherapy*. New York: Holt, Rinehart and Winston, 1964.

Loose, Rik. *The Subject of Addiction: Psychoanalysis and the Administration of Enjoyment*. London: Karnac, 2006.

MacArthur, John, ed. *Think Biblically!: Recovering a Christian Worldview*. Wheaton, IL: Crossway, 2003.

MacArthur, John H., and Wayne A. Mack. *Introduction to Biblical Counseling*. Dallas: Word, 1994.

Mackay, Priscilla W., and G. Alan Marlatt. "Maintaining Sobriety: Stopping Is Starting." *International Journal of the Addictions* 25.9 (1991): 1257.

Mallea, Paula. *War on Drugs: A Failed Experiment*. Toronto: Dundurn, 2016.

Malony, H. Newton. *Psychology and Faith: The Christian Experience of Eighteen Psychologists*. Washington, DC: University Press of America, 1978.

Bibliography

Manser, Martin H. *Dictionary of Bible Themes: The Accessible and Comprehensive Tool for Topical Studies.* London: Martin Manser, 2009.

Marion, Nancy E., and Willard M. Oliver. *Drugs in American Society: An Encyclopedia of History, Politics, Culture, and the Law.* Santa Barbara, CA: ABC-CLIO, 2015.

Marlatt, G. Alan, and William H. George. "Relapse Prevention: Introduction and Overview of the Model." *Addiction* 79.3 (1984): 261–73.

Marshall, E. Jane, Keith Humphreys, David M. Ball, and Griffith Edwards. *The Treatment of Drinking Problems: A Guide for the Helping Professions.* Cambridge, MA: Cambridge University Press, 2011.

Martin, Scott C. *The SAGE Encyclopedia of Alcohol Social, Cultural, and Historical Perspectives.* Los Angeles: SAGE Reference, 2015.

Mayes, Rick, and Allan Horwitz. "Correction to the DSM-III and the Revolution in the Classification of Mental Illnesses." *Journal of the History of the Behavioral Sciences* 43.4 (2007): 249–267.

Mayoclinic.org. "Generalized Anxiety Disorder." https://www.mayoclinic.org/diseases-conditions/generalized-anxiety-disorder/diagnosis-treatment/drc-20361045.

McCarthy, K. "Early Alcoholism Treatment: The Emmanuel Movement and Richard Peabody." *Journal of Studies on Alcohol* 45.1 (1984): 59–74.

McCarty, Dennis, Milton Argeriou, Robert B. Huebner, and Barbara Lubran. "Alcoholism, Drug Abuse, and the Homeless." *American Psychologist* 46.11 (1991): 1141.

McCarty, Dennis, Yael Caspi, Lee Panas, Milly Krakow, David H. Mulligan. "Detoxification Centers: Who's in the Revolving Door?" *Journal of Behavioral Health Services & Research* 27.3 (August 2000): 245–56.

McHugh, R. Kathryn, Suzanne Nielsen, and Roger D. Weiss. "Prescription Drug Abuse: From Epidemiology to Public Policy" *Journal of Substance Abuse Treatment* 48.1 (2015): 1–7.

McLellan A. T., D. C. Lewis, C. P. O'Brien, and H. D. Kieber. "Drug Dependence: A Chronic Medical Illness: Implications for Treatment, Insurance, and Outcomes Evaluation." *Journal of the American Medical Association* 284.13 (October 4, 2000): 1689–95.

McPeake, J. D. *William D. Silkworth, M.D., and the Origin and Development of Alcoholics Anonymous (A.A.).* Dublin, NH: Dublin Group, 2012.

Meil, William M., and Christiana L. Ruby, eds. *Recent Advances in Drug Addiction Research and Clinical Applications.* London: InTechOpen, 2016.

Mendelson, J. "Clinical and Pharmacological Evaluation of Buprenorphine and Naloxone Combinations: Why the 4:1 Ratio for Treatment?" *Drug and Alcohol Dependence* 70.2 (2003): 29–37.

Mendelson, Jack H., and Nancy K. Mello. *The Diagnosis and Treatment of Alcoholism.* New York: McGraw-Hill, 1979.

Merriam-Webster's Medical Dictionary. Springfield, MA: Merriam-Webster, 1999.

Mersy, David J. "Recognition of Alcohol and Substance Abuse." *American Family Physician* 67.7 (April 2003): 1529.

Metlay, Grischa. "Federalizing Medical Campaigns against Alcoholism and Drug Abuse." *Milbank Quarterly* 91.1 (2013): 123–62.

Midgley, Steve. "The Biblical Counseling Movement: History and Context." *Themelios* 35.3 (November 2010): 561–62.

Miller, Geraldine A. *Learning the Language of Addiction Counseling.* Hoboken, NJ: John Wiley & Sons, 2015.

Bibliography

Miller, Michael Craig. "How Addiction Hijacks the Brain." *Harvard Mental Health Letter* 28.1 (2011): 1–3.

Miller, Norman S., and Mark S. Gold. "The Disease and Adaptive Models of Addiction: A Re-Evaluation." *Journal of Drug Issues* 20.1 (1990): 29–35.

Miller, Robert Moats. *Harry Emerson Fosdick: Preacher, Pastor, Prophet*. New York: Oxford University Press, 1985.

Miller, William R. *Treating Addictive Behaviors: Processes of Change*. New York: Plenum, 1988.

Miller, William R., Alyssa A. Forcehimes, and Allen Zweben. *Treating Addiction: A Guide for Professionals*. New York: Guilford, 2011.

Millon, Theodore. *Disorders of Personality: DSM-III, Axis II*. New York: Wiley, 1981.

Milton, Joyce. *The Road to Malpsychia: Humanistic Psychology and Our Discontents*. San Francisco: Encounter, 2002.

Mitchel, Dale. *Silkworth: The Little Doctor Who Loved Drunks*. Center City, MN: Hazelden, 2002.

Moore, David. "Is Alcoholism Really a Disease?" *NY Daily News*, December 10, 2009.

Moore, Russell, Rick Warren, and Tony Rose. "Dealing with Mental Health Issues as a Christian." https://www.youtube.com/watch?v=9BzoVnUw1PI.

Moore, Thomas J., and Donald R. Mattison. "Adult Utilization of Psychiatric Drugs and Differences by Sex, Age, and Race." *JAMA Internal Medicine* 177.2 (2017): 274.

Moraff, Christopher. "Suboxone Creator's Shocking Scheme to Profit off of Heroin Addicts." https://www.thedailybeast.com/suboxone-creators-shocking-scheme-to-profit-off-of-heroin-addicts.

Morreim, Dennis C. *The Road to Recovery: Bridges between the Bible and the Twelve Steps*. Minneapolis: Augsburg, 1990.

Mowrer, Orval Hobart. *Abnormal Reactions or Actions? An Autobiographical Answer*. Dubuque, IA: W. C. Brown, 1966.

Mulford, Harold A. "Rethinking the Alcohol Problem: A Natural Processes Model." *Journal of Drug Issues* 14.1 (1984): 31–43.

Myers, David G. *Psychology in Modules with Updates on DSM-V*. New York: Worth, 2014.

"NAMI." NAMI. Accessed August 6, 2019. https://www.nami.org/learn-more/mental-health-by-the-numbers.

Narramore, Bruce. "Perspectives on the Integration of Psychology and Theology." *Journal of Psychology and Theology* 1.1 (1973): 3.

National Institute on Alcohol Abuse and Alcoholism. "Alcohol Use Disorder: A Comparison Between DSM–IV and DSM–5." https://www.niaaa.nih.gov/publications/brochures-and-fact-sheets/alcohol-use-disorder-comparison-between-dsm.

National Institute on Alcohol Abuse and Alcoholism. "Neuroscience: Pathways to Alcohol Dependence." https://pubs.niaaa.nih.gov/publications/AA77/AA77.htm.

National Institute on Drug Abuse. "Effective Treatments for Opioid Addiction." https://nida.nih.gov/publications/effective-treatments-opioid-addiction

National Institute on Drug Abuse. "Principles of Drug Addiction Treatment: A Research-Based Guide." https://nida.nih.gov/publications/principles-drug-addiction-treatment-research-based-guide-third-edition/principles-effective-treatment.

Nelstrop, Louise, and Kevin Magill. *Christian Mysticism: An Introduction to Contemporary Theoretical Approaches*. London: Taylor and Francis, 2016.

Ness, Immanuel. *Encyclopedia of American Social Movements*. Armonk, NY: M. E. Sharpe, 2004.

Bibliography

North, Robert L. "Benjamin Rush, MD: Assassin or Beloved Healer?" *Baylor University Medical Center Proceedings* 13.1 (2000): 45-49.

Nutt, David J. *Drugs and the Future: Brain Science, Addiction and Society.* Burlington, MA: Academic, 2006.

Offord, Robert. *Jerry Mcauley: An Apostle to the Lost.* Charleston, SC: Nabu, 2010.

Olson, Steve, and Dean R. Gerstein. *Alcohol in America: Taking Action to Prevent Abuse.* Washington, DC: National Academic, 1985.

Orcutt, James D., and David R. Rudy. *Drugs, Alcohol, and Social Problems.* Lanham, MD: Rowman & Littlefield, 2003.

Paris, Joël, and James Phillips. *Making the DSM-5 Concepts and Controversies.* New York: Springer, 2013.

Pattison, E. Mansell, Mark B. Sobell, and Linda C. Sobell. *Emerging Concepts of Alcohol Dependence.* New York: Springer, 1977.

Peabody, Richard R. *The Common Sense of Drinking.* Ventura, CA: Binghamus, 2013.

———. "Psychotherapeutic Procedure in the Treatment of Chronic Alcoholism." *Journal of Nervous and Mental Disease* 78.1 (1933): 91.

———. "Psychotherapy for Alcoholics." *New England Journal of Medicine* 202.25 (1930): 1199-1202.

Pearcey, Nancy. *Total Truth: Liberating Christianity from Its Cultural Captivity.* Wheaton, IL: Crossway, 2008.

Peck, M. Scott. *People of the Lie: The Hope for Healing Human Evil.* New York: Simon and Schuster, 1983.

Pedlar, James E. "Universal Atonement or Ongoing Incarnation?: Comparing the Missional Theologies of William Booth and Isaac Hecker." *Wesleyan Theological Journal* 50.1 (2015): 134-52.

Peele, Stanton. *7 Tools to Beat Addiction.* New York: Three Rivers, 2004.

———. *Diseasing of America: How We Allowed Recovery Zealots and the Treatment Industry to Convince Us We Are out of Control.* San Francisco: Jossey-Bass, 1999. Kindle.

———. *The Meaning of Addiction: Compulsive Experience and Its Interpretation.* Lexington, MA: Lexington Books, 1985.

Peele, Stanton, Archie Brodsky, and Mary Arnold. *The Truth about Addiction and Recovery: The Life Process Program for Outgrowing Destructive Habits.* New York: Simon & Schuster, 1991.

Perritt, Henry H. *Americans with Disabilities Act Handbook.* New York: Wolters Kluwer, 2018.

Petersen, Melody. *Our Daily Meds: How the Pharmaceutical Companies Transformed Themselves into Slick Marketing Machines and Hooked the Nation on Prescription Drugs.* New York: Picador, 2009.

Petty, James C. *Step by Step: Divine Guidance for Ordinary Christians.* Phillipsburg, NJ: P&R, 1999.

Phillips, Laura. "A FAILED Experiment." *Cobblestone* 38.4 (2017): 14.

Phillips, Patricia Pulliam, and Jack J. Phillips. *Return on Investment (ROI) Basics: A Complete How-to Guide.* Alexandria, VA: ASTD, 2005.

Pickard, Hannah, Serge H. Ahmed, and Bennett Foddy. "Alternative Models of Addiction." *Frontiers in Psychiatry* 6 (2015).

BIBLIOGRAPHY

Pilecki, B. C., J. W. Clegg, and D. Mckay. "The Influence of Corporate and Political Interests on Models of Illness in the Evolution of the DSM." *European Psychiatry* 26.3 (2011): 194–200.

Piper, John, and Rick Warren. "John Piper Interviews Rick Warren on Doctrine." https://www.youtube.com/watch?v=LImVHzy7WtU.

Playfair, William L., and George Bryson. *The Useful Lie*. Wheaton, IL: Crossway, 1991.

Pomeroy, John N. *The New York State Inebriate Asylum: Its Objects, Its System, and Its Results*. New York: Direction of the Superintendent, 1870.

Pop, Micheal M. *Misunderstanding Addiction: Overcoming Myth, Mysticism, and Misdirection in the Addictions Treatment Industry*. New York: iUniverse, 2010.

Porter, Roy. "The Drinking Man's Disease: The 'Pre-History' of Alcoholism in Georgian Britain." *Addiction* 80.4 (1985): 385–96.

———. *Madmen: A Social History of Madhouses, Mad-Doctors & Lunatics*. Cheltenham, UK: Tempus, 2006.

Potenza, M. N., M. Sofuuoglu, K. M. Carroll, and B. J. Rounsaville. "Neuroscience of Behavioral and Pharmacological Treatments for Addictions." *Neuron* 69.4 (February 24, 2011): 695–712.

Powlison, David. *The Biblical Counseling Movement: History and Context*. Greensboro, NC: New Growth, 2010.

———. *Overcoming Anxiety: Relief for Worried People*. Greensboro, NC: New Growth, 2012. Kindle.

———. *Seeing with New Eyes: Counseling and the Human Condition through the Lens of Scripture*. Phillipsburg, NJ: P&R, 2003.

Pratt, A. D. "A Mandatory Treatment Program for Skid Row Alcoholics: Its Implication for the Uniform Alcoholism and Intoxication Treatment Act." *Journal of Studies on Alcohol* 36.1 (1975): 166–70.

Prevention and Treatment of Alcohol Problems: Research Opportunities. Washington, DC: National Academy, 1989.

Priolo, Lou. "Presupposition Five: Sickness and Sin." *Journal of Modern Ministry* 2.2 (2005): 63.

———. "Presupposition Four: The Bible and Psychology." *Journal of Modern Ministry* 2.1 (2005): 63.

———. "Sin and Misery: Connecting the Dots." *Journal of Modern Ministry* 1.2 (2004): 97.

Proceedings and Address of the Washingtonian Mass Convention: Held in the City of Boston, at Tremont Temple, Thursday May 29, 1845. Boston: Printed at the New England Washingtonian Office, 1845.

Prochaska, James O., and Wayne F. Velicer. "The Transtheoretical Model of Health Behavior Change." *American Journal of Health Promotion* 12.1 (1997): 38–48.

Prohibition Briefs: Eighteenth Amendment and Volstead Act. Washington, DC: G. P. O., 1919.

Randall, Ian M. *Evangelical Experiences: A Study in the Spirituality of English Evangelicalism, 1918–1939*. Carlisle, Cumbria: Paternoster, 1999.

Rehabs.com, "Choosing the Best Dual Diagnosis Rehab Program." https://rehabs.com/dual-diagnosis-rehabs/.

Rehm, Jürgen. "The Risks Associated with Alcohol Use and Alcoholism." *Alcohol Research & Health: Journal of the National Institute on Alcohol Abuse and Alcoholism* 34.2 (2011): 135–43.

Bibliography

Reichenberg, Lourie W. *DSM-5 Essentials: The Savvy Clinician's Guide to the Changes in Criteria.* Hoboken, NJ: Wiley, 2014.

Reis, Alessandra Diehl, and Ronaldo Laranjeira. "Halfway Houses for Alcohol Dependents: From Theoretical Bases to Implications for the Organization of Facilities." *Clinics (Sao Paulo, Brazil)* 63.6 (2008): 827–32.

Reznek, Laurie. *Peddling Mental Disorder: The Crisis in Modern Psychology.* Jefferson, NC: McFarland, 2016.

Richardson, Robert D. *William James in the Maelstrom of American Modernism: A Biography.* Boston: Mariner, 2007.

Riedman, Sarah Regal, and Clarence C. Green. *Benjamin Rush: Physician, Patriot, Founding Father.* London: Abelard-Schuman, 1964.

Rigg, Khary K., Samantha J. March, and James A. Inciardi. "Prescription Drug Abuse & Diversion: Role of the Pain Clinic." *Journal of Drug Issues* 40.3 (2010): 681–702.

Roberts, Robert C. "The Idea of a Christian Psychology." *Journal of Psychology and Theology* 40.1 (2012): 37–40.

Robinson, Sean, and Bryon Adinoff. "The Classification of Substance Use Disorders: Historical, Contextual, and Conceptual Considerations." *Behavioral Sciences* 6.3 (2016): 18.

Rohan, W. P. "Comment on 'The N.C.A. Criteria for the Diagnosis of Alcoholism: An Empirical Evaluation Study.'" *Journal of Studies on Alcohol* 39.1 (1978): 211–18.

Rokeach, Milton. *The Open and Closed Mind: Investigations into the Nature of Belief Systems.* New York: Basic Books, 1960.

Room, Robin. "Mutual Help Movements for Alcohol Problems in an International Perspective." *Addiction Research* 6.2 (April 1998): 131.

Rorabaugh, W. J. *The Alcoholic Republic: An American Tradition.* Oxford: Oxford University Press, 1981.

Rowe, Craig. "Getting Christ off the Couch." *Journal of Modern Ministry* 5.2 (2008): 74.

Rush, Benjamin. *An Enquiry into the Effects of Ardent Spirits upon the Human Body and Mind: With an Account of the Means of Preventing, and of the Remedies for Curing Them.* New Brunswick: A. Blauvelt, 1805.

———. *An Enquiry into the Effects of Spirituous Liquors upon the Human Body and Their Influence upon the Happiness of Society.* Philadelphia: John M'Culloch, 1791.

———. *Medical Inquiries and Observations upon the Diseases of the Mind.* Birmingham, AL: Classics of Medicine Library, 1979.

Rutjens, Bastiaan T., Frenk Van Harreveld, and Joop Van Der Pligt. "Step by Step." *Current Directions in Psychological Science* 22.3 (2013): 250–55.

S., Igor. "What We Were Like: Emmet Fox and Alcoholics Anonymous." *AA Grapevine: The International Journal of Alcoholics Anonymous* (February 1996).

Sadock, Benjamin J. *Kaplan & Sadock Concise Textbook of Clinical Psychiatry.* Philadelphia: LWW, 2008.

Salty Current, "Review of *Cracked* by James Davies." http://saltycurrent.blogspot.com/2013/12/review-of-cracked-by-james-davies.html.

Schalow, Frank. *Toward a Phenomenology of Addiction: Embodiment, Technology, Transcendence.* Contributions to Phenomenology, vol. 93. N.p: Springer Cham, 2017.

Saloner, Brendan, Rachel Landis, Bradley Stein, and Colleen L. Barry. "The Affordable Care Act in the Heart of the Opioid Crisis: Evidence from West Virginia." *Health Affairs* 38.4 (2019): 633–42.

Bibliography

Sanford, Mark, and Donald Avoy. *Professional Perspectives on Addiction Medicine: Understanding Opioid Addiction and the Function of Methadone Treatment.* N.p.: CreateSpace, 2007.
Satel, Sally, and Scott O. Lilienfeld. "Addiction and the Brain-Disease Fallacy." *Frontiers in Psychiatry* 4.141 (2014).
Schaer, Hans. *Religion and the Cure of Souls in Jung's Psychology.* New York: Pantheon Books, 1950.
Schaler, Jeffery A. *Addiction Is a Choice.* Chicago: Open Court, 2000.
Schatz, Mona Struhsaker, and Evelyn Mallea. *Fetal Alcohol Syndrome: Crack and AIDS Babies. Fostering Families. A Specialized Training Program Designed for Foster Care Workers & Foster Care Parents.* Boulder, CO: Colorado State Department of Social Services, 1992.
Seixas, Frank A. "The NCA Criteria for the Diagnosis of Alcoholism—Intent, Use, and Practicality." *Psychiatry* (1985): 71.
Sessel, T. V. "Beyond the Supreme Court Ruling on Alcoholism as Willful Misconduct: It Is up to Congress to Act." *JAMA* 260.2 (1988): 248.
Shaw, Mark E. *The Heart of Addiction: A Biblical Perspective.* Bemidji, MN: Focus, 2008. Kindle.
Shellnutt, Kate and John Baker. "How Celebrate Recovery Helped Evangelicals Open Up about Addiction." https://www.christianitytoday.com/ct/2016/august-web-only/how-celebrate-recovery-helped-evangelicals-open-up-about-ad.html.
Sikorsky, Igor I. *AA's Godparents: Three Early Influences on Alcoholics Anonymous and Its Foundation, Carl Jung, Emmet Fox, Jack Alexander.* Minneapolis: CompCare, 1990.
Silkworth.net. "Bill W.'s Letter to Dr. Carl Gustav Jung." https://silkworth.net/alcoholics-anonymous/bill-w-s-letter-to-dr-carl-gustav-jung/.
Silkworth, William D. *Alcoholism as a Manifestation of Allergy.* New York: Medical Journal and Record, 1937.
———. "A New Approach to Psychotherapy in Chronic Alcoholism." *Lancet* 46 (July 1939): 3–4.
———. "The Prevention of Alcoholism: A Challenge to the Catholic Clergy." Lecture presented at the National Clergy Conference of Alcoholism, New York City, 1950.
Siluk, Dennis K. *A Path to Relapse Prevention: A Common Sense Book on Understanding the Sensitivity, Thinking and Repair Work Needed for the Alcoholic and Drug Inflicted.* New York: iUniverse, 2003.
Singer, Merrill. "Anthropology and Addiction: An Historical Review." *Addiction* 107.10 (October 2012): 1747–755.
Sire, James W. *The Universe Next Door: A Guidebook to the World Views.* Downers Grove, IL: InterVarsity, 1998.
Skinner, B. F. *Beyond Freedom and Dignity.* New York: Knopf, 1971.
———. "What Religion Means to Me." *Free Inquiry* 7.2 (1987): 13.
Slomski, Anita. "Opioid Agonist and Antagonist Therapies Prevent Opioid Relapse." *JAMA* 319.4 (2018): 333.
Smith, Christian, and Michael Emerson. *American Evangelicalism: Embattled and Thriving.* Chicago: University of Chicago Press, 1998.
Smith, David. "The Evolution of Addiction Medicine as a Medical Specialty." *Virtual Mentor* 13.12 (2011): 900–905.

Bibliography

Smith, Robert D. *The Christian Counselor's Medical Desk Reference*. Stanley, NC: Timeless Texts, 2000.
Snetzer, Michael. "Steps Week Two: The Remedy." Lecture presented at The Village Church, Flower Mound, TX, September 11, 2013.
Snoek, Anke, and Steve Matthews. "Introduction: Testing and Refining Marc Lewis's Critique of the Brain Disease Model of Addiction." *Neuroethics* 10.1 (February 2017): 1–6.
Soeiro-De-Souza, Marcio G., Vasco Videira Dias, Giovani Missio, Vicent Balanza-Martinez, Leandro Valiengo, Andre Carvalho, and Ricardo Alberto Moreno. "Role of Quetiapine beyond Its Clinical Efficacy in Bipolar Disorder: From Neuroprotection to the Treatment of Psychiatric Disorders (Review)." *Experimental and Therapeutic Medicine* 9.3 (2015): 643–52.
Solomon, Joel. *Alcoholism and Clinical Psychiatry*. New York: Springer, 2012.
Spencer, Mark G. *The Bloomsbury Encyclopedia of the American Enlightenment*. New York: Bloomsbury Academic, 2015.
Spickard, Anderson, and Barbara R. Thompson. *Dying for a Drink: What You Should Know about Alcoholism*. Waco, TX: Word, 1985.
Spitzer, Robert L. "The Psychiatric Status Schedule." *Archives of General Psychiatry* 23.1 (1970): 41.
———. "The Trap: What Happened to Our Dream of Freedom." https://watchdocumentaries.com/the-trap-what-happened-to-our-dream-of-freedom/.
———. "Utility of a New Procedure for Diagnosing Mental Disorders in Primary Care." *JAMA* 272.22 (1994): 1749.
Spitzer, Robert L., and Jean Endicott. "DIAGNO II: Further Developments in a Computer Program for Psychiatric Diagnosis." *American Journal of Psychiatry* 125.7S (1969): 12–21.
Spitzer, Robert L., Kurt Kroenke, and Janet B. W. Williams. "The PHQ-9." *Journal of General Internal Medicine* 16.9 (2001): 606–13.
Spitzer, Robert L., Joseph R. Calabrese, Laurie Flynn, Paul E. Keck, Lydia Lewis, Robert Hirschfeld, B. W. Williams, and S. L. McElroy. "Development and Validation of a Screening Instrument for Bipolar Spectrum Disorder: The Mood Disorder Questionnaire." *American Journal of Psychiatry* 157.11 (2000): 1873–75.
Statista.com. "Prescription Drug Expenditure U.S., 1960–2017." https://www.statista.com/statistics/184914/prescription-drug-expenditures-in-the-us-since-1960/.
Stein, Murray. *Jung on Christianity*. Princeton, NJ: Princeton University Press, 2012.
Steingard, Sandra. *Critical Psychiatry Controversies and Clinical Implications*. New York: Springer International, 2019.
Stern, Alexandra Minna. "STERILIZED in the Name of Public Health." *American Journal of Public Health* 95.7 (2005): 1128–38.
Stohler, R., and Wulf Rössler, eds. *Dual Diagnosis: The Evolving Conceptual Framework*. Key Issues in Mental Health.172. Edited by A. Riecher-Rössler and M. Steiner. Basel: Karger, 2005.
Stolberg, Victor B. "Narcotic Addict Rehabilitation Act." In *Encyclopedia of Drug Policy*. Thousand Oaks, CA: SAGE, 1982.
Stone, Bob. *My Years with Narcotics Anonymous*. Joplin, MO: Hulon Pendleton, 1997.
Stöppler, Melissa Conrad, and William C. Shiel. *Webster's New World Medical Dictionary*. 3rd ed. Boston: Houghton Mifflin, 2009.

Bibliography

Strecker, Edward A., and Francis T. Chambers. *Alcohol: One Man's Meat*. New York: Macmillan, 1938.

Street, John D. "Market-Driven Madness: What's Behind Purpose-Driven Churches?" *Journal of Modern Ministry* 2.1 (2005): 19.

Strickland, Bonnie B. *The Gale Encyclopedia of Psychology*. Detroit: Gale Group, 2001.

Strozier, Charles B. "Benjamin Rush: Revolutionary Doctor." *American Scholar* 64.3 (1995): 415.

Sultan, Ryan S., Christoph U. Correll, Michael Schoenbaum, Marrisa King, John T. Walkup, and Mark Olfson. "National Patterns of Commonly Prescribed Psychotropic Medications to Young People." *Journal of Child and Adolescent Psychopharmacology* 28.3 (2018): 158.

Surís, Alina, Ryan Holliday, and Carol North. "The Evolution of the Classification of Psychiatric Disorders." *Behavioral Sciences* 6.1 (2016): 5.

Switzer, Charles Irvin. "The Political, Philosophical, and Religious Thought of Dr. Benjamin Rush." PhD diss., University of Michigan, East Lansing, MI, 1966.

Szalavitz, Maia. *Unbroken Brain: A Revolutionary New Way of Understanding Addiction*. New York: Picador, 2017.

Szasz, Thomas. *The Manufacture of Madness: A Comparative Study of the Inquisition and the Mental Health Movement*. New York: Harper & Row, 1970.

———. *The Myth of Psychotherapy: Mental Healing as Religion, Rhetoric, and Repression*. Syracuse, NY: Syracuse University Press, 1988.

Tappert, Theodore G., trans. and ed. *Luther: Letters of Spiritual Counsel*. Vancouver: Regent College, 2003.

Taylor, David W. *Like A Mighty Army?: The Salvation Army, the Church, and the Churches*. Cambridge, MA: James Clarke, 2015.

Tekin, Şerife. "Brain Mechanisms and the Disease Model of Addiction." *Routledge Handbook of Philosophy and Science of Addiction* (2018): 401–10.

Terry, W. Clinton. *The Early Drug Courts Case Studies in Judicial Innovation*. Thousand Oaks, CA: SAGE, 1998.

Thecabinchiangmai.com. "Do I Need Recovery Meetings to Stay Sober?" https://www.thecabinchiangmai.com/blog/do-i-need-recovery-meetings-to-stay-sober/.

Thombs, Dennis L., and Cynthia J. Osborn. *Introduction to Addictive Behaviors*. New York: Guilford, 2013.

Thornton, Edward E. *Professional Education for Ministry: A History of Clinical Pastoral Education*. Nashville: Abingdon, 1970.

Timimi, Sami. "No More Psychiatric Labels: Why Formal Psychiatric Diagnostic Systems Should Be Abolished." *International Journal of Clinical and Health Psychology* 14.3 (2014): 208–15.

Tobey, J. A. "Historical, Legal, and Statistical Review of Eugenical Sterilization in the United States." *American Journal of Public Health* 16.7 (1926): 725–26.

Towns, Charles Barnes. *The Work of the Charles B. Towns Hospital and Its Relation to the Medical Profession: With Special Reference to the Now Widened Scope of Its Service to and Co-Operation with the Physician in Private Practice*. New York: Charles B. Towns Hospital, 1918.

Towns, Charles Barnes, and Alexander Lambert. *Habits that Handicap: The Menace of Opium, Alcohol, and Tobacco, and the Remedy*. New York: Century, 1917.

Tracy, Sarah W. *Alcoholism in America From Reconstruction to Prohibition*. Baltimore: Johns Hopkins University Press, 2009.

Bibliography

Travis, Trysh. *The Language of the Heart: A Cultural History of the Recovery Movement from Alcoholics Anonymous to Oprah Winfrey*. Chapel Hill, NC: University of North Carolina Press, 2009.

Turner, J. Edward. *History of the First Inebriate Asylum in the World*. New York: Rarebooksclub, 2012.

Unger, Harlow G. *Dr. Benjamin Rush: The Founding Father Who Healed a Wounded Nation*. New York: Da Capo, 2018.

US Congress, House of Representatives. SUPPORT for Patients and Communities Act. H.R.6, 115th Cong., 2nd sess., *Congressional Record* 163, daily ed. (June 6, 2018): H.Prt. 115–76. H.Prt. 115–78.

US Congress. Compilation of Treasury Decisions Relating to Act of Dec. 17, 1914, Known as Harrison Narcotic Law, Issued during Period Feb. 2, 1915 to May 11, 1917. Washington, DC: U.S. G.P.O., 1917.

Vaillant, George E. *The Natural History of Alcoholism*. Cambridge, MA: Harvard University Press, 1983.

Valverde, Mariana. *Diseases of the Will: Alcohol and the Dilemmas of Freedom*. Cambridge, MA: Cambridge University Press, 1998.

Van Auken, Philip. *The Well-Managed Ministry*. Wheaton, IL: Victor, 1989.

Veatch, Robert M. *Disrupted Dialogue: Medical Ethics and the Collapse of Physician-Humanist Communication (1770–1980)*. Oxford: Oxford University Press, 2010.

Velander, Jennifer. "Suboxone: Rationale, Science, Misconceptions." *Ochsner Journal* 18.1 (Spring 2018): 23–29.

Vogel, Steven R. "Finding the Whole Person: A Thumbnail Anthropology: Part 1." *Journal of Modern Ministry* 2.3 (2005): 181–82.

Volkow, Nora D. "Addiction: A Disease of Free Will." Lecture presented at the 168th Annual Meeting of the American Psychiatric Association, Toronto, Canada, July 1, 2015.

Volkow, Nora D., and Anat Biegon. *Sites of Drug Action in the Human Brain*. Boca Raton, FL: CRC, 1995.

Volkow, Nora D., George F. Koob, and A. Thomas Mclellan. "Neurobiologic Advances from the Brain Disease Model of Addiction." *New England Journal of Medicine* 374.4 (2016): 363–71.

Vonasch, Andrew J., Cory J. Clark, Stephan Lau, Kathleen D. Vohs, and Roy F. Baumeister. "Ordinary People Associate Addiction with Loss of Free Will." *Addictive Behaviors Reports* 5 (2017): 56–66.

W., Bill. "12 STEPS in 30 Minutes." *AA Grapevine: The International Journal of Alcoholics Anonymous* (July 1953).

———. "After Twenty-Five Years." *AA Grapevine: The International Journal of Alcoholics Anonymous* (March 1960).

———. *Alcoholics Anonymous*. 1st ed. New York: Works, 1945.

———. *Alcoholics Anonymous: The Big Book: The Original 1939 Edition*. Mineola, NY: Ixia, 2019.

———. *Alcoholics Anonymous: The Story of How Many Thousands of Men and Women Have Recovered from Alcoholism*. New York: Alcoholics Anonymous, 1939.

———. *Alcoholics Anonymous: The Story of How Many Thousands of Men and Women Have Recovered from Alcoholism*. New York: Alcoholics Anonymous World Services, 1976.

Bibliography

———. *Alcoholics Anonymous: The Story of How Many Thousands of Men and Women Have Recovered from Alcoholism.* New York: Alcoholics Anonymous, 2013.

———. *Alcoholics Anonymous Comes of Age: A Brief History of A.A.* New York: Alcoholics Anonymous World Services, 1985.

———. "A Benediction from Bill . . . Memo to the Folks Back Home—Progress, Humility, Unity, Mark Sessions of Delegates." Lecture presented at the Second General Service Conference, New York City, April 27, 1952.

———. "Coming of Age." Lecture presented at Twentieth A.A. Anniversary, St. Louis, July 3, 1955.

———. "Good Reading." *AA Grapevine: The International Journal of Alcoholics Anonymous* (July 1948).

———. "How the Twelve Steps Were Born." *AA Grapevine: The International Journal of Alcoholics Anonymous* (September 1962).

———. "The Power of One Alcoholic Talking to Another." Lecture presented at A.A. Meeting, Atlanta, July 1951.

———. "Thirty-Third AA Anniversary Party." Lecture presented at Thirty-Third AA Anniversary Party, New York, October 7, 1967.

———. "Transformation." Lecture presented at Twentieth A.A. Anniversary Dinner, New York, 1955.

Wakefield, J. C. "DSM-5 Substance Use Disorder: How Conceptual Missteps Weakened the Foundations of the Addictive Disorders Field." *Acta Psychiatrica Scandinavica* 132.5 (2015): 327–34.

Wakeman, Sarah E. "Language and Addiction: Choosing Words Wisely." *American Journal of Public Health* 103.4 (2013): 1–2.

Ward, Judith, William Bejarano, Thomas F. Babor, and Nicholas Allred. "Re-Introducing Bunky at 125: E. M. Jellinek's Life and Contributions to Alcohol Studies." *Journal of Studies on Alcohol and Drugs* 77.3 (2016): 375–83.

Warner, J. "'Resolv'd to Drink No More': Addiction as a Preindustrial Construct." *Journal of Studies on Alcohol* 55.6 (1994): 685–91.

Warren, Kay. "Psychiatry and Faith." https://www.youtube.com/watch?v=LlvlZyHn5CY.

Warren, Rick. *The Purpose Driven Life.* Chagrin Falls, OH: Zondervan, 2006.

Warren, Rick, and John Baker. *Celebrate Recovery: A Program for Implementing a Christ-centered Recovery Ministry in Your Church.* Grand Rapids, Zondervan, 1998.

Warsh, Cheryl Krasnick. "Adventures in Maritime Quackery: The Leslie E. Keeley Gold Cure Institute of Fredericton, N.B." *Acadiensis* 17.2 (1988): 109.

———. *Drink in Canada: Historical Essays.* Montréal: McGill-Queen's University Press, 2014.

Washton, Arnold. *Cocaine Addiction: Treatment, Recovery, and Relapse Prevention.* New York: W. W. Norton, 1991.

Watts, Thomas D. "The Uneasy Triumph of a Concept: The 'Disease' Conception of Alcoholism." *Journal of Drug Issues* 11.4 (1981): 451–60.

Welch, Edward T. *Addictions: A Banquet in the Grave: Finding Hope in the Power of the Gospel.* Phillipsburg, NJ: P&R, 2001.

———. *Blame It on the Brain?: Distinguishing Chemical Imbalances, Brain Disorders, and Disobedience.* Phillipsburg, NJ: P&R, 1998.

———. *When People Are Big and God Is Small: Overcoming Peer Pressure, Codependency, and the Fear of Man.* Phillipsburg, NJ: P&R, 1997.

Bibliography

Welch, Robert H. *Church Administration: Creating Efficiency for Effective Ministry.* Nashville: B&H Academic, 2011.

Whitaker, Robert. *Anatomy of an Epidemic: Magic Bullets, Psychiatric Drugs, and the Astonishing Rise of Mental Illness in America.* New York: Crown, 2010.

White, William. *Addiction Recovery Mutual Aid Groups in the United States: A Chronology of Founding Dates.* Bloomington, IL: Chestnut Health System, 2015.

White, William L. "Pre-A.A. Alcoholic Mutual Aid Societies." *Alcoholism Treatment Quarterly* 19.2 (2001): 1–21.

White, William L., and John William Crowley. *Drunkard's Refuge: The Lessons of the New York State Inebriate Asylum.* Amherst, MA: University of Massachusetts Press, 2004.

———. *Slaying the Dragon: The History of Addiction Treatment and Recovery in America.* Bloomington, IL: Chestnut Health Systems, 2014.

———. *William White Papers.* Bloomington, IL: Chestnut Health Systems, 1998.

Wieczner, Jen. "Drug Companies Look to Profit from DSM-V." https://www.marketwatch.com/story/new-psych-manual-could-create-drug-windfalls-2013-06-05.

Williams, R. "The Biblical Counseling Movement: History and Context." *Edification: The Transdisciplinary Journal of Christian Psychology* 5.1 (November 2011): 78–79.

Williamson, Kristy, and Graeme Johanson. *Research Methods: Information, Systems, and Contexts.* Oxford: Chandos, 2017.

Winskill, Peter T. *The Temperance Movement and Its Workers: A Record of Social, Moral, Religious, and Political Progress.* London: Blackie, 1892.

Winslow, Lyttleton. *Journal of Psychological Medicine and Mental Pathology.* Vol. 13. Ann Arbor, MI: University of Michigan Library, 2010.

———. "On Habits of Intoxication as Causing a Type of Disease." *Journal of Psychological Medicine and Mental Pathology* 13 (April 1, 1850): 127.

Woolley, John Granville. *Temperance Progress of the Century.* Brantford, ON: Linscott, 2012.

Wormald, Benjamin. "U.S. Public Becoming Less Religious." www.pewforum.org/2015/11/03/u-s-public-becoming-less-religious/.

Wyatt, Richard Jed. *Wyatt's Practical Psychiatric Practice: Forms and Protocols for Clinical Use.* Philadelphia, American Psychiatric Association, 2004.

Xavier, N. S. *Fulfilling Heart and Soul: Meeting Psychological and Spiritual Needs with Conscience.* Bloomington, IN: AuthorHouse, 2007.

Younger, Jarred, Noorulain Noor, Rebecca McCue, and Sean Mackey. "Low-Dose Naltrexone for the Treatment of Fibromyalgia: Findings of a Small, Randomized, Double-Blind, Placebo-Controlled, Counterbalanced, Crossover Trial Assessing Daily Pain Levels." *Arthritis & Rheumatism* 65.2 (2013): 529–38.

Zagon, I., and P. Mclaughlin. "Naltrexone Modulates Tumor Response in Mice with Neuroblastoma." *Science* 221.4611 (1983): 671–73.

Zuvekas, S. H. "Prescription Drugs and the Changing Patterns of Treatment for Mental Disorders, 1996–2001." *Health Affairs* 24.1 (2005): 195–205.

www.ingramcontent.com/pod-product-compliance
Lightning Source LLC
Chambersburg PA
CBHW072144160426
43197CB00012B/2244